OECD Reviews of Risk Management Policies

JAPAN

LARGE-SCALE FLOODS AND EARTHQUAKES

OECD

119715 25

ORGANISATION FOR ECONOMIC CO-OPERATION AND DEVELOPMENT

The OECD is a unique forum where the governments of 30 democracies work together to address the economic, social and environmental challenges of globalisation. The OECD is also at the forefront of efforts to understand and to help governments respond to new developments and concerns, such as corporate governance, the information economy and the challenges of an ageing population. The Organisation provides a setting where governments can compare policy experiences, seek answers to common problems, identify good practice and work to co-ordinate domestic and international policies.

The OECD member countries are: Australia, Austria, Belgium, Canada, the Czech Republic, Denmark, Finland, France, Germany, Greece, Hungary, Iceland, Ireland, Italy, Japan, Korea, Luxembourg, Mexico, the Netherlands, New Zealand, Norway, Poland, Portugal, the Slovak Republic, Spain, Sweden, Switzerland, Turkey, the United Kingdom and the United States. The Commission of the European Communities takes part in the work of the OECD.

OECD Publishing disseminates widely the results of the Organisation's statistics gathering and research on economic, social and environmental issues, as well as the conventions, guidelines and standards agreed by its members.

This work is published on the responsibility of the Secretary-General of the OECD. The opinions expressed and arguments employed herein do not necessarily reflect the official views of the Organisation or of the governments of its member countries.

Foreword

This third volume of the OECD Futures Project on Risk Management Policies contains two case study reviews on natural disaster management in Japan: the first focusing on large-scale floods and the second concentrating on earthquakes. It follows the publication of two previous risk management reviews: "Norway: Information Security" and "Sweden: The Safety of Older People".

Launched in October 2003, the OECD Futures Project on Risk Management Policies aims to assist countries to identify the challenges of managing risks in the 21st century, and to contribute to their reflection on how best to address those challenges. The Project is monitored by a Steering Group consisting of representatives from participating Ministries and Agencies. Its focus is placed on the consistency of risk management policies and on their ability to detect and adapt to changes in the risk landscape. The Project follows a multidisciplinary approach in its analysis of how participating countries deal with the challenges, present and future, created by various risks such as natural disasters, critical infrastructures and vulnerable populations. The country reviews are based on a background study prepared, discussed and adopted during the first phase of the Project; a self-assessment of policy by national authorities using an ad hoc questionnaire; and a second phase in which a series of interviews are carried out in the country by the OECD review teams.

The reviews of Japan's risk management policies for large scale floods and earthquakes were set up at the request of the Japanese Cabinet Office and the Ministry of Land, Infrastructure and Transport (MLIT). These issues are of particular importance in Japan due to a confluence of hazardous climatic and seismic conditions in its national territory and the unique exposure of its population to these hazards. In recent years, Japan has witnessed a significant increase in precipitation levels and in the frequency of extreme climatic events such as typhoons, which have raised the likelihood of flood disasters. In addition, Japan is one of the most earthquake prone countries in the world. The most recent example of this on a catastrophic scale was the Kobe (Great Hanshin-Awahi) earthquake in 1995 which caused the death of more than 6 000 persons.

Results of the Phase 1 background studies prepared the ground for Phase 2 in-depth reviews carried out by two teams of international experts from May 14-19, 2007 and May 20-26, 2007 respectively. The review teams appraised the complete range of Japanese disaster management policies related to large scale floods and earthquake, herein referred to as Japan's risk management system. The review teams submitted interim reports of findings and recommendations to the Japanese authorities and two draft reports. This final report, in two "Parts", contains the findings, conclusions and recommendations of both reviews. Both Part I (large scale floods) and Part II (earthquakes) consist of five sections that consider in turn the different components of Japan's risk management system: the first section addresses Japan's integrated approach to policy framework, the second deals with risk assessment and communication, the third considers protection, i.e. physical and structural disaster prevention measures, the fourth investigates emergency preparedness and response policies and the fifth is about post-disaster issues, from reconstruction to damage compensation.

Each section is further divided into several sections, in which the review team proposes a short analysis of the general context, presents its findings and its policy recommendation with regard to a specific policy issue, together with some opportunities to put the policy recommendations in practice. The report does not only focus on areas where flood and earthquake risk management can be improved, but also tries to identify areas where Japan's instruments and policies can be considered best practices and promoted in other OECD countries.

Japan is renowned worldwide for its engineering feats in earthquake-resistant buildings and construction of flood defences – channels and embankments, retention basins, dams, super levees, and so on. It is also a world leader in the use of highly sophisticated technologies in advance warning of floods and tremors, data collection and analysis, risk assessment and communication. Hence, Japan's structural flood and earthquake defences have progressed considerably, and this despite significant reductions in capital budgets in recent years.

As the country has accumulated ever more experience in tackling floods, it has continually adapted and updated its laws and regulations on the basis of lessons learned, and has modernised and refined its flood management and earthquake risk management techniques. Japan has now developed a Total Disaster Management System that is a seamless cycle of prevention, mitigation, preparedness, response, recovery and rehabilitation – a system that encourages strong national leadership and multi-sectoral co-ordination, and serves Japan well in dealing with the small and medium sized floods that frequently occur.

However, in several respects, Japan is now entering a new era. Against the backdrop of climate change sea levels are expected to rise, while at the same time the country's vulnerability to flooding and earthquakes is expected to grow due to the denser occupation of affected urban areas, and its ageing population. At the same time, responsibilities for risk assessment, preparedness, prevention and response tend to become fragmented as a result of government decentralisation, privatisation and regulatory reform. Japan therefore increasingly needs to turn its attention to the likelihood and consequences of large-scale floods and major earthquakes in the future, and its capacity to manage them. This will mean better targeted investment in structural defences and flood control technologies. But it will particularly entail improving the non-structural aspects of flood disaster management and earthquake risk, notably in the areas of policy coherence, co-ordination among and between the different levels of government, transparency of legislation, vulnerability assessment, organisation and communication in emergency response, as well as the planning and preparation of the recovery phase.

Allocating resources optimally amongst competing social and infrastructure needs, against a background of fiscal consolidation and mounting pressure to reduce public investment expenditures, is not easy. Nonetheless the case can be made to maintain, re-allocate and even increase in some situations the resources to cope with natural disasters in Japan. Indeed, in the light of the prospect of significant increases in the cost of recovery from major disasters, efforts to enhance prevention and mitigation and to improve non-structural measures do need to be stepped up.

Such efforts would include:

1. A better anticipation of the potential negative consequences stemming from climate change with respect to the frequency and scale of damages in case of natural disasters, particularly in the case of floods, typhoons, windstorms, tsunamis, even if the population of Japan is due to decline in the decades to come.

2. Better integration of risk management policies regarding emerging risks, as well as consideration of worst-case hypotheses – for example, what would happen if a severe earthquake was to trigger a large-scale flood or in the case of a co-occurrence of a large-scale flood and a serious epidemic?

3. Sustaining investment and maintenance via structural measures such as tremor-resistant installations, dykes, levees, locks or other protective measures needs to remain a high priority. But at the same time non-structural measures such as the clarification of roles and responsibilities, capacity building at local level, evacuation procedures, consultations with stakeholders, use of building codes, etc. should receive both more attention and in some cases more resources.

In the context of the current budgetary constraints in Japan, a number of options remain open:

● Consider ways in which the excellent horizontal approaches already in place for earthquakes and floods, in the form of such mechanisms as the Disaster Management Council, Technical Investigation Committees, etc., might be applied to other risk areas (pandemics, terrorism, technological accidents, certain financial or social risks).

● Reinforce the roles of Cabinet Office and Cabinet Secretariat in monitoring the threats and coordinating policy measures across risk areas.

● Use the opportunity presented by large investment needs in tangible infrastructure (water, transportation, gas distribution, power generation and transmission, telecommunications) to enhance long-term measures for disaster risk management, in light of the challenges stemming from new risks; such measures might include a more proactive approach to land use and city planning on the basis of existing risks and vulnerabilities, better adaptation of infrastructures to vulnerable groups, a more energetic search for cost efficiency and greater resilience of systems.

For each review, interviews were conducted with civil servants from the national government's Cabinet Office, relevant ministries and agencies, as well as the regional and local level organisation of the Ministry of Land Infrastructure and Transport (MLIT). For the review on floods, representatives from local government authorities were also interviewed, including the City of Tokyo and the Saitama Prefecture. Among the businesses that participated in the reviews were construction, manufacturing and insurance companies. The review team also attended a large-scale and ambitious emergency management drill against flooding in the Tone River.

The team that carried out the review on risk management policies for large scale floods was led by Dr. Yves Kovacs, Consulting Engineer and Expert in Flood Management. Team members included: Ulf Bjurman, Senior Advisor on Civil Protection and Crisis Management, Previously Head of Department, Swedish Rescue Services Agency; Reza Lahidji, Consultant in Risk Management Policy for the OECD Secretariat; and Dr. Tsujimoto, Professor at Nagoya University in flood countermeasures studies. The team that conducted the review on risk management policies for earthquakes was led by Reza Lahidji. Team members included Ulf Bjurman, Professor Yoshiaki Kawata, Director of the Disaster Prevention Research Institute at the Kyoto University, and Nikolaï Malyshev, Senior Economist at the OECD Secretariat. Pierre-Alain Schieb of the OECD Secretariat was the project manager and together with Barrie Stevens provided guidance and overall direction. Their dedicated counterparts in Japan were Mr. Kazuhisa Ito and Mr. Ichizo Kobayashi. Anita Gibson and Lucy Krawcsyk provided technical support throughout the project. Jack Radisch and Jenny Leger helped to edit and shape the publication.

The review teams are indebted to representatives of the Cabinet Office, several central government ministries and agencies, as well as their regional and local affiliates, local government authorities, including the City of Tokyo and Saitama Prefecture, several municipalities, businesses, a research institute and organisations, who provided valuable information during the interviews. The review team thanks in particular the Disaster Management Bureau, Cabinet Office and the River Planning Division of the Ministry of Land Infrastructure and Transport for providing advice and comments at the meeting of the OECD Steering Group on Risk Management Policies.

Both reports benefited from the guidance of the Steering Group to the OECD Futures Project (see list of members in Annex II.4) and editorial assistance from the staff of the OECD International Futures Programme.

Table of Contents

Part II
Earthquakes

List of boxes

List of tables

List of figures

Acronyms and Organisations Cited

AIST	National Institute of Advanced Industrial Science and Technology
ANSI/NFPA	American National Standard for Disaster/Emergency Management and Business Continuity Programs

Bank of Japan

BCP	Business Continuity Planning
BS	British Standard
BZK	Ministry of the Interior and Kingdom Relations (Netherlands)
CalARP	California Accidental Release Prevention
CAO	Cabinet Office (Japan)
CAT bond	Catastrophe Bond
CCS	Civil Contingencies Secretariat (United Kingdom)
CDF	Contingent debt facility
CDMC	Central Disaster Management Council
CEMAGREF	French Institute for Agriculture, Rural Engineering, Water and Forests – Centre d'Etude du Machinisme Agricole, du Génie Rural, des Eaux et des Forêts (France)
CND Plan	Comprehensive National Development Plan
DEFRA	Department for Environment and Rural Affairs (United Kingdom)
DHI	Danish Hydraulic Institute
Diet	Japanese Parliament

Disaster Prevention Research Institute, Kyoto University

DSB	Norway's Directorate for civil Protection and Emergency planning
EC	European Commission
EEA	European Economic Area
EPTB	Basin Territory River Administration (Établissement Public Territorial de Bassin)
ESPACE	European Spatial Planning Adapting to Climate Events
FDMA	Fire and Disaster Management Agency (Japan)
FEMA	Federal Emergency Management Agency (United States)
GBP	Great Britain Pounds
GDP	Gross Domestic Product

GEONET	GPS Earth Observation Network System
GNP	Gross National Product
GSI	Geographical Survey Institute
HERP	Headquarters for Earthquake Research Promotion
HIC	International Conference on Hydro-informatics
ICHARM	International Centre for Water Hazards and Risk Management
ICPR	International Commission for the Protection of the Rhine
ICT	Information and Communication Technologies
IDI	International Development Institute (Japan)
IPPC	Intergovernmental Panel on Climate Change (Japan)

Japanese Red Cross Society

JMA	Japan Meteorological Agency.
JPY	Japanese Yen
MLIT	Ministry of Land, Infrastructure and Transport (Japan)
NCC	National Coordination Centre (Netherlands)
NFIP	National Flood Insurance Program (United States)
NFPA	National Fire Protection Association
NGO	Non Government Organisation
NIED	National Research Institute on Earth Science and Disaster Prevention
NVC	National Public Information Center (Netherlands)
OECD	Organisation for Economic Co-operation and Development
PES	Policy Evaluation system
PRP	Preferred Risk Program (United States)
PWRI	Public Works Research Institute (Japan)
RIA	Regulatory Impact Analysis
RMS	Risk Management Solutions Inc.
SME	Small and Medium Enterprise

Swedish Rescue Services Agency

UK	United Kingdom
UNEP	United Nations Environment Programme
UNESCO	United Nations Educational, Scientific and Cultural Organization
UN/ SDR	United Nations/International Strategy for Disaster Reduction
UN/WWAP	United Nations/World Water Assessment Program
USA	United States of America

ISBN 978-92-64-05639-8
OECD Reviews of Risk Management Policies
Japan: Large-Scale Floods and Earthquakes
© OECD 2009

PART I

Large-Scale Floods

Japan's risk management policies for large scale floods have achieved a high level of technical expertise and coordination across government. These policies, however, will face new challenges from climate change and increased concentration of Japan's population and valuable assets.

ISBN 978-92-64-05639-8
OECD Reviews of Risk Management Policies
Japan: Large-Scale Floods and Earthquakes
© OECD 2009

Executive Summary

Japan is in a unique situation compared with other OECD countries. Due to its geography, topography and climate, it is subject to frequent typhoons, torrential rains and heavy snow falls, and has a long history of serious flooding. About half the population and full three-quarters of its economic assets are concentrated in flood-prone areas, and almost five and a half million people live in areas below sea level.

Over the centuries, Japan has developed an extraordinarily high level of expertise in dealing with floods. It is renowned worldwide for its engineering feats in the construction of flood defences – channels and embankments, retention basins, river floodways, dams, super levees, and more recently its integrated strategies combining flood control, water use and environmental protection. It is also a world leader in the use of highly sophisticated technologies in advance flood warning, data collection and analysis, risk assessment, communication, and protection of critical infrastructures. Hence, Japan's structural flood defences have progressed considerably, and this despite significant reductions in capital budgets in recent years

As the country has accumulated ever more experience in tackling floods, it has continually adapted and updated its laws and regulations on the basis of the lessons learned, and has modernised and refined its flood management techniques. Japan has now developed a Total Disaster Management System that is a seamless cycle of prevention, mitigation, preparedness, response, recovery and rehabilitation – a system that encourages strong national leadership and multi-sectoral co-ordination, and serves Japan well in dealing with the small and medium sized floods that frequently occur.

But in several respects, Japan is now entering a new era. Against the backdrop of climate change, sea levels are expected to rise, precipitation patterns to change, and extreme weather events to increase. At the same time, the country's vulnerability to flooding is expected to grow due to the denser occupation of flood-prone urban areas, and its ageing population. Thus, Japan increasingly needs to turn its attention to the likelihood and consequences of major, large-scale floods in the future, and its capacity to manage them. This will mean more and better targeted investment in structural defences and flood control technologies. But equally, it will also entail careful review of the scope for improving the non-structural aspects of flood disaster management, notably in the areas of policy coherence, co-ordination among and between the different levels of government, transparency of legislation, vulnerability assessment, organisation and communication in emergency response, as well as the planning and preparation of the recovery phase.

Integrated approach to flood risk management

1. A cross-sectoral approach to flood control at the central level

Japan possesses a comprehensive and strategic disaster management system elaborated in the Disaster Countermeasures Basic Act, which has been enhanced following lessons learned from different large scale disasters. The system covers all phases of disaster management: prevention, mitigation and preparedness, emergency response, recovery and rehabilitation. Further, it clarifies the roles and responsibilities both of government at national and local levels and relevant stakeholders in the public and private sectors who cooperate in implementing various disaster countermeasures.

The overall national strategy for flood risk management is defined at the highest level by the combined work of the Cabinet, the Cabinet Office and since 2001 the Central Disaster Management Council. These public bodies collaborate in the development of the national strategy and co-ordination of actions and policies that are implemented on a practical level by various ministries and agencies.

Findings

The necessity to involve various ministries and agencies to achieve a holistic flood disaster management requires that strong coordination and leadership is exercised. Although central government bodies control implementation of national policies, the use of inspections and evaluations to review the strategies and to monitor the coherence and efficiency of action taken within the holistic flood risk management system should be used more systematically.

Opportunities for action

At present, the separation in central administrations between responsibility for protection measures, prevention and preparedness measures and response measures should be addressed to achieve stronger co-operation under the co-ordination of the Cabinet Office. Closer collaboration between bureaus of the same ministry, for example the River bureau and Land Use bureau of the MLIT, should be fostered to achieve more integrated implementation of policies. Certain aspects of central and local government relations could benefit from more developed co-operation. Evaluation of measures taken by separate ministries should be conducted to assess and control their coherence with the national overall strategy for flood risk management within the overall disaster management cycle.

Recommendation 1. The Central Government needs to have a stronger co-ordination role and more effective tools for enforcing implementation of coherent disaster management policies.

2. Co-ordination of actions and strategies between central and local level

Under the Disaster Counter Measure Act, prefectures and municipalities implement local disaster management plans in line with global strategies of the overall national strategy for flood risk management under the leadership of the central government.

Specific laws constitute the legal framework setting-out the responsibilities of central and local levels of government. For example, the Disaster Relief Act tackles the response stage, whereas the River Law deals with river improvement projects, which include the construction of flood protective devices such as dykes or dams.

A system classifying rivers according to their importance determines the level of government administration involved. For medium and small size rivers, flood management is fully the responsibility of local governments, namely prefectures and municipalities.

For Class A rivers, which are considered of national importance due to the high number of people and economic assets at stake, the Ministry of Land, Infrastructure, and Transport (MLIT) is in charge both of developing protection strategies and managing the necessary flood protection measures. Responsibility for implementation of prevention, preparedness and emergency response measures mainly falls to local governments.

Findings

For large-scale floods prevention and management strategies, cooperation between various concerned administrations at central and local levels to implement prevention, preparedness and emergency response should be strengthened. Though the current structure is consistent with the high level of risk in Japan for specific rivers, there is room for more involvement of local governments, river basin committees, stakeholders and interest groups.

Successive development of new laws based on evaluation and integration of past experience has proven to be very successful in improving disaster management policies. At the same time it has led to a somewhat piece-meal and dispersed legislation, which could stand to advance a clearer overview of roles and responsibilities and overall transparency. The density of the legal framework, in conjunction with its high level of economic and technical exigencies, compels the introduction of capacity building for local actors to foster the implementation of disaster management policies. For its part, the central government needs to be given more appropriate tools to evaluate and inspect local policies and offer them feedback and advice.

Opportunities for action

Co-operation between the central government authorities and local governments needs to be strengthened. To this end, the capacity of local government administrations to react to floods needs to be enhanced through designated training and education programs.

In parallel, a system could be introduced through which a designated central administrative body such as the Central Disaster Management Council collects and monitors local experience and schemes for co-ordination, as well as evaluates and analyses local needs and proposals for improvements.

In order to make the National Risk Management Strategy more accessible to local governments and to help them understand their precise roles and responsibilities, a review with the aim of improving transparency and streamlining the current legislation could be considered. The further development and introduction of River Basin committees should also be considered taking into account the success such committees have proven to have in other OECD countries.

Finally, given the possibility that embankments could be damaged by an earthquake, leading to serious flooding of inhabited land areas below sea level, coherent management is needed.

Recommendation 2. There is a need for more integrated flood risk management of river basins supported by local capacity building, a clarification of roles and responsibilities, an increased exchange of information and co-ordination between all sectors and levels of government, and a systematic evaluation and analysis of results by central government authorities.

3. The budget for structural measures

Notwithstanding an observable increase in recovery expenditures over the last ten years due to the increase of extreme flood events, Japan's severe fiscal crisis in the middle of the 1990's led to a decrease of the central budget for flood protection measures. Such fiscal constraints may prove hard to overcome in a persistently tight national budget context, even though climate change may increase the risks for major flood disasters.

Findings

As a consequence of the limited budget and the growing challenge to flood protection generated by climate change, there is a need to set priorities and to search for new funds. Though initial evaluation including cost benefit analyses is already partly used and communicated to the general public before the initiation of a new project, there is a growing need to implement systematically these types of instruments.

In addition, the need to combine non-structural measures together with structural measures should be defined more clearly when a project is initiated, and integrated into the cost-benefit analysis in order for the appropriate budget to be evaluated and allocated.

Opportunities for action

The use of cost-benefit or multi-criteria analysis should be used more systematically in the flood risk management decision-making process and communicated to citizens. This will promote the involvement of each individual citizen during the planning of structural and non structural measures as well as general planning and building development projects. Such elements in risk communication can also form a basis for budgetary allocation or decision making at local government level regarding local taxes. The added value of integrating non-structural measures in development projects or flood risk management projects should also be evaluated.

Recommendation 3. Tools such as multi-criteria studies or cost-benefit analyses are needed to promote communication and dialogue in reaching consensus on the acceptable levels of protection and budgets for flood risk management through both structural and non-structural measures and appropriate budget allocations.

Risk assessment and communication

1. Data collection and information technologies
for early-warning

Responsibility for collecting and monitoring rainfall and water levels falls to the MLIT and the Japan Meteorological Agency (JMA). Flood forecasts are provided to sub-levels of flood disaster management both for the implementation of long-term strategies through flood modelling and for the organisation of emergency response through real-time early-warning.

Special attention is already paid to the likely consequences of climate change through scenario building carried out by the Intergovernmental Panel on Climate Change (IPCC).

Findings

Technologies used by the Japanese Government for both collection and communication of weather and flood forecasting are of very high quality and allow for an efficient early-warning system.

A systematic integration of the increased risk of large-scale floods induced by climate change is already underway for policy setting at the protection level, response level and for early-warning. Still, the process is only in its initial phase and should be brought even more into focus.

Opportunities for action

Collaboration between central policy-makers and scientific experts at a national and international level could be strengthened in order to keep updating information technologies and situation awareness systems in respect to large-scale floods, taking account of the increasing risk for major impacts related to climate change.

With regard to communication of information for the purpose of organising the crisis management system, the opportunity to issue guidelines together with technical data in order to allow for more holistic and efficient cross sector cooperation amongst the different levels of response at the early-warning stage could be considered.

Recommendation 4. Continued efforts should be made to maintain the very high quality of the information technology research, risk assessment, and communication, including means for early warning, to take into account risks of large scale flooding related to climate change.

---

2. Combination of hazard, exposure and vulnerability towards an integrated risk assessment and mapping

---

Hazard assessment is on the right path and has been implemented through hazard maps by many municipalities. On the other hand, vulnerability assessment has been conducted for medium-size events both by local governments and economic stakeholders including public service network companies.

Findings

At the three levels of public administration, there is a lack of vulnerability assessment, both for damage assessment and safety assessment concerning vulnerable groups. Some private companies have decided to leave flood-prone areas and to move to safer zones, when restructuring their plants.

Opportunities for action

Vulnerability assessment should be carried out by local governments to draw up risk maps which combine hazard and vulnerability assessment. Such risk awareness is a good way to promote vulnerability assessment to individuals and economic stakeholders. The real need is to promote vulnerability assessment at the very local and individual level (to each household, building, company, or any stakeholder installed in flood-prone areas), in order to stimulate every decision maker involved to take structural measures to mitigate damage, and initiate non-structural measures such as action plans to reduce damage when large-scale floods occur.

Recommendation 5. Vulnerability assessment needs to be conducted by local government in support of natural hazard evaluation and risk communication with citizens to achieve a more efficient system of flood risk management and damage mitigation through both structural and non-structural measures.

Flood prevention and damage mitigation

1. A strong long-term structural flood defence strategy

In view of the country's high exposure to floods, Japan has worked persistently towards the implementation of structural defences. Attention has been paid particularly to the construction of protective engineering works both for river improvements such as dykes, dams and control basins, and for runoff control to counterbalance increased soil proofing with urbanisation.

Benefits of these structures have become apparent in many cases and have led to a decrease in damages and recovery costs.

Efforts have been promoted recently by the government to integrate flood prevention works in the social and natural environment.

Findings

Long-term goals set up by the government and more specifically the MLIT aim at a protection against 30 to 200-year floods depending on the size of the river and on the assets at stake.

Currently targets fall short of these goals and are likely to be harder to achieve in view of budget restrictions, further construction in urban flood-prone areas and in the context of climate change, the rising number of extreme flood events that could overwhelm the capacity of existing structures.

Adaptation to severe impacts of climate change indicated by the IPCC 4th report, such as sea level rise and severe heavy rainfall, has lead to basic studies and the creation of expert panels. But these findings have not yet been taken into consideration in the current programmes to strengthen structural measures.

Opportunities for action

Work on structural protection measures needs to be continued both for maintenance and construction in order to approach long-term goals. Meanwhile, priorities need to be established. The integration of physical infrastructures into the landscape and into the social environment needs also to be continued and strengthened.

Non-structural measures should be implemented further to reinforce the efficiency of structural works.

Recommendation 6. The highly vulnerable situation in respect to floods and increasing flood risks, not least due to climate change, requires a much higher level of investments in structural protection measures as well as continued comprehensive integration of physical flood defences into the natural and social environment.

2. Further development of mitigation measures

Non-structural measures to mitigate flood damages should continue to be sought through the implementation of measures in land use, city planning and building requirements.

The City Planning Law and local master plans require that flood-prone areas should not, in principle, be considered for new urban development.

Regulations on building standards which take into account natural risks are also provided for in the legal framework.

Findings

Local authorities and stakeholders already seem quite concerned with and involved in damage mitigation activities. There are many instances of vulnerability reduction and damage mitigation measures that are undertaken voluntarily.

On the other hand, people living in areas where protective mega-infrastructures (such as dykes, dams, or super levees) are already in place may be inclined toward a sense of safety that does not correspond to the seriousness of the risks. Lack of awareness and advance mitigation measures in these areas, which are perceived as being secure, could be especially problematic in case of large-scale floods. Therefore, risk communication and non structural mitigation measures should be more focused in such areas. Building standards are fully taken into account for earthquakes, and increasingly also for floods as a growing number of districts are declared possible hazard areas.

Opportunities for action

Risk communication and dialogue with citizens should be encouraged to enhance acceptance of land use restrictions and prescription of building standards.

Reduction of vulnerability could be emphasised by avoiding the utilisation of flood-prone areas for purposes related to vulnerable population groups, and the facilities they use (hospitals, retirement homes etc).

There is scope to raise awareness of the need to mitigate damage from possible large-scale floods.

Recommendation 7. There is an urgent need for efficient non-structural measures to combat flood risks through a more holistic approach to prevention and damage mitigation.

---

3. The particular flood risks related to hazardous activities

---

Floods are likely to spread pollutants and harmful substances. Thus, risks emanating from industrial sites need to be considered with special care.

In Japan, just as in other OECD countries, the location and activities of hazardous industries are carefully regulated. Such regulations include mandatory safety measures, security measures and risk assessment considerations, especially for natural disasters such as earthquakes.

Findings

The definition of industrial zones is subject to a detailed legal framework which supports a cross-sectoral approach and encourages urban planning to take economic and environmental considerations into account.

Still, no particular restrictions are directed toward land-owners in areas subject to large-scale floods when protective devices are considered to already secure the area. Further, mitigation measures towards flood risk reduction for hazardous industries are not systematically promoted.

Opportunities for action

Through active communication on the likely costs of a disaster, the government should enhance the good will of industries toward directives to relocate to areas less exposed to floods.

Industries that can trigger special harm in case of flood accidents, such as chemical and nuclear industries, should be required by law to move to safer areas.

In addition, further use of calamity danger districts based on the Building Standards Act to mitigate the impacts of floods could be encouraged.

Recommendation 8. Regulations applicable to hazardous industrial activities should include requirements for operators to assess and manage risks related to floods

Emergency response

1. Co-ordination during flood events

Emergency response to floods in Japan has to be seen as a part of the Total Disaster Management System, which has been developed through a seamless cycle of prevention, mitigation, preparedness, response, recovery and rehabilitation i.e. protection against floods and river management on the one side and emergency management on the other. The system ensures strong national leadership and multi-sectoral coordination. Operational responsibility for emergency response however falls mainly to municipalities, which are usually the most relevant for undertaking emergency actions. Inter-municipal agreements exist to enhance wider capacity at the local level when needed.

In the event of large-scale floods, the central authorities are responsible for providing situation awareness and decision support. The central government authorities become involved to provide general support and guidance to the local governments, to ensure necessary co-operation and co-ordination and to provide the additional resources required to manage the disaster. An emergency team at the national government level gathers immediately at the Crisis Management Centre to take stock of and analyse the disaster situation. The Cabinet Office ensures the overall co-ordination of disaster reduction activities. Meanwhile, the Cabinet Secretariat provides situation awareness and incident information to the Cabinet, based on the data collected 24 hours a day by the Cabinet Information Collection Centre.

The Red Cross deploys its aid force at its discretion or upon request from the prefecture. The MLIT may launch immediate repairs on protective works through the assistance of private companies or volunteers as needed. Critical public infrastructure providers and essential service utilities have undertaken business continuity planning. Response organisations, including volunteer groups, participate in joint exercises or drills on a regular basis.

Strategies are also developed ahead of time to facilitate emergency response, such as issuing guidelines for business continuity planning, or drills and exercises for volunteer citizens.

OECD REVIEWS OF RISK MANAGEMENT POLICIES – ISBN 978-92-64-05639-8 – © OECD 2009

Findings

The organisation of emergency response in Japan seems to take into consideration the different possible scales of flood disasters and to be well synchronised with other layers of the crisis management cycle which include emergency mitigation and risk assessment.

Local governments are responsible for organising the emergency response. When the damages caused by floods exceed their response capacities, the central government will supply additional support.

In the event of large scale disasters, the Cabinet Office and Cabinet Secretariat are merged into a united body to ensure a higher efficiency.

The shifting of the organisational structure with the size of the disaster event is consistent with the limited local capacities and the need for a broader approach for large-scale floods. On the other hand, it requires a very high level of advance preparation and a clear definition of how the various administrations will interact together to ensure that the shifting between the organisational structures will not provoke confusion. Though the general division of roles and responsibilities defined in the Disaster Countermeasures Basic Act can be considered relevant, clarifications on the legal provisions for interactions between the different levels involved in emergency response is needed. More specifically, the leadership of the national government needs to be made more visible both for local decision makers and for the general public.

The chain of command and the interfaces between the national government level and the local governments thus need to be made clearer to all involved in the crises management system, not least the personnel involved at the local government level. The personnel in the different bodies demonstrated during the interviews a strong commitment to their tasks and an excellent capability in their own area of responsibility. Nevertheless, some administrative bodies appeared to be insufficiently concerned by or involved in other authorities' responsibilities within the Total Disaster Risk Management System in general.

Opportunities for action

Especially in the event of large scale floods, the chain of command and the interfaces between the national government bodies and the local governments need to be clarified. The tools for providing coordination and support to the local governments to increase their capacities could be bolstered and made more transparent.

To reinforce the coordination and consistency of the national leadership in crises, there is also a need for strong preparedness through planning and joint exercises. Crisis communication with citizens and local actors should be enhanced.

A more coherent and transparent system is needed in respect of co-operation, as well as roles and responsibilities of various authorities in the event of a crisis.

Further development of training citizens and volunteers could be strengthened by drills and other educational programs in addition to dissemination of information.

Agreements on flood-fighting activities could be promoted more systematically between municipalities.

Recommendation 9. The emergency chain of command needs to be streamlined, and the roles and responsibilities of organisations involved in emergency response at various levels to be clarified and made transparent.

2. Sheltering and evacuation for large-scale floods

In the event of a flood, information is communicated to citizens on how to evacuate and where to find shelter through the dissemination of hazard maps for each municipality and the use of real-time information techniques at the early warning stage.

Findings

In efforts to organise evacuations, local relief actors use hazard maps to identify water levels, zones of high exposure and vulnerability, and shelters. Flood brigades at the prefectural level and municipal fire and rescue services are involved in the co-ordination of evacuation operations. Cooperation between these entities is not fully achieved and knowledge is usually limited to each competent authority's specific role without an overview of the Total Disaster Management System.

Though emergency response exercises are conducted in advance to raise citizen awareness and their ability to undertake individual evacuation in case of floods, the involvement of citizens is not complete, especially in areas where floods have not been experienced for many years.

Another challenge is linked to large-scale evacuations for which it is difficult to provide appropriate training and preparation.

Opportunities for action

For large-scale evacuations that are likely to involve the deployment of numerous emergency response forces and require co-ordinated action between various administrative bodies and levels of government, there is a need for a stronger cooperation between municipalities and prefectures through the definition of appropriate legal procedures and agreements.

Awareness of local stakeholders with regard to the methods of individual evacuation should also be raised more systematically.

Recommendation 10. There is an urgent need to make adequate provision for sheltering and evacuation of local populations that could be affected by large-scale flood events, including through enhanced cooperation between local governments.

---

3. Emergency response regarding the most vulnerable groups of population

---

Physical, economic and cultural vulnerability may impact on people's ability to react to disasters such as floods.

In addition to increased urbanisation in flood-prone areas, social factors such as ageing of the population and an increasing number of dependent people, change the conditions of emergency response.

Findings

The Flood-fighting Act was amended in 2005 to take more specific account of vulnerable population groups in emergency situations, including during flood events. The new law requires municipalities to confirm information regarding vulnerable people's facilities, such as nursing homes for elderly people, and to set up local disaster prevention plans to provide disaster information.

Maps have been established at the municipal level in order to identify vulnerable people such as the handicapped, the sick, invalids or the elderly and to allow them to be integrated into rescue plans instead of relying only on mutual help. The efficiency and comprehensiveness of these maps, however, may be limited due to the reluctance of some people to communicate their weakness.

Opportunities for action

Co-operation between municipal welfare services and risk management authorities should be enhanced to better consider the needs of vulnerable groups at the response stage.

Recommendation 11. Municipal services in charge of disaster response and health and welfare need to be better prepared to reach out to the most vulnerable groups of the population.

Recovery

---

1. The implementation of optimal reconstruction schemes

With the enactment of the Act on Support for Livelihood Recovery and Disaster Victims in 1998, and the issuing of Business Continuity Guidelines, the Central

Government of Japan has already made an important step towards the definition and implementation of national strategies for recovery measures.

Findings

Current policies do not devote attention to the question of preparedness and need for general guidelines for reconstruction. The complexity of dealing with reconstruction after a natural disaster usually makes it difficult to find an appropriate balance between early reconstruction measures, such as building temporary housing or shelters, and long-term recovery of society as well as undertaking measures to evaluate experiences and learn lessons from the crisis or disaster management. There is a need for better preparedness for speeding up the more general reconstruction and of an appropriate use of the experiences of civil protection personnel to integrate preventative or mitigation measures against floods in the planning and building in reconstruction zones and general development of society.

Opportunities for action

It would be of great use to consider the practical experience of civil protection services regarding successful or inappropriate preventative and mitigation measures for emergency response and standards before reconstruction plans are undertaken in city planning and building standards and general development.

Integrating recovery model plans with city plans before the occurrence of disasters could provide a basis for better-prepared, faster and more far-sighted reconstruction.

Recommendation 12. In order to facilitate reconstruction, agreements need to be reached in advance. After the disaster, the detailed organisation of reconstruction should be discussed between civil protection and planning services.

2. The collection and communication of experiences

Strategies to counteract floods, mitigate damages and organise protection and relief actions have continuously been updated in Japan based on past disasters. Information sharing events have been organised in order to collect lessons learned both at the central and local levels.

Findings

The follow-up of past major disasters and the consequent updating of the legislation have proven very successful in Japan. However, there is a need for a more systematic collection of data and experience, evaluation of experiences from the natural disasters that occur quite frequently in Japan, and a strengthened communication with citizens to enhance the general and individual risk culture. In order to facilitate the understanding of roles and responsibilities and to improve disaster risk management there is a need to review the successively developed legislation and thereby make it more transparent and accessible for citizens.

Opportunities for action

A systematic framework for the collection, analysis and communication of past experiences from floods disasters and lessons learned needs to be introduced and implemented in order to keep on improving existing policies, including risk communication with the public and all other stakeholders. There is also a clear need for reviewing the dispersed legislation related to flood risk management to enhance its transparency and to facilitate the understanding and implementation of the legislation by the competent authorities and decision makers at local government level.

Recommendation 13. Risk management experiences should be systematically collected, evaluated and disseminated widely to all stakeholders to enhance the development of an overall risk culture. In addition, an overall review of successively developed legislation should be conducted to improve transparency.

3. The recovery costs and insurance

Recovery costs are borne by municipalities and prefectures for the most part, although such costs may also be borne by the central government when the extent of damages exceeds local financial resources. An important part of recovery costs are borne by individuals, which highlights the need for an efficient insurance scheme. Floods are usually covered by householders' comprehensive insurance policies.

Findings

Transfers of public funds to flood victims are relatively small in Japan. Indeed, there is no flood reinsurance scheme in which the Japanese government is involved. The Japanese government does not act as a re-insurer, in contrast to many other OECD countries.

Currently, insurance against floods in Japan is handled by the private sector, and is determined by supply and demand. Thus, while in Japan fire insurance is wide-spread, insurance coverage against floods is not considered necessary for areas with low flood risks or for by residents in high-rise apartments. For this reason, the penetration rate of householders' comprehensive insurance remains only around 70% according to estimates by a major Japanese insurance company.

With the recovery costs for losses from floods anticipated to rise due to climate change and further concentration of economic assets in flood-prone areas, the capacity of private insurance companies is expected to be insufficient and this may have a negative impact on financial markets.

Moreover, as Japanese cities go vertical and underground malls develop, accumulated risks increase.

Following the liberalisation of insurance premiums, private insurance companies are responding to requests from clients to extend coverage of flood risks. There is concern that risks will increase due to climate change and to the concentration of assets in urban areas, even in areas which have not been considered risky until now.

Opportunities for action

Because flood losses can be overwhelming, there is an opportunity for the government to become more active in the insurance and reinsurance schemes.

The current Japanese insurance system, which accepts flood risks by depending on foreign private reinsurance markets, is not well prepared for large-scale floods, and the government needs to become more involved through reinsurance or other tools.

Recommendation 14. In order to help citizens and private companies cope with the financial costs of major events, the insurance system regarding floods should be improved, with the aim to increase both the population coverage and the capacity of insurance companies. This could be achieved through a stronger involvement of the national government as reinsurer.

ISBN 978-92-64-05639-8
OECD Reviews of Risk Management Policies
Japan: Large-Scale Floods and Earthquakes
© OECD 2009

Synthèse

Par rapport aux autres pays de l'OCDE, le Japon se trouve dans une situation unique. En raison de sa géographie, de sa topographie et de son climat, il est sujet à de fréquents typhons, à des pluies torrentielles et à de fortes chutes de neige, et connaît depuis longtemps de graves inondations. La moitié environ de la population et trois bons quarts de ses actifs économiques sont concentrés dans des zones sujettes aux inondations, et près de 5.5 millions d'individus vivent dans des zones situées en dessous du niveau de la mer.

Au fil des siècles, le Japon a acquis des compétences spécialisées en gestion des inondations d'un niveau tout à fait extraordinaire. Le pays est connu dans le monde entier pour ses exploits techniques dans le domaine de la construction d'ouvrages anti-inondations – canaux et remblais, bassins de rétention, canaux d'évacuation des crues, barrages, super-digues – et, plus récemment, pour ses stratégies intégrées conjuguant la maîtrise des inondations, l'utilisation de l'eau et la protection environnementale. Le Japon est également un leader mondial du recours à des technologies très avancées en matière d'alerte précoce, de recueil et d'analyse des données, d'évaluation des risques, de communication et de protection des infrastructures critiques. Ainsi, les défenses structurelles du Japon contre les inondations ont considérablement progressé, et ce malgré les nettes réductions des budgets d'investissement de ces dernières années.

Accumulant de plus en plus d'expérience dans la prise en charge des inondations, le pays n'a pas cessé d'adapter et d'actualiser ses lois et règlements sur la base des enseignements tirés des événements, et a modernisé et affiné ses techniques de gestion des inondations. Il a aujourd'hui mis au point un Système total de gestion des catastrophes qui se présente comme un cycle parfaitement continu de prévention, d'atténuation, de préparation, d'intervention, de redressement et de reconstruction, et incite fortement à un commandement national fort et à une coordination multisectorielle, et aide beaucoup le Japon à gérer les inondations de petite et moyenne ampleur qui se produisent fréquemment.

À plusieurs titres, le Japon entre toutefois aujourd'hui dans une nouvelle ère. En effet, dans un contexte de changement climatique, le niveau des mers devrait monter, les régimes de précipitations changer, et les épisodes climatiques extrêmes se faire plus nombreux. Parallèlement, la vulnérabilité du pays aux inondations devrait croître en raison de la densification des zones urbaines sujettes aux inondations et du vieillissement de la population. Ainsi, le Japon doit de plus en plus se préoccuper de la probabilité et des conséquences d'inondations futures de grande ampleur, et de son aptitude à les gérer. Il lui faudra pour cela consentir des investissements plus nombreux et mieux ciblés dans des moyens de défense structurels et des technologies de maîtrise des inondations. Mais le pays devra tout autant se soucier des possibilités d'amélioration des aspects non structurels de la gestion des inondations catastrophiques, à savoir notamment : cohérence des politiques, coordination des différents échelons de l'action publique, transparence de la législation, évaluation des vulnérabilités, organisation et communication durant la phase d'intervention d'urgence, planification et préparation de la phase de redressement.

Une approche intégrée de la gestion des risques d'inondation

1. Une approche intersectorielle de la maîtrise des inondations au niveau central

Le Japon dispose d'un système exhaustif et stratégique de gestion des catastrophes naturelles élaboré dans le *Disaster Countermeasures Basic Act*, qui a été amélioré grâce aux enseignements tirés de différentes catastrophes de grande ampleur. Ce système couvre toutes les phases de la gestion des catastrophes : prévention, atténuation et préparation, intervention d'urgence, redressement et reconstruction. En outre, il tire au clair les rôles et les responsabilités des pouvoirs publics nationaux et locaux et des parties prenantes publiques et privées qui coopèrent à la mise en œuvre des différentes mesures de lutte contre les catastrophes.

La stratégie nationale globale de gestion des risques d'inondation est définie au plus haut niveau sous l'égide combinée du Cabinet, de l'Office du Cabinet et, depuis 2001, du *Central Disaster Management Council*. Ces organes publics collaborent pour mettre au point la stratégie nationale et coordonner les actions et les politiques mises en œuvre de manière concrète par différents ministères et organismes.

Constats

L'implication nécessaire de différents ministères et organismes afin de parvenir à une gestion complète des inondations catastrophiques suppose une coordination et un commandement sans failles. Bien que les autorités centrales contrôlent la mise en œuvre des politiques nationales, le recours à des inspections et des évaluations permettant de passer les stratégies en revue et de surveiller la cohérence et l'efficience des actions décidées dans le cadre du système total de gestion des inondations catastrophiques devrait être plus systématique.

Opportunités d'action

Actuellement, il conviendrait, pour renforcer la coopération coordonnée par l'Office du Cabinet, de distinguer au niveau de l'administration centrale la responsabilité des mesures de protection, celle des mesures de prévention et de préparation, et celle des mesures d'intervention. Il faudrait stimuler une collaboration plus étroite entre les départements d'un même ministère, par exemple ceux des voies navigables et de l'aménagement du territoire du MLIT, afin de mieux intégrer la mise en œuvre des politiques. Certains aspects des relations entre l'échelon central et l'échelon local de la puissance publique tireraient profit d'une coopération accrue. L'évaluation des mesures prises par différents ministères devrait être effectuée afin d'apprécier et de contrôler leur cohérence par rapport à la stratégie nationale globale de gestion des risques d'inondation faisant partie du cycle général de gestion des catastrophes naturelles.

Recommandation 1. Les autorités centrales doivent renforcer leur rôle de coordination et disposer d'outils plus efficaces pour assurer la mise en œuvre de politiques cohérentes de gestion des catastrophes naturelles.

---

*2. Coordination des actions et des stratégies
entre l'échelon central et l'échelon local*

En application du *Disaster Countermeasures Basic Act*, les préfectures et les municipalités mettent en œuvre les plans locaux de gestion des catastrophes sous l'égide de l'autorité centrale conformément aux dispositions générales de la stratégie nationale globale applicable à la gestion des risques d'inondation.

Des lois spécifiques composent le cadre juridique fixant les responsabilités des échelons central et locaux de la puissance publique. Par exemple, le *Disaster Relief Basic Act* s'occupe de la phase d'intervention, tandis que le *River Law* prend en charge les projets d'amélioration des cours d'eau, dont fait partie la construction d'ouvrages anti-inondations tels que des digues ou des barrages.

Un système de classification des cours d'eau selon leur importance détermine l'échelon administratif concerné. La gestion des inondations incombe entièrement aux autorités locales, à savoir les préfectures et les municipalités, lorsqu'il s'agit de cours d'eau de petite ou de moyenne importance.

S'agissant des cours d'eau de classe A, considérés comme d'importance nationale compte tenu de l'ampleur de la population et des actifs économiques en jeu, c'est le ministère du Territoire, des Infrastructures et des

Transports (MLIT) qui est chargé à la fois de l'élaboration des stratégies de protection et de la gestion des mesures nécessaires de protection contre les inondations. La charge de la mise en œuvre des mesures de prévention, de préparation et d'intervention d'urgence incombe aux autorités locales.

Constats

S'agissant des stratégies de prévention et de gestion des inondations de grande ampleur, il conviendrait de renforcer la coopération entre les différents échelons administratifs concernés, centraux et locaux, pour la mise en œuvre des mesures de prévention, de préparation et d'intervention d'urgence. Même si la structure actuelle correspond bien au niveau élevé de risque qui caractérise certains fleuves japonais, une implication accrue des autorités locales, des comités de bassins fluviaux, ainsi que de certaines parties prenantes et certains groupes d'intérêts, reste possible.

Le travail législatif continu fondé sur l'évaluation et l'intégration de l'expérience acquise a beaucoup contribué à améliorer les politiques de gestion des catastrophes. Simultanément, il a suscité une législation quelque peu morcelée et disparate, qui pourrait évoluer vers une plus grande clarté des rôles et des responsabilités et une transparence globale accrue. La densité du cadre juridique, conjuguée à un niveau élevé d'exigences économiques et techniques, impose le renforcement des capacités des acteurs locaux si l'on veut améliorer la mise en œuvre des politiques de gestion des catastrophes. Il convient par ailleurs de fournir aux autorités centrales des outils mieux adaptés à l'évaluation et à l'inspection des politiques locales, et à l'échange de réactions et de conseils.

Opportunités d'action

La coopération entre les autorités centrales et les instances locales doit être renforcée. À cette fin, il convient d'améliorer les capacités de réaction des administrations locales aux inondations par le biais de programmes de formation et d'éducation spécifiques.

En parallèle, on pourrait mettre en place un système par lequel un organe administratif central spécifique tel que le *Central Disaster Management Council* collecterait et suivrait les expériences et les dispositifs locaux en matière de coordination, et évaluerait et analyserait les besoins locaux et les propositions d'améliorations.

On pourrait, pour améliorer l'accès des instances locales à la Stratégie nationale de gestion des risques et les aider à comprendre leurs rôles et leurs responsabilités précis, envisager de conduire un examen visant à améliorer la transparence et à simplifier la législation en vigueur. Il faudrait par ailleurs étudier la possibilité d'instaurer et de développer davantage les comités de bassins fluviaux en prenant en compte leur réussite dans d'autres pays de l'OCDE.

Enfin, compte tenu des dommages que les digues peuvent subir en cas de séisme et, partant, des risques de grave inondation de zones habitées situées en dessous du niveau de la mer, il convient d'assurer une gestion cohérente de ces ouvrages.

Recommandation 2. La nécessité se fait sentir d'une gestion plus intégrée des risques d'inondation des bassins fluviaux grâce à un renforcement des capacités locales, une clarification des rôles et responsabilités, un accroissement des échanges d'informations et de la coordination entre tous les secteurs et tous les niveaux de la puissance publique, et l'évaluation et l'analyse systématiques des résultats par les autorités centrales.

3. Le budget des mesures structurelles

Nonobstant l'augmentation des dépenses de redressement qui a pu être observée ces dix dernières années en raison de la recrudescence d'inondations d'une gravité extrême, la sévère crise budgétaire qu'a connue le Japon au milieu des années 90 a entraîné une baisse du budget central disponible pour les mesures de protection contre les inondations. Ces contraintes pourraient s'avérer difficiles à surmonter dans un contexte budgétaire national qui reste tendu, même si le changement climatique est susceptible d'accroître les risques de catastrophes majeures dues à des inondations.

Constats

En raison des limitations budgétaires et du défi croissant que représente la protection contre les inondations face au changement climatique, il convient de fixer des priorités et de rechercher de nouveaux crédits. Les autorités ont certes déjà partiellement recours à des évaluations initiales comprenant des analyses coûts-avantages, et les communiquent au grand public avant de lancer un nouveau projet ; mais la mise en œuvre systématique d'instruments de ce type est une nécessité croissante.

Il conviendrait en outre de définir plus clairement, au lancement d'un projet, la nécessaire association de mesures non structurelles et structurelles, et de les intégrer à l'analyse coûts-avantages afin d'évaluer et d'allouer le budget adéquat.

Opportunités d'action

Il faudrait avoir plus systématiquement recours aux analyses coûts-avantages ou multicritères dans le processus décisionnel de gestion des risques d'inondation, et les communiquer aux citoyens. Cette systématisation favoriserait l'implication de chaque individu dans le travail de planification des mesures structurelles et non structurelles, ainsi que dans les projets d'aménagement et de construction. De tels éléments de communication sur les risques peuvent aussi servir de socle aux allocations budgétaires ou aux décisions fiscales des autorités locales. Il conviendrait également d'évaluer la valeur ajoutée d'une intégration de mesures non structurelles aux projets de construction ou aux projets de gestion des risques d'inondation.

Recommandation 3. Des outils tels que les études multicritères et les analyses coûts-avantages sont nécessaires si l'on souhaite promouvoir une communication et un dialogue propices à un consensus sur les niveaux acceptables de protection et les budgets de gestion des risques d'inondation au moyen de mesures tant structurelles que non structurelles et d'allocations budgétaires adéquates.

Gestion des risques et communication

1. Alerte avancée : collecte des données et technologies de l'information

Ce sont le MLIT et la JMA (Agence météorologique du Japon) qui sont chargés de recueillir et de suivre les niveaux des précipitations et des eaux. Les prévisions d'inondations sont fournies aux échelons inférieurs de la gestion des catastrophes pour leur permettre à la fois de mettre en œuvre des stratégies de long terme à travers une modélisation des inondations et d'organiser des interventions d'urgence grâce à des alertes précoces en temps réel.

Une attention spéciale est déjà portée aux conséquences probables du changement climatique au travers de l'élaboration de scénarii par le GIEC (Groupe d'experts intergouvernemental sur l'évolution du climat).

Constats

Les technologies utilisées par le gouvernement japonais pour collecter et communiquer les prévisions météorologiques et d'inondations sont de très haute qualité et ouvrent la voie à un système efficient d'alerte avancée.

L'intégration systématique du risque accru d'inondations de grande ampleur provoquées par le changement climatique aux politiques est déjà en cours au niveau de la protection, des interventions et de l'alerte avancée. Encore dans sa phase initiale, le processus devrait cependant bénéficier d'une attention encore plus grande.

Opportunités d'action

La collaboration entre les responsables centraux des politiques et les experts scientifiques nationaux et internationaux pourrait être renforcée afin de poursuivre la mise à jour des systèmes informatiques et des dispositifs de sensibilisation aux situations d'inondation de grande ampleur, en prenant en compte le risque accru de répercussions majeures liées au changement climatique.

S'agissant de la communication d'informations visant à organiser le dispositif de gestion de crise, on pourrait étudier la possibilité d'émettre des lignes directrices assorties de données techniques afin de permettre, au stade de l'alerte avancée, une coopération intersectorielle plus complète et efficiente entre les différents niveaux d'intervention.

Recommandation 4. Il convient de poursuivre les efforts visant à maintenir la qualité très élevée de la recherche informatique, de l'évaluation des risques et de la communication – moyens d'alerte avancée compris – afin de prendre en compte les risques d'inondations de grande ampleur liés au changement climatique.

---

*2. Conjuguer aléas, exposition et vulnérabilité
pour évaluer et cartographier les risques
de manière intégrée*

L'évaluation des aléas est menée comme il convient et prend la forme de cartes d'aléas établies par de nombreuses municipalités. D'un autre côté, l'évaluation de la vulnérabilité a été conduite pour des événements d'ampleur moyenne à la fois par des instances locales et des acteurs économiques tels que des exploitants de réseaux de services publics.

Constats

On note aux trois niveaux des administrations publiques une insuffisance d'évaluation de la vulnérabilité, tant du point de vue de l'appréciation des dommages que de celle de la sûreté des groupes vulnérables. Au moment de restructurer leurs usines, certaines entreprises privées ont décidé de quitter des zones sujettes aux inondations au profit de zones plus sûres.

Opportunités d'action

L'évaluation de la vulnérabilité devrait être menée par les instances locales afin de tracer des cartes des risques conjuguant aléas et vulnérabilité. Ce type de sensibilisation aux risques est une bonne manière de promouvoir l'évaluation de la vulnérabilité auprès des individus et des parties prenantes économiques. La mise en avant de l'évaluation de la vulnérabilité à un niveau très local et individuel (pour chaque foyer, bâtiment, entreprise ou partie prenante des zones sujettes aux inondations) est tout à fait nécessaire, afin d'inciter tous les décideurs concernés à prendre des mesures structurelles susceptibles d'atténuer les dommages, et, lorsque des inondations de grande ampleur se produisent, lancer des mesures non structurelles visant, à l'instar de plans d'action, à diminuer les dommages.

Recommandation 5. Les échelons locaux doivent mener des évaluations de la vulnérabilité à l'appui de celle des aléas naturels et du travail de communication sur les risques effectué auprès des citoyens, afin d'aboutir à un dispositif plus efficient de gestion des risques d'inondation et d'atténuation des dommages au moyen de mesures tant structurelles que non structurelles.

Prévention des inondations et atténuation des dommages

1. Une solide stratégie de défense structurelle à long terme contre les inondations

Compte tenu de sa forte exposition aux inondations, le Japon n'a pas cessé de créer des défenses structurelles. Il a prêté une attention particulière à la construction d'ouvrages protecteurs visant à la fois à améliorer les cours d'eau (digues, barrages et bassins de rétention) et à maîtriser les débordements de façon à contrebalancer l'imperméabilisation croissante des sols liée à l'urbanisation.

Les avantages de ces structures se sont manifestés dans de nombreux cas et ont suscité un recul des dommages et des coûts de remise en état.

Récemment, les autorités ont mis en exergue des efforts visant à intégrer les travaux de prévention des inondations à l'environnement social et naturel.

Constats

Les objectifs à long terme fixés par les pouvoirs publics et plus particulièrement par le MLIT sont d'assurer une protection contre 30 à 200 inondations par an, selon la taille des cours d'eau et les actifs en jeu.

Actuellement, ces objectifs ne sont pas remplis et devraient être de plus en plus difficiles à satisfaire compte tenu des restrictions budgétaires, de l'apparition de constructions nouvelles dans les zones urbaines sujettes aux inondations et, dans le contexte du changement climatique, du nombre croissant d'inondations extrêmes qui pourraient saturer la capacité des structures existantes.

L'adaptation aux graves impacts du changement climatique mentionnés par le 4e rapport du GIEC (montée du niveau des mers et pluies particulièrement fortes) a entraîné la réalisation d'études de base et l'instauration de groupes d'experts. Mais ces éléments n'ont pas encore été pris en considération dans les programmes actuels pour renforcer les mesures structurelles.

Opportunités d'action

Il convient, afin de progresser en direction des objectifs de long terme, de poursuivre les efforts relatifs aux mesures de protection structurelle tant du point de vue de la maintenance que de la construction. Dans l'intervalle, il faut fixer des priorités. L'intégration d'infrastructures physiques à l'environnement naturel et social doit également être poursuivie et renforcée.

Il faudrait mettre en œuvre de nouvelles mesures non structurelles afin de renforcer l'efficience des ouvrages structurels.

Recommandation 6. La situation de forte vulnérabilité aux inondations et aux risques accrus d'inondation, en particulier du fait du changement climatique, nécessite un niveau bien plus élevé d'investissement dans des mesures de protection structurelle, ainsi que la poursuite de l'intégration complète des défenses matérielles contre les inondations à l'environnement naturel et social.

---

2. Poursuite de l'élaboration de mesures d'atténuation

Il convient de continuer à rechercher l'atténuation non structurelle des dommages dus aux inondations par la mise en œuvre de mesures d'aménagement du territoire, d'urbanisme et de réglementation de la construction.

Les textes d'urbanisme et les plans locaux d'occupation des sols interdisent, en principe, tout nouvel aménagement urbain dans les zones sujettes aux inondations.

Le cadre juridique prévoit par ailleurs des réglementations qui fixent des normes de construction prenant en compte les risques naturels.

Constats

Les autorités locales et les parties prenantes semblent déjà tout à fait investies et impliquées dans des activités de limitation des dommages. On rencontre de nombreux exemples de mesures de réduction de la vulnérabilité et d'atténuation des dommages mises en œuvre de manière spontanée.

D'un autre côté, la population des zones dans lesquelles de très grandes infrastructures de protection (digues, barrages ou remblais) sont déjà en place peut éprouver un sentiment de sécurité qui ne correspond pas à la gravité des risques. Dans ces zones perçues comme sûres, ces carences au niveau de la sensibilisation et des mesures préventives d'atténuation pourraient s'avérer particulièrement problématiques en cas d'inondation de grande ampleur. Il faudrait donc axer davantage la communication portant sur les risques et les mesures d'atténuation non structurelles sur ces zones. Les normes de construction sont parfaitement prises en compte pour les séismes, mais également de plus en plus pour les inondations, car un nombre croissant de districts entrent dans la liste des zones potentielles d'aléas.

Opportunités d'action

Il convient d'encourager la communication portant sur les risques et le dialogue avec les citoyens pour renforcer l'adhésion de ces dernières aux restrictions foncières et la prescription de normes de construction.

La réduction de la vulnérabilité pourrait être mise en avant en évitant l'emploi de zones sujettes aux inondations pour tout objectif concernant des catégories vulnérables de la population, ainsi que les installations qu'elles utilisent (hôpitaux, maisons de retraite, etc.).

Il est enfin possible de sensibiliser la population à la nécessité d'atténuer les dommages imputables à de possibles inondations de grande ampleur.

Recommandation 7. Il faut de manière urgente mettre en place des mesures non structurelles efficientes de lutte contre les risques d'inondation à travers une approche de prévention et d'atténuation des dommages plus complète.

3. Risques particuliers liés aux activités dangereuses en cas d'inondation

Les inondations sont susceptibles de répandre des polluants et des substances dangereuses. Il convient donc d'envisager avec un soin tout particulier les risques posés par les sites industriels.

Au Japon, tout comme dans d'autres pays de l'OCDE, l'emplacement et les activités des industries dangereuses sont soigneusement réglementés. La réglementation prévoit des mesures obligatoires de sûreté, des mesures de sécurité et une évaluation des risques, notamment pour les catastrophes naturelles telles que les séismes.

Constats

La définition des zones industrielles s'inscrit dans un cadre juridique détaillé qui soutient une approche intersectorielle et incite les urbanistes à prendre en compte des considérations économiques et environnementales.

Pourtant, aucune restriction particulière ne vise les propriétaires de terrains situés dans des zones sujettes à des inondations de grande ampleur que l'on estime sécurisées par des ouvrages de protection. En outre, les mesures d'atténuation des risques que présentent les inondations pour les industries dangereuses ne sont pas systématiquement mises en avant.

Opportunités d'action

Grâce à une communication sur les coûts probables d'une catastrophe, les autorités devraient renforcer la bonne volonté des industriels à l'égard des directives de déplacement de leurs activités dans des zones moins exposées aux inondations.

La loi devrait contraindre les activités susceptibles de causer des dommages particulièrement importants en cas d'inondation (industries chimiques et nucléaires, par exemple) à déménager dans des zones plus sûres.

En outre, il conviendrait, pour atténuer les conséquences des inondations, d'encourager un recours accru à la notion de district présentant des dangers extrêmes prévue dans le *Building Standards Act*.

Recommandation 8. La réglementation applicable aux activités industrielles dangereuses devrait comporter pour les exploitants l'obligation d'évaluer et de gérer les risques liés aux inondations.

Interventions d'urgence

1. Coordination en cas d'inondation

Au Japon, les interventions d'urgence en cas d'inondation doivent être considérées comme un volet du Système global de gestion des catastrophes, qui représente un cycle parfaitement continu de prévention, d'atténuation, de préparation, d'intervention, de redressement et de reconstruction, assurant d'un côté la protection contre les inondations et la gestion des cours d'eau, et de l'autre la gestion des urgences. Ce dispositif garantit un commandement national fort et une coordination multisectorielle. La responsabilité opérationnelle des opérations d'urgence, toutefois, incombe principalement aux municipalités, qui sont habituellement les mieux à même de les mener. Des accords intercommunaux permettent de renforcer les capacités locales en cas de besoin.

Lorsque se produisent des inondations de grande ampleur, les autorités centrales sont chargées d'informer sur la situation et d'aider à la prise de décisions. Elles apportent un soutien général et des conseils aux autorités locales afin d'assurer la coopération et la coordination nécessaires et de fournir les ressources complémentaires utiles pour gérer la catastrophe. Elles réunissent immédiatement une équipe d'urgence au Centre de gestion de crise pour apprécier et analyser la situation. L'Office du Cabinet assure la coordination globale des activités de lutte contre la catastrophe et ses effets. Dans l'intervalle, le Secrétariat du Cabinet fournit à celui-ci des informations sur la situation et les incidents sur la base de données recueillies 24 heures sur 24 par le Centre de collecte d'informations du Cabinet.

La Croix Rouge déploie ses moyens d'assistance de son propre chef ou sur demande de la préfecture. Le MLIT peut mettre en chantier des réparations immédiates des ouvrages de protection, avec l'aide le cas échéant d'entreprises privées ou de volontaires. Les fournisseurs d'infrastructures publiques essentielles et les principales entreprises de services publics ont mis en place des dispositifs visant à assurer la continuité de l'exploitation. Des structures d'intervention – dont des groupes de volontaires – participent de manière régulière à des exercices conjoints d'entraînement.

Par ailleurs, des stratégies sont élaborées par avance afin de faciliter les interventions d'urgence : ont ainsi été publiées des lignes directrices utiles pour la continuité opérationnelle, ou des exercices d'entraînement de citoyens volontaires.

Constats

L'organisation des interventions d'urgence semble au Japon prendre en considération les différentes ampleurs possibles des inondations catastrophiques et paraît bien synchronisée avec les autres volets du cycle de gestion des crises, y compris ceux de l'atténuation d'urgence des conséquences et de l'évaluation des risques.

Les autorités locales sont chargées d'organiser les interventions d'urgence. Lorsque les dommages provoqués par les inondations dépassent leurs capacités d'intervention, les autorités centrales viennent à leur rescousse.

Dans le cas de catastrophes de grande ampleur, l'Office du Cabinet et le Secrétariat du Cabinet fusionnent en un organe unique afin de gagner en efficience.

L'ajustement de la structure organisationnelle à l'ampleur de la catastrophe est cohérente avec les limites des capacités locales et la nécessité d'une approche plus globale des inondations importantes. D'un autre côté, il nécessite un degré très élevé de préparation en amont et une définition claire de la manière dont les différentes administrations interagiront, afin d'éviter toute confusion due aux transferts de responsabilités entre les différentes structures. Bien que l'on puisse considérer comme pertinente la répartition générale des rôles et des responsabilités définie dans le *Disaster Countermeasures Basic Act*, il conviendrait de préciser les dispositions juridiques s'appliquant aux interactions entre les différents niveaux impliqués dans les interventions d'urgence. Il faut en particulier affirmer le commandement des autorités nationales au niveau tant des décideurs locaux que du grand public.

La chaîne de commandement et les interfaces entre l'échelon national et les autorités locales doivent donc être précisées à l'intention de tous ceux qui sont impliqués dans le système de gestion des crises, et notamment du personnel concerné au niveau local. Durant les entretiens, le personnel des différents organismes a fait montre d'une détermination sans faille à l'égard de ses tâches et de capacités de très bon niveau dans ses domaines de responsabilité. Néanmoins, certains organes administratifs ont paru insuffisamment concernés par les responsabilités d'autres autorités du Système global de gestion des catastrophes.

Opportunités d'action

Dans le cas en particulier des inondations de grande ampleur, il convient de clarifier la chaîne de commandement et les interfaces existant entre les organismes nationaux et les autorités locales. Les outils de coordination et d'appui visant à renforcer les capacités de ces dernières pourraient être mis en avant et rendus plus transparents.

Afin d'accroître la coordination et la cohérence du commandement national en cas de crise, il conviendrait également d'assurer une solide préparation au moyen d'activités de planification et d'exercices conjoints. La communication de crise visant les citoyens locaux doit être renforcée.

Un système plus cohérent et transparent s'avère nécessaire dans le domaine de la coopération, mais aussi dans celui des rôles et des responsabilités des différentes autorités en cas de crise.

Une formation plus approfondie des citoyens et des volontaires pourrait être renforcée par des exercices et d'autres programmes de formation venant s'ajouter au travail d'information.

Il serait possible de promouvoir de manière plus systématique des accords intercommunaux portant sur les activités de lutte contre les inondations.

Recommandation 9. La chaîne de commandement des interventions d'urgence doit être simplifiée et les rôles et les responsabilités des organismes concernés à différents niveaux par ces interventions doivent devenir plus clairs et transparents.

2. Mise sous abri et évacuation en cas d'inondation de grande ampleur

En cas d'inondation, des informations sont fournies aux citoyens sur la manière d'évacuer et de se rendre dans des abris grâce à la diffusion de cartes d'aléas dans chaque municipalité et l'emploi de techniques d'information en temps réel au stade de l'alerte avancée.

Constats

Soucieux d'organiser les évacuations, les acteurs locaux des secours ont recours à des cartes d'aléas pour préciser le niveau des eaux, les zones de forte exposition et de vulnérabilité, et les abris à rejoindre. Des brigades chargées des inondations au niveau préfectoral et les services municipaux d'incendie et de secours sont impliqués dans la coordination des opérations d'évacuation. La coopération entre ces entités n'est pas complète et les connaissances de chacune d'elles se limitent en général au rôle spécifique de l'autorité compétente, sans vision globale du Système général de gestion des catastrophes.

Malgré la conduite en amont d'exercices d'intervention d'urgence destinés à sensibiliser les citoyens et à renforcer leur capacité d'évacuation en cas d'inondation, l'implication de la population n'est pas parfaite, notamment dans les zones qui n'ont pas connu d'inondations depuis de nombreuses années.

Les évacuations à grande échelle pour lesquelles il est difficile d'assurer une formation et une préparation adéquates constituent un autre défi.

Opportunités d'action

S'agissant des évacuations à grande échelle qui ont toutes les chances de requérir le déploiement de forces d'intervention d'urgence nombreuses ainsi qu'une action coordonnée entre les divers organes et niveaux administratifs, on constate un besoin de renforcement de la coopération entre les municipalités et les préfectures qui passe par la définition de procédures juridiques et d'accords adéquats.

La sensibilisation des parties prenantes locales aux méthodes d'évacuation individuelles devrait également faire l'objet d'un renforcement plus systématique.

Recommandation 10. Le besoin est urgent de prévoir de manière appropriée la mise sous abri et l'évacuation des populations locales susceptibles d'être touchées par des inondations de grande ampleur, y compris au travers d'une coopération renforcée entre les organes locaux.

3. Interventions d'urgence concernant les catégories de la population les plus vulnérables

La vulnérabilité physique, économique et culturelle peut peser sur la capacité de réaction des individus à des catastrophes naturelles telles que les inondations.

Outre l'urbanisation accrue dans les zones sujettes aux inondations, des facteurs sociaux tels que le vieillissement de la population et le nombre croissant de personnes dépendantes peuvent modifier les conditions des interventions d'urgence.

Constats

Le Flood-fighting Act a été modifié en 2005 afin de prendre en compte de façon plus précise les catégories vulnérables de la population dans les situations d'urgence, y compris en cas d'inondation. La nouvelle législation impose aux municipalités de confirmer les informations relatives aux installations où vivent les personnes vulnérables, telles que les maisons d'accueil des personnes âgées, et de mettre en place des plans locaux de prévention des catastrophes susceptibles de fournir des informations sur ces dernières.

Des cartes ont été établies au niveau municipal pour recenser les personnes vulnérables (handicapés, malades, invalides ou personnes âgées) et leur permettre d'être intégrées à des plans de secours au lieu de ne devoir compter que sur une assistance mutuelle. L'efficience et l'exhaustivité de ces cartes peuvent toutefois pâtir de la réticence de certains à faire part de leur état de faiblesse.

Opportunités d'action

Il convient de renforcer la coopération entre les services municipaux de secours et les autorités chargées de la gestion des risques afin de mieux prendre en compte les besoins des catégories vulnérables au stade de l'intervention d'urgence.

Recommandation 11. Les services municipaux en charge des interventions en cas de catastrophe et des questions de santé et de bien-être doivent être mieux préparés à desservir les catégories les plus vulnérables de la population.

Opérations de redressement

1. Mise en œuvre de dispositifs optimaux de reconstruction

Avec la promulgation en 1998 de la loi sur le soutien au rétablissement des moyens de subsistance et aux victimes de catastrophes, et la publication de lignes directrices pour la continuité opérationnelle, le gouvernement du Japon a déjà fait un pas important vers la définition et la mise en œuvre de stratégies nationales dans les domaines des mesures de redressement.

Constats

Les politiques actuelles n'accordent pas assez d'attention à la question de la préparation et à la nécessité d'instaurer des lignes directrices générales pour la reconstruction. La complexité de cette dernière après la survenue d'une catastrophe naturelle, alourdit en général la tâche consistant à trouver un équilibre adéquat entre les premières mesures de reconstruction (logements, abris temporaires) et le redressement à long terme de la société, ainsi que la mise en œuvre de mesures permettant d'évaluer les expériences et de tirer des enseignements de la gestion de crise ou de catastrophe. Il faudrait mieux se préparer, afin d'accélérer la reconstruction en général, mais aussi utiliser à bon escient l'expérience acquise par la protection civile pour intégrer des mesures de prévention ou d'atténuation des inondations à l'aménagement des zones de reconstruction, ainsi qu'au développement sociétal général.

Opportunités d'action

Avant de mettre en œuvre des plans de reconstruction au niveau de l'urbanisme, des normes du bâtiment et de l'aménagement du territoire en général, il serait très utile de prendre en compte l'expérience pratique qu'ont les services de la protection civile des mesures de prévention et d'atténuation utiles ou au contraire inadéquates en matière d'intervention d'urgence et de normes.

L'intégration de plans types de redressement aux plans d'urbains avant même la survenue des catastrophes pourrait fournir les bases d'une reconstruction mieux préparée, plus rapide et prenant mieux en compte le long terme.

Recommandation 12. Afin de faciliter la reconstruction, il convient de nouer des accords à l'avance. Après la catastrophe, la protection civile et les services d'urbanisme et d'aménagement doivent débattre de l'organisation détaillée de la reconstruction.

2. Recueil et communication des expériences

Au Japon, les stratégies de lutte contre les inondations, d'atténuation des dommages et d'organisation de la protection et des secours ont été sans cesse actualisées sur la base des catastrophes survenues. Des réunions visant à partager les informations ont été organisées afin de collecter les enseignements tirés aux niveaux tant central que local.

Constats

Le suivi des grandes catastrophes passées et l'actualisation consécutive de la législation sont au Japon de grandes réussites. Néanmoins, il conviendrait de recueillir de manière plus systématique les données et les expériences, d'évaluer les expériences de catastrophes naturelles qui surviennent très fréquemment dans le pays, et de renforcer la communication avec les citoyens afin de développer une culture générale et individuelle du risque. Il faudrait, pour faciliter l'appréhension des rôles et des responsabilités et améliorer la gestion des risques dus aux catastrophes, passer en revue la législation modifiée par ajouts successifs et, ainsi, la rendre plus transparente et accessible pour les citoyens.

Opportunités d'action

Il faut instaurer et mettre en œuvre un cadre systématique de recueil, d'analyse et de communication de l'expérience acquise des inondations catastrophiques et des enseignements qui ont pu en être tirés, afin de continuer à améliorer les politiques en vigueur, y compris en matière de communication sur les risques avec le public et toutes les autres parties prenantes. À l'évidence, il faudrait également revoir la législation quelque peu morcelée qui régit la gestion des risques d'inondation, afin de renforcer sa transparence et de faciliter sa compréhension et sa mise en œuvre par les autorités compétentes et les décideurs locaux.

Recommandation 13. Il convient de collecter, d'évaluer et de diffuser largement les expériences de gestion du risque, de manière systématique et à toutes les parties prenantes, dans le but de renforcer le développement d'une culture générale du risque. En outre, il faudrait procéder à une étude globale d'une législation quelque peu morcelée et établie par ajouts successifs afin d'en améliorer la transparence.

---

3. Coûts de redressement et assurance

Les coûts de redressement sont en majorité supportés par les municipalités et les préfectures, bien qu'ils puissent aussi incomber aux autorités centrales lorsque l'ampleur des dommages excède les ressources financières locales. Une part importante de ces coûts est assumée par les personnes physiques, ce qui met en lumière la nécessité d'un dispositif assurantiel efficient. En général, les inondations sont couvertes par l'assurance multirisques habitation.

Constats

Au Japon, les transferts de fonds publics au profit de victimes d'inondations sont relativement réduits. De fait, il n'existe pas de dispositif de réassurance en cas d'inondation dans lequel le gouvernement japonais soit impliqué. À la différence de la règle en vigueur dans de nombreux autres pays de l'OCDE, l'État japonais ne joue pas le rôle de réassureur.

Actuellement, l'assurance contre les inondations est gérée au Japon par le secteur privé, et soumise aux lois de l'offre et de la demande. Ainsi, alors que l'assurance incendie est très répandue dans le pays, la prise en charge assurantielle des inondations n'est pas considérée comme une nécessité dans les zones où les risques d'inondation sont faibles ou pour les habitants d'étages élevés. C'est pourquoi, selon les estimations d'une grande compagnie japonaise, le taux de pénétration de l'assurance multirisques habitation reste voisin de 70 % seulement.

Compte tenu de la hausse attendue du coût de la prise en charge des dommages dus aux inondations que devraient provoquer le changement climatique et la concentration accrue des actifs économiques dans des zones sujettes aux inondations, on s'attend à ce que la capacité des compagnies d'assurance privées soit insuffisante, ce qui pourrait avoir un impact négatif sur les marchés de capitaux.

En outre, les risques cumulés s'accroissent au fil de la verticalisation des villes japonaises et de l'essor des centres commerciaux souterrains.

À la suite de la libéralisation des primes d'assurance, les compagnies d'assurance privées répondent à la demande de clients désireux d'étendre la prise en charge aux risques d'inondation. D'aucuns s'inquiètent d'un éventuel accroissement de ces risques en raison du changement climatique et de la concentration des actifs dans les zones urbaines, y compris dans des lieux qui, jusqu'ici, n'avaient pas été considérés comme à risque.

Opportunités d'action

Le caractère potentiellement colossal des dommages dus aux inondations donne l'occasion aux autorités centrales de s'impliquer davantage dans les dispositifs d'assurance et de réassurance.

Le système d'assurance actuel du Japon, qui prend en charge les risques d'inondation en s'appuyant sur les marchés étrangers de la réassurance privée, n'est pas bien préparé aux inondations de grande ampleur, et le gouvernement doit s'impliquer davantage par le biais de la réassurance ou d'autres outils.

Recommandation 14. Afin d'aider les citoyens et les entreprises privées à faire face au coût financier des grandes catastrophes, le système d'assurance applicable aux inondations devrait être amélioré, dans le but d'accroître à la fois la couverture des risques pour la population et la capacité de prise en charge des compagnies d'assurance. Ces progrès pourraient consister à renforcer le rôle de réassureur de l'État.

ISBN 978-92-64-05639-8
OECD Reviews of Risk Management Policies
Japan: Large-Scale Floods and Earthquakes
© OECD 2009

Chapter 1

Introduction – Flood Risks in Japan

1. Facing flood disaster risks in Japan

The geographical, topographical and meteorological conditions of Japan subject the country to frequent natural disasters such as typhoons, torrential rains and heavy snow. These conditions require a high capacity for emergency and disaster management. Japan's history of floods has left thousands of people dead and triggered extensive damages to property and the national economy.

Although Japan has worked continuously towards the implementation of disaster management systems, there is scope for further improvement, especially in view of evolving challenges such as the increased risk of exposure due to climate change, densification of urban areas protected by flood defences, and an ageing population.

2. Land use conditions and occupation of flood-prone areas

Japan's national territory covers approximately 378 000 km^2, 70% of which is mountainous and uninhabitable. This means that the land which can be used for exploitation and living space by the country's more than 120 million inhabitants is very restricted.

In fact about half of the population and 75% of the assets in Japan are concentrated in flood-prone areas and 5.4 million people live in areas below sea level. The assets in areas below sea level are concentrated around Japan's three largest bays, Tokyo, Osaka and Nagoya.[1] The population living in flood-prone areas is much higher than in the United Kingdom and the United States.

The 173 km long Arakawa River, which flows through an area inhabited by 10 million people in Saitama Prefecture and Tokyo, provides a good example of the extremely high concentration of people and assets in Japan. Approximately 1.4 million inhabitants in this area live in flood-prone areas below sea level at high tide. The value of assets located in this river basin and downstream is approximately JPY 100 trillion (20% of Japan's GNP).[2] A continued increase in exploitation and urbanisation, as well as more intensive use of vulnerable urban structures such as underground transport, aggravate the situation. A comparison between the flood-prone areas in Tokyo and London illustrates the present situation.

Figure 1.1. **Percentage of the population living in flood-prone areas in Japan compared to the United Kingdom and the United States**

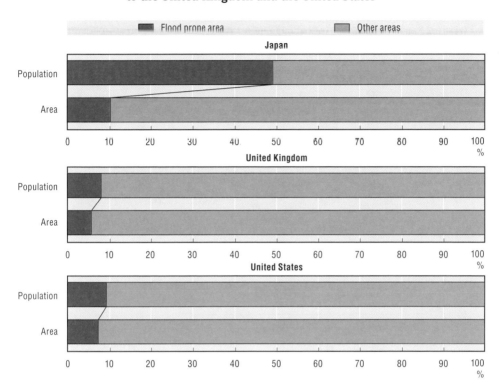

Source: Japanese Ministry of Land, Infrastructure and Transport (MLIT), May 2007, Power Point Presentation, "Existing Conditions and Tasks of River Administration in terms of Flood Control".

3. Climatic changes and river characteristics

Japan has a temperate climate, with three periods of heavy precipitations. Floods are frequent events occurring primarily during the rainy season in June and July, or when typhoons hit the country in the late summer and autumn.

In the last thirty years, rainfall recordings above 50 mm per hour have increased by about 50% and those exceeding 100 mm have increased more than doubled.

There has been an observable decrease in the annual rainfall in Japan over the last century, while at the same time the range of variation between light rains and heavy rains has increased, trends that can be considered in the overall context of climate change.

Moreover, despite a lack of consensus on the exact extent of global warming, a rise in sea level is likely to occur, placing greater pressure on Japan's coastal areas.

Figure 1.2. **Tokyo and London flood-prone areas**

These conditions leave Japan very vulnerable to flood disasters.

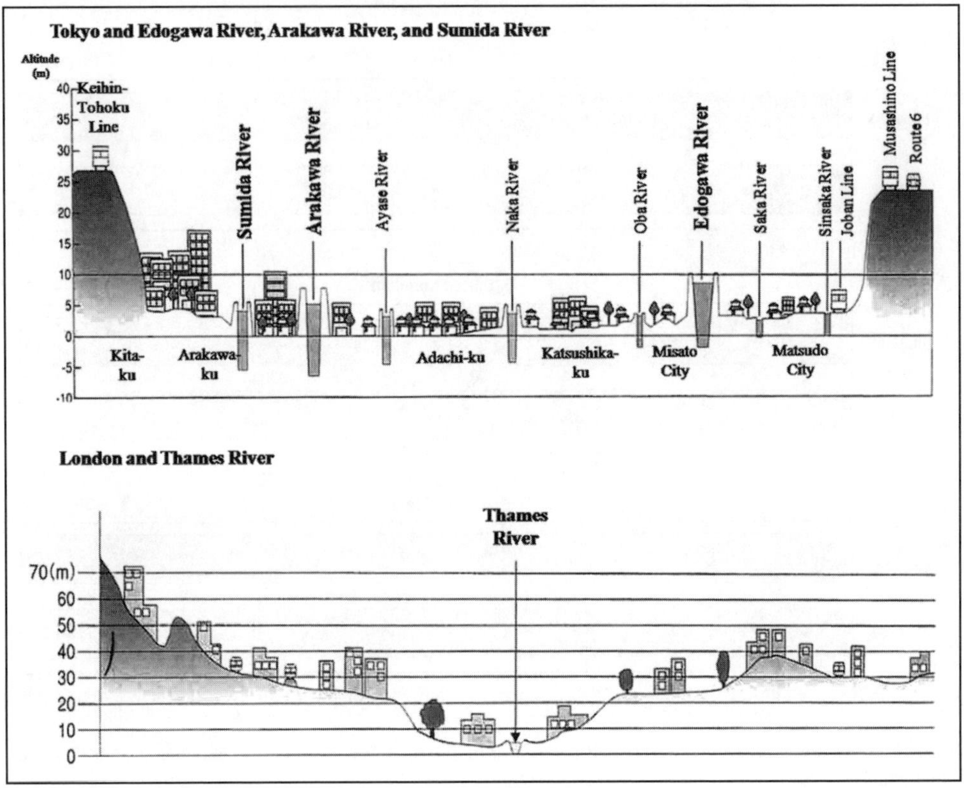

Source: MLIT, May 2007, Power Point Presentation, "Existing Conditions and Tasks of River Administration in terms of Flood Control".

A sea level rise of 60 cm in 100 years, as forecast in the worst case scenario calculated by the Inter-governmental Panel on Climate Change (IPCC), would result in a 50% increase of inhabited land area below sea level (located along three major bays: Tokyo, Nagoya and Osaka). In this case Japan would face drastically increased vulnerability to storm surges.

A recent cross country analysis of port cities estimated exposure to coastal flooding due to storm surges and damage due to high winds (OECD, 2008). Its analysis focuses on the exposure of population and assets to a 1 in 100 year surge-induced flood event, although it does not address the statistical risk of flooding. According to the report, Osaka-Kobe figures among the top 10 world port cities in terms of exposed population; Osaka-Kobe and Tokyo both figure among the top 10 world port cities in terms of assets exposed; and both Tokyo and Osaka figure among the top 10 most exposed to wind damage from

Figure 1.3. **Increasing torrential rain**

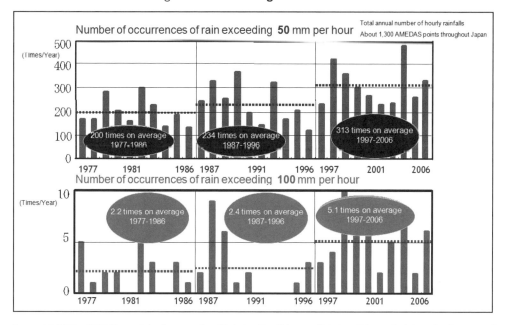

Source: MLIT, May 2007, Power Point Presentation, "Existing Conditions and Tasks of River Administration in terms of Flood Control".

tropical and extra tropical cyclones, with Tokyo at the top of the list in terms of wind damage index. Among other cities in the study, only a few in the United States and China come close to such combined risk exposures.

Japan proves to be a unique case in terms of its topographical and hydrological characteristics that can give rise to severe flood conditions. Its rivers are short and steep upstream, flowing rapidly and violently from mountain to sea (see Figure 1.4).

Moreover, the ratio between the normal volume of flow and that during a storm is extreme. A striking example is the Tone River, which has a maximum discharge of about one hundred times the minimum discharge. By comparison, this ratio is roughly thirty to one for the Mekong, four to one for the Danube and three to one for the Mississippi (see Figure 1.5).

4. Experiences of floods

Due to land and climate conditions, Japan has on many occasions and in many parts of the country experienced serious flood damage. Ten typhoons struck in 2004 causing damage throughout the country, the largest number in a single year on record.[3] In 1947 Typhoon Katherine caused a dyke of the Tone River to break and left 1 930 persons dead or missing in Tokyo. Only 12 years

Figure 1.4. **Increasing fluctuation of annual precipitation**

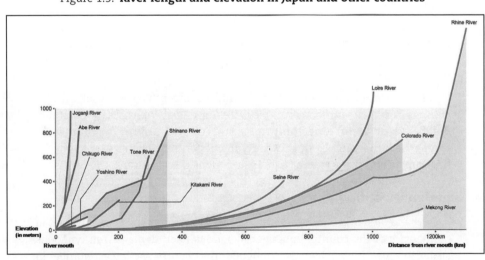

Source: MLIT, May 2007, Power Point Presentation, "Existing Conditions and Tasks of River Administration in terms of Flood Control".

Figure 1.5. **River length and elevation in Japan and other countries**

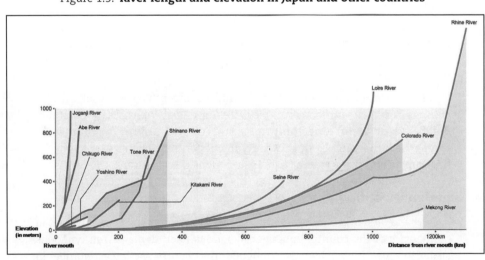

Source: MLIT, River Bureau, September 2006, "Rivers in Japan".

Figure 1.6. **Ratio of flood duration per unit area of catchment discharge**

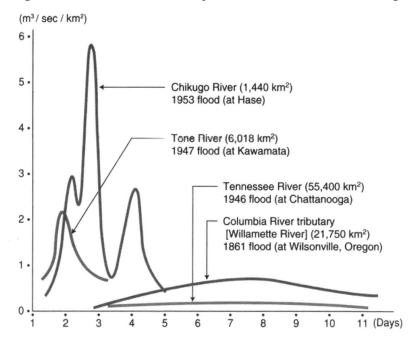

Source: MLIT, River Bureau, September 2006, "Rivers in Japan".

later, in 1959, the worst floods in Japan's modern history occurred with Typhoon Ise-Wan causing more than 5 000 fatalities.[4]

5. Cost of floods

In the last few years there have been several major floods related to typhoons, and every year there is significant loss of life and property as a result of natural disasters. There are considerably fewer lives lost due to floods than to earthquakes, yet the resulting damage to property and loss in productivity has a high impact on the national economy.

Despite Japan's policy to improve protection against major flooding and the progressive reduction of the total inundated area, flood damages continue to rise due to the strong and increasing concentration of economic assets in flood- prone areas.

6. Increasingly vulnerable population

Even though Japan has been successful in reducing areas vulnerable to floods, the government still faces growing challenges related to the

Table 1.1. **Significant flooding events in Japan, 2000-04: economic and social cost**

Event	Description	Economic loss		Human loss
		Insured loss	Total damage	
Tokai Heavy Rain, September 2000	Floods and landslides in the Nagoya area	USD 990 million (2001 value)	USD 7 billion**	18
Fukui Niigata-Fukushima Torrential Rain, July 2004	More than 12 500 hectares damaged, 5 800 homeless	USD 279 million	USD 1.95 billion	20 dead, 1 missing
Typhoon Songda/No. 18 September 2004	Winds up to 212 km/h, torrential rain	USD 3.59 billion *	USD 7.17 billion	41 dead, 4 missing *
Typhoon Meari/No. 21 September 2004	Winds up to 160 km/h, rain, floods, landslides	USD 291 million	USD 798 million	26 dead, 1 missing
Typhoon Ma-On/No. 22 October 2004	Winds up to 162 km/h, rain, floods	USD 241 million	USD 603 million	7 dead, 4 missing
Typhoon tokage/No. 23 October 2004	Winds up to 229 km/h, 23 210 houses destroyed	USD 1.12 billion	USD 3.2 billion	94 dead, 3 missing

** Figures from Japan Institute of Construction Engineering.

Source: Swiss R., 2001 and 2005.

Figure 1.7. **Increase of elderly households in Japan, 1975-2003**

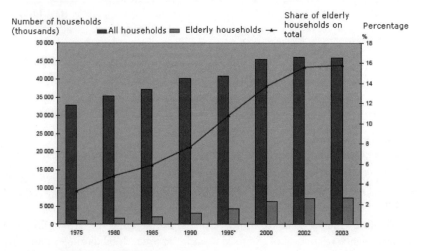

Source: Japanese Statistics Bureau (2005).

densification of urban areas protected by flood defences, climate change and an ageing and more vulnerable Japanese population.

In the event of a disaster, the population's physical and economic characteristics have a statistically significant important impact on their ability to protect themselves and recover.

The rising share of the elderly in Japan's population (and in other OECD countries), together with mounting differences in economic conditions between social groups, indicate a likely increase in the vulnerability of the elderly. Elderly women, for example, who suffer more often from physical deficiency and limited economic means, are likely to be less able to protect themselves and be more vulnerable.

Japan has a clear need to maintain its high level of ambition to improve risk management associated with natural disasters, in particular with regard to the already high and increasing probability of – and vulnerability to – flood events.

7. Decades of solid progress in flood control

Disaster damage, in particular loss of human life, has declined in Japan despite the magnitude of challenges it faces and the considerable yet nonetheless limited economic resources available to meet these. Japan's capacity to address disasters and mitigate vulnerability to disasters has progressed. There has been substantial improvement in the development of disaster management systems, national land conservation and weather forecasting technologies. Furthermore, disaster information communication systems have been upgraded.

Experience has led to decades of successive improvements both in flood protection capability including river management, and in disaster preparedness and response capability for dealing with natural disasters. The immense damage caused by the Ise-wan Typhoon in 1959 was a turning point that significantly strengthened the disaster management system and lead to the Disaster Countermeasures Basic Act was of 1961. Through this legislation, a comprehensive and strategic disaster management system was formulated, which has been further enhanced following lessons learned from other large scale disasters such as the Great Hanshin-Awaji Earthquake. The system addresses all disaster phases and clarifies the roles and responsibilities of the national and local governments, with the relevant stakeholders of the public and private sectors cooperating in implementing various disaster countermeasures.

Notes

1. *Source:* Japanese Ministry of Land, Infrastructure and Transport (MLIT) and the Cabinet Office (2005): PowerPoint Presentation at 4th meeting of OECD Risk Management Project Steering Group, unpublished, Paris

2. *Source:* Interview of the OECD Review Team with the Arakawa downstream office, 15/05/07.

3. *Source:* MLIT, 2006, Rivers in Japan.

4. *Source:* MLIT, 2007, "Existing Conditions and Tasks of River Administration in terms of Flood Control".

ISBN 978-92-64-05639-8
OECD Reviews of Risk Management Policies
Japan: Large-Scale Floods and Earthquakes
© OECD 2009

Chapter 2

Integrated Approach to Flood Risk Management

Risk management of floods in Japan has to be seen as part of the Total Disaster Management System which has been developed through a seamless cycle of prevention, mitigation, preparedness, response, recovery and rehabilitation. The system ensures strong national leadership and multi-sectoral coordination. According to the Disaster Countermeasures Basic Act introduced in 1961, the central government, local government and public corporations are all responsible at their respective levels for protecting the land, life and limb of people and property against natural disasters. The level and type of administration involved in flood management depends on two variables: the significance of the river or of the event, and the phase of the management cycle. A systematic difference is to be made between preventive and protective actions on the one hand and disaster management in the event of floods on the other.

In the European Union, policies are based on a holistic approach to the different phases of the disaster management cycle, illustrated by Figure 2.1:

Under this scheme, overall coordination and leadership is exercised at the highest, central government, level. Implementation and practical operational responsibility is in most respects decentralised to the local level.

1. A cross-sectoral approach to flood control at the central level

Coordination of actions and strategies at the national level is guaranteed by the strong role of the Prime Minister and, since 2001, by the Cabinet Office and the Central Disaster Management Council.

The central administrations dealing with flood disaster management include the Cabinet Office, the Cabinet Secretariat, the Minister of State for Disaster Management, the Central Disaster Management Council, and a number of relevant Ministries and Agencies, as can be seen in Figure 2.2.

Along with a series of reforms of the Japanese central government system in 2001, the post of Minister of State for Disaster Management was established to integrate and coordinate disaster reduction policies and measures undertaken by ministries and agencies. The Cabinet Office is responsible for securing cooperation and collaboration amongst related government organisations on a wide range of issues, and has a role in supporting the Cabinet Secretariat in disaster management matters. The Cabinet Office in the United Kingdom also provides an example of coordination of flood risk

Figure 2.1. **The integrated risk management cycle**

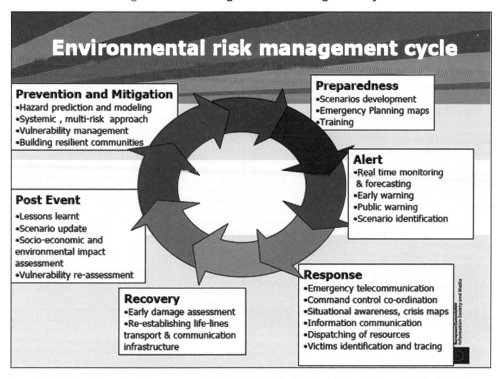

Source: Weets, Guy, "Improving risk management", DG INFSO-ICT for Sustainable Growth, Brussels, May 31, 2007.

management at the highest level of government (see Annex I.2). In Japan, the Cabinet Secretariat system and risk management functions have been strengthened, including the establishment of a Cabinet Information Collection Centre to address emergencies such as large-scale disasters and serious accidents (Cabinet Office, Government of Japan, 2007, *Disaster Management in Japan*).[1]

In the Cabinet Office, the Central Disaster Management Council (CDMC) is one of the bodies that deal with crucial policies of the Cabinet. As shown in Figure 2.3, the Council is chaired by the Prime Minister and is composed of the Minister of State for Disaster Management, responsible for coordination, and the cabinet ministers, heads of major public institutions (Japanese Red Cross Society, Bank of Japan and public utility providers) and academic experts. Its main responsibilities include the definition of the nation's strategy against disasters (Basic Disaster Management Plan and Plan of Emergency Measures for a Major Disaster) and the promotion of comprehensive disaster measures according to requests from the Prime Minister and the Minister of State for Disaster Management.

Figure 2.2. **Organisation of central government**

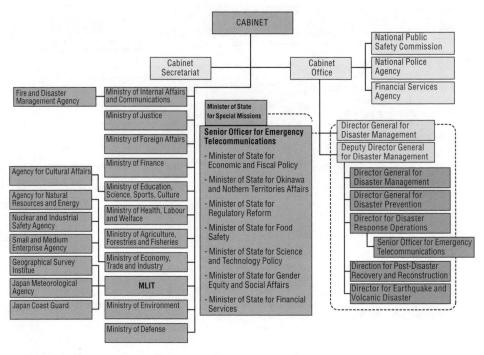

Source: Cabinet Office, Government of Japan, 2007, *Disaster Management in Japan.*

The Central Disaster Management Council thus provides help in the coordination of advanced measures and real-time emergency strategies towards enhanced coherence and integration of actions in the risk management cycle. Its responsibilities are especially critical in the elaboration of response and emergency strategies, including warning and evacuation schemes.

National responsibilities for protection measures against floods mainly fall under the responsibility of the Ministry of Land, Infrastructure and Transport (MLIT). Since the merger of four ministries in January 2001, the MLIT is in charge of construction standards, transport infrastructures (roads, railways, bridges, ports, airports), as well as water and river management facilities such as dams and levees.

The main bureaus of the MLIT concerned with flood management are the River Bureau, the Land and Water Bureau, the City and Regional Development Bureau and the Housing Bureau. Each Bureau implements a plan in accordance with a legal framework, including the River Law, the City Planning Law, the Buildings Standards Law, the Land Use Fundamental Law, the Natural Land Use Planning Law, and others not specifically mentioned. These laws

Figure 2.3. **Central Disaster Management Council**

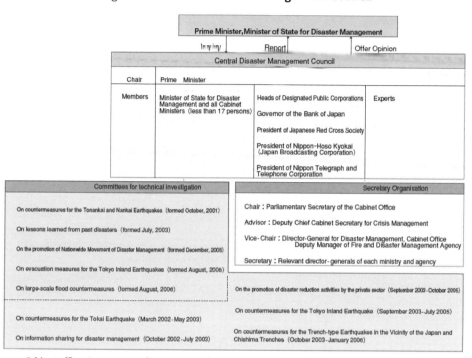

Source: Cabinet office, Government of Japan, 2007, *Disaster Management in Japan.*

have been supplemented with numerous ordinances and guidelines that provide details for their application.

Findings

The Japanese disaster management system is in principle holistic and coherent. The Cabinet Office exercises a coordination function and delegates responsibilities to different sectors and administrative levels. The Central Disaster Management Council (CDMC) plays an important and positive role in the development of policies. The close linkage of the CDMC to the head of government, who is its Chair, and the strong involvement in disaster management at the central level help decisions to be taken with a holistic overview. There is, however, room for improvement in respect both of the countermeasures and advising the ministries involved on major flood events.

Some coordination of the different central ministries involved in the risk management cycle and the control of how national strategies are implemented. The central administration system in Japan, as in some other OECD countries, is characterised by a high level of independence in each ministry. This is not only perceptible in practical matters such as separate buildings, equipment and

Figure 2.4. **Organisation of the MLIT**

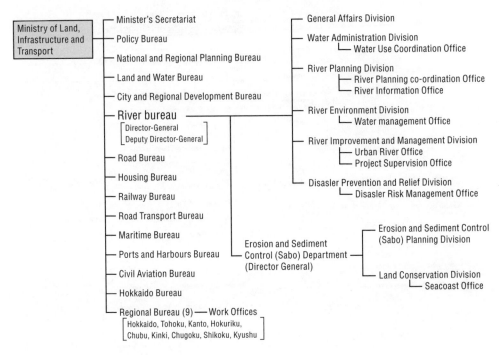

Source: MLIT, September 2006, *Rivers in Japan*.

staff, but also in the management of central government activities such as awareness-raising and public-private partnerships.

These natural barriers between central government bureaus remain even though the system has opened up somewhat over the last ten years, as shown by the fact that civil servants may now change bureaus from one ministry to another, which was very rarely the case in the past.

Due to the complexity of flood risk management there is a strong need for involvement of, and close collaboration between, the different ministries in order to achieve the necessary integration of management within the whole disaster management cycle. This requires strong leadership to ensure coordination.

To ensure the integration of the different strategies across ministries in respect to disaster management, the Prime Minister and Cabinet Office exercise a strong role in coordination and cooperation between ministries and promote the development of common cross-sectoral policies.

However, the tools available to the Cabinet Office for this task need to be bolstered as they seem in certain respects to lack some power in exercising the necessary influence on the implementation of flooding policies at the central level.

Though the Central Disaster Management Council also plays an essential role in integrating disaster management countermeasures on holistic flood prevention and response policy, its action is limited to planning ministries have the role of exercising control and audit in general within the Japanese public administration, such as the Evaluation Authority of the Ministry of General Affairs, the Accounting Office and the Ministry of Finance. But they are not systematically involved in the auditing of the risk management plans. The work between bureaus of the same Ministry and across authorities is not traditionally governed by evaluation of cross-sectoral collaboration.

For example, the Housing Bureau as well as the Land and Water Bureaus could play a much stronger and more active role in collaboration with local government with respect to prevention and mitigation of vulnerabilities in flood-prone areas. The present shortcomings could be attributed to the lack of sufficient requirements for coordinating work across the various bureaus concerned. Vertical barriers between central administrative sectors need to be addressed by a stronger co-ordinating body at central government level, which should be mandated to encourage well-developed cross sectoral collaboration across all ministries. This would contribute actively to cover the needs for active cooperation between central and local authorities at the different functional or administrative layers of flood risk management.

Opportunities for action and recommendations

The various policies contributing to flood risk management need to be better integrated into a holistic approach and the coordinating role of central government needs to be strengthened considerably. The Cabinet Office could be entrusted with this enhanced, more extensive leading role by being given a clearer responsibility with regard to evaluation of different ministries' policies. Collaboration between sectors, and cooperation between the different layers of administration would be improved by collecting and disseminating information, conducting evaluations and comparing the implementation of disaster management policies.

The Government could also consider creating an independent body in charge of auditing and evaluating disaster management activities across sectors and at different administrative levels. This responsibility could be given to an existing government entity with similar duties, providing it does not have any disaster management responsibilities at operational level. Various OECD governments have already developed such an internal evaluation capacity.

Recommendation 1. The central government needs to have a stronger coordination role and more effective tools for enforcing implementation of coherent disaster management policies.

2. Co-ordination of actions and strategies between central and local level

In Japan there are three layers in the administrative system: central government and two levels of local government (prefectures and municipalities). According to the Disaster Countermeasures Basic Act formulated in 1961, ministerial departments and prefectures are responsible for elaborating their own disaster management plans, provided these are in line with the Basic Disaster Management Plan. Likewise, municipalities develop their plans in line with their corresponding prefecture's plan.[2]

According to the Disaster Relief Act (1947) prefectures are responsible for the provision of relief services on an emergency basis: rescue, shelter and temporary housing, health care, provision of basic supplies and emergency repairs. At that point, the role of national ministries and agencies is essentially to secure the necessary resources, if necessary by requiring the support of other prefectures or private actors. The governor of a prefecture can delegate his mission to heads of municipalities. The costs of relief activities are borne by the prefecture up to a certain amount, and shared between the prefecture and the central government if costs exceed this threshold.

Although the Disaster Countermeasures Basic Act provides the legal basis for an integrated disaster management strategy and especially for the definition of responsibility at the response stage, various specific laws are relevant with regard to flood prevention strategies.

The River Law is at the core of flood control legislation. This law was enacted in 1964 to reorganise the role of the river administrations and to change the conventional section-by-section river management into a more integrated approach. It was then amended in 1997 to take into account economic and social changes, to emphasise the need for sound river environments, and to incorporate the opinions of local residents through river improvement planning systems (MLIT 2006). Whereas the River Law insists more specifically on flood prevention structural measures, the Flood-fighting Law, first established in 1949 and revised in 2005, focuses on flood-fighting activities at the local level in reaction to flood events.

Rivers are divided into Class A, B and C in Japan. Class A rivers are those considered to be of national significance due to the considerable assets and population in their flood plain. Particularly important sections of Class A rivers are administered by the Ministry of Land, Infrastructure and Transport (MLIT) River Bureau.

Certain sections of Class A rivers designated by the MLIT and Class B rivers are administered by Prefectures. Class C rivers are administered by municipalities. The regional river offices of the MLIT River Bureau are responsible for improvements in flood protection for the 109 Class A rivers– 7% of the total river length (MLIT 2006).

Figure 2.5. **The River Law**

Administrative responsibility for flood control depends on the type of river involved.

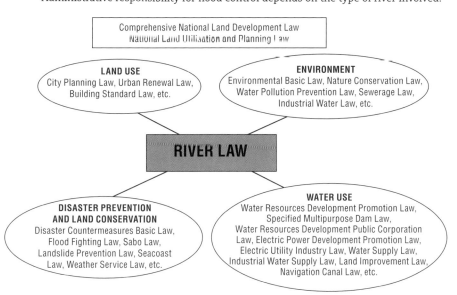

Source: MLIT, September 2006, *Rivers in Japan.*

Organised Prefectures and municipalities co-operate to manage the organisation of flood warnings and crisis management (flood-fighting, evacuation, and organisation of relief and recovery). A Flood-fighting Liaison Committee established for each river meets in April, May, or June of every year before the flood season. In addition, municipalities that include potential flood areas are required by law to prepare and disseminate flood hazard maps on the basis of maps of flood-prone areas created by the MLIT and the prefectures.

Findings

The policy defined by Japan forms a Total Disaster Management System in which levels of responsibilities and actions are defined between central and local levels in respect to the importance or size of the events, rivers and potential risks and damage of floods. Both central government and local government bodies are expected to work together towards the implementation of a fully integrated and holistic risk management strategy. Local government focuses on adapting the general schemes in the central government's Basic Disaster Management plan to their particular needs and conditions.

Currently, central government does not seem to have the necessary tools for effectively coordinating, and when necessary monitoring, local decisions. When duties are delegated within a line of command, assignment should always be accompanied by clear objectives and tasks, and be combined with reporting and evaluation requirements. However, at present no central governmental body has a mandate to enforce corrective actions when necessary.

New legislation enacted over the years has led to improvements in the disaster management system, particularly following large-scale natural disasters. The fundamental legal instrument is the Disaster Countermeasures Basic Act, but there are also a number of different laws applicable to disaster management (7 basic acts, 18 disaster prevention and preparedness acts, 3 disaster emergency response acts and 23 disaster recovery, reconstruction and financial measures acts).

Although the Disaster Countermeasures Basic Act defines the Comprehensive Disaster Management System and addresses all phases of the risk management cycle, indicating roles and responsibilities, the above mentioned legal instruments also cover these matters from different perspectives.

Each law addresses a particular issue or phase of the flood risk management cycle and can be useful in implementing measures within the limited focus of its scope. Such multiplicity in dispersed legislation creates challenges to obtain an overview and understanding of the requirements for those involved in the implementation of the policies, which is of particular concern in a disaster situation. A review to achieve more systematic and transparent legislation is needed to provide a more coherent platform for coordinated action.

As far as the division of responsibilities between central and local government is concerned, a distinction needs to be drawn between how disaster management for major rivers (class A Rivers) and small rivers is administered.

For class A Rivers, protective works and data collection fall under the responsibility of the MLIT through its regional bureaus, whereas most of the prevention and preparedness measures are implemented at the local level. Though it is very sensible that the MLIT maintain responsibility for Class A river improvement works and administration considering their importance at the national level, there is a need for more systematic and active cooperation between MLIT and the local authorities so that clearer linkages are established between protection measures on the one hand, and prevention and preparedness on the other.

As far as class B and C rivers are concerned, the problem is less one of coordination than political and economic capacity. Small municipalities may encounter both technical and economic difficulties in the implementation of adequate protective measures and actions against floods, as well as insufficient capability to respond efficiently and effectively to disasters.

The commendable efforts already made this last decade towards a more appropriate risk management process at the local level have to be strengthened. More specifically, enhancing the capacity of local actors for prevention, preparedness and emergency response, together with allowing them to have an integrated understanding of the risk management cycle is of specific importance.

The thorough knowledge local authorities regarding local constraints and conditions as well as their operational capability have been taken into account more extensively in the risk management system, but they have still to strengthen their role in the overall flood prevention strategy.

Opportunities for action

By collecting regional-level flood-fighting schemes and checking their consistency with the Basic Disaster Management Plan, the Central Disaster Management Council could systematically re-evaluate its global Disaster Management Plan and help local bodies in their decision-making process. This could help clarify the scope of each structure's area of responsibility, support the implementation of a system for monitoring, and help local governments by providing a basis for improvements through much needed inspections and evaluations.

More efficient collaboration between administrative bodies can also be better achieved by a more coherent and consolidated body of legislation. Such legislation should be targeted to, and thereby be better understood by, a very wide group of authorities, organisations, and stakeholders in the public and private sectors, as well as by the general public. In the European Union, the trend in recent years has been towards more holistic framework legislation, supplemented by regulation of particular issues, to provide a clear overview and greater transparency. A single document, the European Flood Directive, tackles all levels of flood risk management in order to facilitate the understanding of entrusted roles, responsibilities and objectives for all relevant stakeholders including the public and local authorities.

Improved coordination implies the collection of local proposals and the evaluation of local strategies by the central government, in order both to meet specific needs of each prefecture or municipality more accurately, and to check the effectiveness of local plans.

There is evidently a strong need for capacity building and more support to local government in line with current trends elsewhere in the world. Local capacity building could be achieved by implementing risk management education of local stakeholders through training programs, which can be expected to lead to a more efficient decision-making process. Local government could furthermore be required to communicate draft reports of

Local Disaster Management Plans to the competent central government authorities and receive feedback from these as a basis for further action. It could be useful for central government authorities and prefectures to promote additional inter-municipal agreements.

More focus could also be put on the establishment of coherent river basin management systems. Many countries acknowledge the fact that the river basin is the optimal scale for flood risk management.

In Japan, many examples illustrate the need for coherent river management at the basin level, such as the downstream area where the Arakawa River (A-class river, directly controlled by the minister) and the Nakagawa River (A-class river, controlled by the governor) flow in parallel.

An organisation, Flood-fighting that has the legitimacy to act at the scale of a river basin for instance in the form of a Flood-Fighting Liaison Committee, could better promote the implementation of more adequate prevention and damage mitigation strategies. The implementation of such an approach needs to be supported by standards and guidelines issued by the relevant central government authorities. Some examples and experiences from Europe demonstrate how central government recommendations can be elaborated successfully by drawing from local pilot case studies (See Annex I.1).

Recommendation 2. There is a need for more integrated flood risk management of river basins supported by local capacity building, a clarification of roles and responsibilities, an increased exchange of information and coordination between all sectors and levels of government, and a systematic evaluation and analysis of results by central government authorities.

3. The budget for structural measures

Projects led by the MLIT River Bureau on flood protection structural measures can be broadly classified as national projects and subsidised projects. National projects are carried out by the Ministry of Construction itself in sections of Class A rivers. The major portion of funds for national projects comes from the national budget, and the remainder comes from local budgets. Subsidised projects are projects that receive some funding from the national government, but are carried out by Prefectures in sections of Class A or Class B rivers under their jurisdiction.

The River Bureau budget, which is spent not only on projects related to rivers, but also on sea coasts, slope preservation measures and disaster rehabilitation, has decreased successively in recent years. For the fiscal year 2005 it amounted to about JPY 639 billion, around half of the budget for 1996.[3] The budget presentation in Figure 2.6 indicates the evolution in the share of large scale flood recovery works in the River Bureau budget.

Figure 2.6. **Evolution of the share of large-scale flood recovery works in the River Bureau Budget**

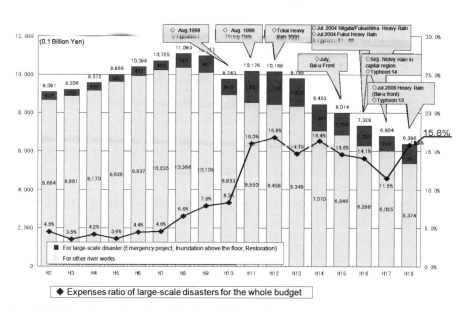

Source: MLIT, River Bureau, November 2007, *River Administration in Japan.*

The rising share of expenditures for damage recovery is related to the numerous extreme climatic events after 1996, i.e. the heavy rains and typhoons which caused large-scale floods. With the rise in extreme climatic events and the continued concentration of people and assets in flood-prone areas as well as the expected consequences of climate change, floods are likely to have an even stronger impact on the economy. Although the protection measures that were taken by the central government after the Second World War have had a very positive impact in limiting both loss of life and assets, and have led to a decrease in recovery costs, the trend now seems to be changing significantly.

The reduction in the central budget is largely accounted for by the severe fiscal crisis that Japan has experienced since the middle of the 1990s. After the 2002 peak of the government's budget deficit and public debt, the decision was made to freeze public investments. This problematic budget situation is unlikely to improve in the short term due to an anticipated rise in spending on social services for the elderly. Within the context of a tight budget, the building of highly expensive infrastructures such as dykes or dams has been slowed down, resulting in delays in achieving the protection goals set by the government.

Findings

Whereas the Government's budget allocations for flood risk reduction have been decreasing continually since the middle of the 1990's, the need to set in motion enhanced protection measures against floods has never been so compelling, given the increasing vulnerability of Japan's population and assets. Budget constraints not only challenge the necessary maintenance of established structural flood defences, but also considerably reduce the scope for new protective infrastructures.

While the financial means available for structural protection are dwindling, damage costs are likely to rise, which puts a higher economic burden on the budget for post-disaster recovery. The advantage of undertaking preventive measures has been calculated and demonstrated in many cases. Investments of JPY 71.6 billion in Nagoya City for installing protection infrastructures were evaluated as translating into a JPY 550 billion damage reduction compared to the 1999 and 2003 floods.[4]

The use of cost-benefit analyses which demonstrate the considerable benefits and added value of undertaking structural protection projects was reinforced through the "Government Policy Evaluations Act" in 2002. Also, public debates to integrate the views of academic experts and general public opinion before the implementation of long-term and mid-term plans for river improvement were organised in order to improve communication on river improvement plans and budgets.

In light of the expected impacts of climate change and current budget restrictions that postpone the financing of satisfactory levels of protection infrastructures, there is a need to further promote the use of integrated cost-benefit analyses both to establish priorities and to take better account of the value added of non-structural measures when a project is initiated so that an appropriate budget is allocated for them.

Strengthened transparency and enhanced public communication could have positive effects on fundraising from locally concerned stakeholders.

Opportunities for action

More systematic use of cost-benefit analyses or multi-criteria studies could thus be a valuable tool for reinforcing the implementation of the integrated risk management approach in Japan. In each particular situation, it would help to identify the most effective measures and to reach an appropriate balance between risk management options. Furthermore, such tools are very efficient for setting adequate priorities and allocating necessary public resources accordingly.

Devolvement of some responsibility for flood risk management should be given consideration in light of the budget situation. For example, local bodies could be given more autonomy in financial appraisal. Public acceptance of a tax levied to finance disaster management planning and infrastructures is likely to increase if the population bearing the tax burden is directly involved in the decision making process and fully informed about the benefits of such measures. Higher goals could be achieved in a shorter time notwithstanding the current budget restrictions. In such cases the public could be more involved and cooperation could be established and emphasised with the private sector, including the insurance industry, which may be interested in reducing insurance recovery costs through more appropriate damage mitigation measures.

Beyond evaluating the economic advantage of a project, there is a need to assess the potential benefits expected from undertaking more efficient non-structural measures. For example, immediately repairing and consolidating damaged dykes or levees is both an efficient and low-cost way of preventing or mitigating flooding and thus reducing damage. Within a development project, the citizens concerned should be involved and become aware of the contribution they can make to improve their own safety. If citizens can be motivated, then they are more likely to support the project, for example by federating into river committees. A combination of local efforts and social consensus on the required safety level could influence the government to allocate a budget sufficient to improve flood risk management. Such an approach could in addition lead to a better balance between structural and non structural protection measures.[5]

Recommendation 3. Tools such as multi-criteria studies or cost-benefit analyses are needed to promote communication and dialogue in reaching consensus on the acceptable levels of protection and budgets for flood risk management through both structural and non-structural measures and appropriate budget allocations.

Notes

1. *Source:* Cabinet Office, Government of Japan, 2007, *Disaster Management in Japan.*

2. *Source:* Cabinet Office, Government of Japan, 2007, *Disaster Management in Japan,* MLIT, 2006, *Flood Fighting in Japan.*

3. *Source:* MLIT, 2007, "Existing Conditions and Tasks of River Administration in terms of Flood Control".

4. *Source:* MLIT, 2007, "Existing Conditions and Tasks of River Administration in terms of Flood Control".

5. Definition of non-structural measures: "Structural measures refer to any physical construction to reduce or avoid possible impacts of hazards, which include engineering measures and construction of hazard resistant and protective structures and infrastructure. Non structural measures refer to policies, awareness, knowledge development, public commitment, and methods and operating practices, including participatory mechanisms and the provision of information, which can reduce risk and related impacts", UN/ISDR, Geneva, 2004.

ISBN 978-92-64-05639-8
OECD Reviews of Risk Management Policies
Japan: Large-Scale Floods and Earthquakes
© OECD 2009

Chapter 3

Risk Assessment and Communication

1. The early-warning system

The Japan Meteorological Agency (JMA) issues warnings, such as forecasts of heavy rain which could lead to serious flooding disasters. In addition, the MLIT and prefectures work hand in hand with the JMA to provide flood forecasts. The JMA observes and predicts rainfall for Class A and Class B rivers, and the MLIT provides hydrological assessments. Risk-level assessments are made using local data for small rivers which are managed by municipalities.

Rainfall and river levels are monitored through radar, rain gauges and telemeters, and are communicated directly to the government divisions mentioned above. Through active cooperation, they provide flood forecasts to the sub-level, meaning the city, town, or village flood-fighting management entities through the use of various high capacity networks (wireless, optical fibre and satellite). Disaster prevention information, such as the river water level, rainfall and dam storage levels, is supplied in real time on the website *www.river.go.jp*. Data are updated every ten minutes. Real time information also includes on-site filming. In the case of some main rivers such as the Tone, real-time simulations of flood development are also created and supplied to affected municipalities as support for their crisis management plan.

The MLIT and the JMA use a very accurate, reliable observation system to jointly provide information on water levels and flood forecasts for the main rivers in Japan. The JMA constantly collects precipitation data at about 1300 spots throughout the country, while the MLIT River Bureau is in charge of the collection and dissemination of nearly 2000 river-related data. In order to continually upgrade the scientific accuracy of risk assessment, particular attention is paid to cooperation between the national government and major research institutes, committees and experts, such as the Public Works Research Institute (PWRI) and the International Centre for Water Hazards and Risk Management (ICHARM).

The flood forecasts issued by the JMA are used for two purposes. One is to organise long-term strategies based on past experiences of floods, meteorological data, and flood modelling. The information gathered by the MLIT and the JMA are necessary for the implementation of structural protection measures, including gauging engineering works, and for the realisation of flood hazard maps. These data will be communicated to decision makers of each administration through special radio networks when needed to start organising emergency response. For example, the Fire Disaster Management Radio Communication System connects fire fighting organisations across the country. In cases of immediate risk, citizens are contacted through the combined use of various mass media, including internet, mobile phones, television and radio.

The MLIT or the prefectures designate the rivers, lakes and marshes or sea coasts where the flood-fighting warnings are to be provided. Co-operation has increased between the river administrations and the JMA, but there is a great and growing demand for information also from the public. The MLIT Regional Bureaus, which are linked together in a network, handle the information on floods.

In the Flood-fighting Act, administrative bases are detailed regarding the organisation and communication of early-warning and immediate response at the local level. They also define the cooperative entities for flood-fighting. The 2005 amendment of the Flood-fighting Law enabled flood information transmission during the early-warning process for medium and small-size rivers to be improved (MLIT 2006).

A special warning stage based on river water level was set as the guideline for small and medium rivers' flood-fighting managers (head of city/town/village) to launch their emergency strategy. The autonomy of the co-operating flood-fighting entities at the local level has been enhanced through the establishment of flood-fighting plans.

In the event of a large-scale flood disaster, the Central Disaster Management Council (CDMC) is in charge of response management. For this purpose, the Cabinet Information Collection Centre collects disaster information 24 hours a day.

Based on the experiences of the Great-Hanshin-Awaji Earthquake, the Cabinet Office has also developed Disaster Information Sharing Platforms (PF) to augment risk communication during a disaster (Cabinet Office 2007). PF are common information sharing systems with a standardised information format, where disaster information provided by ministries and agencies, local governments, relevant organisations and residents, can be posted and accessed by all.

Findings

The combined use of extremely capable research institutes and governmental agencies in Japan has achieved a very high level of efficiency in the collection of data on flood occurrence, risk assessment and the dissemination of information both to the relevant authorities at different levels and the public.

There is however still a need for enhanced efforts on risk assessment. Japan will most probably be heavily affected by the consequences of global warming and climate change as recognised by the Intergovernmental Panel on Climate Change (IPCC), and a revision of the flood management policy has therefore been initiated to adapt the policy to climate change.

A probable increase in the frequency of inundations and particularly of large-scale flood disasters, together with an expected rise in sea levels, imply a greater need for the Japanese government to go further in the updating of climate data, in the evaluation of the probability of large-scale floods and in the adaptation of the early warning system in respect of these changing conditions.

Opportunities for action

The use of new information technology for data collection, analysis, information and decision support and communication is well established, but needs to be continually maintained and updated. Efforts on research and development in this area should therefore be encouraged. Even if the technology in the command and control centres of each sector or organisation is world class, there is a need from a national perspective for a common cross-sector, situational awareness and information support system as a basis for the necessary collaboration in disaster management decision making.

Risk management policy needs to attach higher priority to very large-scale floods not only in light of the prevailing conditions in Japan, but also – and especially – due to the growing future risk of large-scale floods linked to climate change. In order to improve current knowledge, the government could take further steps to enhance cooperation with national scientific institutes, and foster international collaboration on these matters. The Bavarian adaptation strategies detailed in Annex I.3 demonstrate the benefits of expert consultations on climate change aimed at updating the institutional framework.

Dissemination of information together with a decision support system could provide a practical tool for the stronger collaboration and coordination of the authorities responsible for disaster management. The example of England presented in Box 3.1, where updating of data collection on the coastline was set up together with the definition of how to use the data in local plans is an interesting example of how to efficiently integrate risk assessment into the policy making process. In Japan, the need for stronger collaboration should be considered, especially for large-scale floods where all the layers of administration, both central and local, need to be involved.

Recommendation 4. Continued efforts should be made to maintain the very high quality of information technology research, risk assessment and communication, including means for early warning, to take into account risks of large-scale flooding related to climate change.

Box 3.1. **Coastal monitoring projects in the United Kingdom**

A strategic management framework for flood defence and coastal protection was introduced in England in 1995, and shoreline management plans now exist for the whole country. Each plan typically provides a strategic policy framework for an integrated programme of flood defence and coastal protection, for several hundred kilometres of coast. The purpose of the plans is to provide an economically sustainable management framework that enables a means of coordination of localised schemes and operational management, without adverse environmental impact. Several management tiers exist beneath the policy based shoreline management plan, each requiring more detailed levels of data. Effective planning and implementation of shoreline management requires high quality, long-term, time-series data sets, at appropriate spatial and temporal resolution, to predict long-term coastal evolution and to determine design conditions for coastal protection and flood defence projects.

A large scale pilot regional monitoring programme (including analytical databases, GIS and web delivery) was introduced in 2002 to provide a systematic approach to collection, management and analysis of data for use in strategic and operational management of coastal erosion and flood risk in southeast England; this was expanded in 2006 to cover the whole of southern England. Approximately 2000 kilometres of open sea and estuarine coast are now included in the programme. A wide range of agencies within the region (50), have responsibilities for management of short sections of coastline. The strategic monitoring initiative includes all of these agencies working in partnership, and integrates the requirements of operating-authorities with responsibilities for management of coastal erosion and coastal flood risk, at both strategic and operational levels.

Source: Andrew P. Bradbury, Channel Coastal Observatory 2007, "Application of a large-scale, long-term, regional coastal observation network to coastal management on the English-channel coast".

---

2. Combining hazard, exposure and vulnerability assessment: towards integrated risk assessment and mapping

In Japan, as in many other OECD countries, hazard assessment is communicated to citizens and policy-makers through the use of hazard maps. Normally created by each municipality, hazard maps provide information to residents on flooding levels that could be reached in their street. Together with hazard data, they also include response information such as where the shelters (the high grounds) are located, how to get to them, and when it is necessary to go there (see Figure 3.1). Municipalities are required to provide hazard maps, generally based on data from maps showing the areas where flooding could be expected. The data is provided to municipalities by both

MLIT offices in charge of respective rivers and prefectural governments. The local authorities are endeavouring to meet their obligations.

Medium-scale flood hazards are well assessed by local authorities. Data are used to set up mitigation measures addressed to the citizens or companies at risk, essentially for new constructions. Major companies concerned with people's safety, or assets at stake, use the same data to organise themselves to guarantee personal or public safety and mitigate damage in case of floods. Also, some major buildings have developed their own structural means, such as emergency impervious doors, to cope with medium size floods.

Hazard maps probably exist in most municipalities,[1] but seem to be used only for emergency response, and not for vulnerability assessment and reduction.

Even though there are general figures that concern vulnerability assessments, such as the global population at risk or the value of assets compared to Japanese GNP, these figures have probably been calculated from very global, rough assessments. Neither systematic nor detailed vulnerability assessment seems to be performed by any of the three levels of administration involved.

Vulnerability assessment does seem to be carried out by some economic stakeholders, albeit on a voluntary base. Such is the case of some public services networks, who prepare themselves to mitigate damage and increase

Figure 3.1. **Flood hazard maps : schematic version**

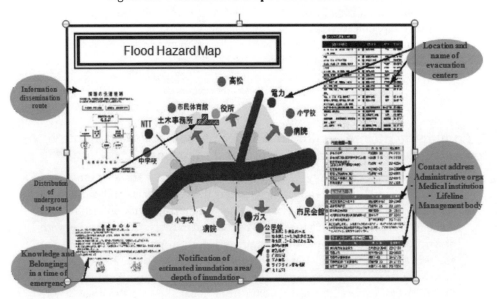

Source: MLIT September 2006 *Rivers in Japan.*

Figure 3.2. **Flood-prone area map of Naka River**

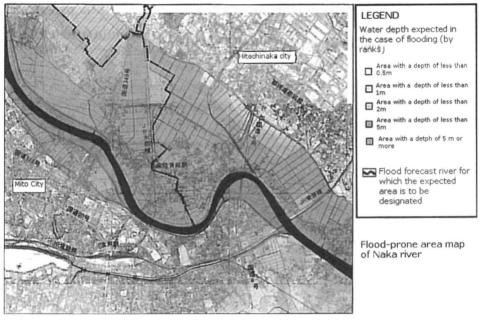

LEGEND

Water depth expected in the case of flooding (by ranks)

☐ Area with a depth of less than 0.5m

☐ Area with a depth of less than 1m

☐ Area with a depth of less than 2m

☐ Area with a depth of less than 5m

☐ Area with a detph of 5 m or more

▨ Flood forecast river for which the expected area is to be designated

Flood-prone area map of Naka river

Source: MLIT September 2006 *Rivers in Japan.*

their users' safety using vulnerability assessment data to design and implement measures. Also, some hazardous industries have moved to safer areas after assessing the vulnerability and the risks for them and the surrounding population.

Findings

Assessing the vulnerability of assets in an area could be a very efficient and necessary way to start mitigating damage in the event of large-scale floods. Several meters of water due to large-scale flooding over an extended territory could create such a disaster that the only issue at stake for the authorities would be to save human life. But in terms of material damage, there is clearly evidence that even if water levels reach several meters in depth, a whole range of measures can be taken in order to reduce damage, provided vulnerability has been assessed. Moreover, vulnerability assessment is also aimed at raising risk awareness, thereby helping to save lives and to enable people to organise themselves better and more safely in the face of large-scale flood risks.

The general objectives of vulnerability assessment are:

● Identify where the most vulnerable population groups and the most vulnerable assets are located.

- Know the risks and evaluate ways to mitigate them.

The second part of the vulnerability assessment, damage mitigation, is based on the following measures:

- Plan the local non-structural measures to enhance the self-organising capacity of the local population in order to mitigate damage and increase the safety of individuals.

- Build local structural measures to mitigate material damage to reduce recovery works and costs as well as to reduce the down time during which the facility is unusable.

Vulnerability diagnosis depends not only on the assessment of the hazard – inundated area, water depth, velocity if important, duration of the inundation, speed of floodwater rise – but also on the facility involved.

Opportunities for action

While information on hazard assessments is good, mainly thanks to hazard maps, the assessment of vulnerability to large-scale floods could be further advanced.

In order to develop vulnerability assessment, hazard assessment should nevertheless be done at a more detailed scale, in order that each individual can really estimate the potential damage in his own vicinity, and think about the possibilities to reduce them. Vulnerability assessments for assets go together with vulnerability mitigation plans that propose structural modifications of buildings or equipment, as well as non-structural measures in terms of how to run affected building or equipment before and after a crisis. These plans have to be elaborated taking into account existing response plans (if any), in order to check the availability of human resources to run the plan from pre-crisis to post-crisis.

Above all, local government should take charge of vulnerability assessment, which in Europe appears to be the appropriate scale. The necessary training and education, initiated by the central government and involving the various bureaus of MLIT, would encourage local government to step into this long-term process. Together with a need for more detailed hazard assessment, hazard maps could be used in order to make cross links with vulnerability assessment.

Using hazard assessment, vulnerability assessment could be carried out, first at the local government scale, and using urban typologies and general categories such as housing, public buildings, offices, and industries. Those general categories can of course be divided into sub-categories, such as for housing: privately owned houses, semi-collective properties, and collective residences, multi-storey buildings, etc. The vulnerability assessment at local government level could be well summarised using mapping tools. It is then possible to realise links with hazard maps, which provide the base for risk assessment.

Risk maps could be used extensively in risk communication with all stakeholders including the public. It is particularly important to raise awareness regarding the risks of very large-scale floods among public risk managers, and to develop a risk communication strategy for the promotion of damage mitigation measures against flood risks, in partnership with all relevant actors. Information on potential impacts and damage reduction strategies regarding large-scale floods should be gathered and communicated to citizens in advance, in order to enforce the efficiency of emergency early-warning, as well as to start individual damage mitigation strategies. An illustration of the use of such maps for the development of an integrated disaster management strategy is given in Annex I.4 which describes the case of the International Commission for the Protection of the Rhine.

As a major part of vulnerability mitigation efforts, priorities should be stipulated concerning for example urban public networks such as electricity, water, transportation and telecommunications. If these services are no longer available, each individual economic actor or citizen is likely to see his or her own damage increase significantly. For instance, not having access to electricity for several days can cause serious damage to many factories, buildings and equipment. While a power outage or subway breakdown could affect people's ability to be warned and evacuated, it could also – if it persists – prevent recovery works from starting on time and slow the upturn of economic activity, drastically increasing the financial losses incurred. Thus, it will be necessary to gradually implement a more systematic vulnerability assessment of public service networks in order to plan non-structural damage mitigation measures or to design and build local structural damage mitigation facilities.

The savings can be considerable. It has been estimated, for example, that a 100-year flood in Paris would now cost only half what it would have cost 10 years ago, thanks mostly to recent efforts by all the network owners and operators to mitigate their own damage and shorten the period of time during which their services are unavailable.

At the individual level, local government has to play a leading role for the major stakeholders, as well as for the public, in order to encourage individuals to perform their own vulnerability assessment of their property. Guidelines could be produced by prefectures or central government bodies. Financing these vulnerability assessments could be a good way to promote them. For instance, from 2008 to 2012, economic stakeholders located in flood-prone areas in the Loire Basin in France will have some 3 000 vulnerability assessments financed (half by the European Union).[2] The aim is to raise awareness, and to encourage them to manage their vulnerability voluntarily by taking the appropriate measures to mitigate the damage they could suffer.

To sum up, vulnerability assessment should be performed at various scales:

- Local government scale where the aim is essentially to draw up risk maps and collect data to raise awareness and encourage private initiative.
- The main stakeholders such as economic actors who have to perform their own vulnerability assessment in order to set up mitigation plans, including local structural and non-structural measures, generally could receive technical and financial help from relevant public bodies.
- All buildings and inhabitants that can also conduct vulnerability assessments and establish mitigation plans, could generally receive technical and financial help from relevant public bodies.

Vulnerability assessment together with hazard assessment creates risk assessment that should be focused on communication and awareness towards citizens. An example of the efficiency of such a combination is given in Box 3.2.

Recommendation 5. Vulnerability assessment needs to be conducted by local government in support of natural hazard evaluation and risk communication with citizens to achieve a more efficient system of flood risk management and damage mitigation through both structural and non-structural measures.

Box 3.2. **How to integrate vulnerability and social perception of risk in flood risk assessment: the CEMAGREF method**

The method developed in France by the CEMAGREF (French Institute for Agriculture, rural Engineering, Water and Forests) is an innovative tool for flood risk management based on the inclusion of two different scales: the local one integrating socioeconomic criteria and the global one respecting river basin coherency. To achieve this goal, a risk map is finalised based on the combination of hazard and vulnerability maps.

The definition of vulnerability for this method takes into account both the economic values of damages and the social cost of floods. A default value, called TOP, is attributed for protective purposes to each plot of land, based on acceptable return periods. The most valuable areas include houses (TOP=50-100), chemical industries and hospitals (TOP=1000), whereas meadows or forest are classified as less valuable areas (TOP=1). A negotiation phase is undertaken in order to allow inhabitants to express their perception of risk, and to include affective values in vulnerability. Though such discussions can help engineering projects to be better adapted to local needs, they can meet difficulties in their implementation since the specific vocabulary and technology used by the method can be hard to understand for a non-expert audience.

OECD REVIEWS OF RISK MANAGEMENT POLICIES – ISBN 978-92-64-05639-8 – © OECD 2009

> **Box 3.2. How to integrate vulnerability and social perception of risk in flood risk assessment: the CEMAGREF method** *(cont.)*
>
> Regarding the design of hazard maps, a detailed hydraulic assessment of the catchment and river behaviour is carried out through rainfall-runoff models such as the DHI MIKE Module. Project hydrographs are estimated thanks to the combined use of calibration based on a past flood experience and theoretical models. The models include the impact of storage structures and the adaptation of return periods for the different tributaries of the main river studied. Flood modelling permits the return period of the first flooding flow, or TAL, to be determined for each plot of land. From the comparison of the estimated values of the TOP and TAL, both expressed as return periods, a single map can be drawn up, the risk map, which gives a coherent and homogenous estimation of the risk, understandable to a non-expert audience. This simplifies the difficult task of deciding where economic efforts should be concentrated.

Figure 3.3. **Examples of risk maps**

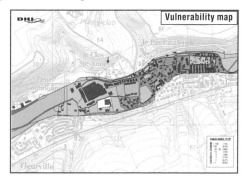

Source: Document prepared by S. MEJDI, DHI Eau & Environnement, for the 7th International Conference on Hydroinformatics HIC 2006, Nice, FRANCE.

Notes

1. Based on estimations from IDI, 700 municipalities out of 1 822 are already equipped with Hazard Maps.

2. *Source: http://www.eptb-loire.fr/publications/newsletter/NL5.htm*, accessed in February 2008.

OECD REVIEWS OF RISK MANAGEMENT POLICIES – ISBN 978-92-64-05639-8 – © OECD 2009

ISBN 978-92-64-05639-8
OECD Reviews of Risk Management Policies
Japan: Large-Scale Floods and Earthquakes
© OECD 2009

Chapter 4

Flood Prevention and Damage Mitigation

1. A strong long-term structural flood defence strategy

Japan's extremely high exposure to floods has lead to a policy of introducing ambitious structural measures to protect its population and assets. These defences have been progressively improved and Japan has become a leader in disaster management, for instance in respect to new information technology systems and protective engineering and construction of secure infrastructures.

Structural measures for flood prevention comprise river or channel improvements, *e.g.* embankment, dredging, construction of retarding basins, floodways and dams. Japan has always devoted great attention to such flood prevention measures, which have contributed to a reduction in the population affected by floods.

Another action, especially in respect to decreasing land retention properties as a result of waterproofing of soil through urbanisation, is the runoff control and implementation of comprehensive rainwater management

Figure 4.1. **Examples of physical flood defences**

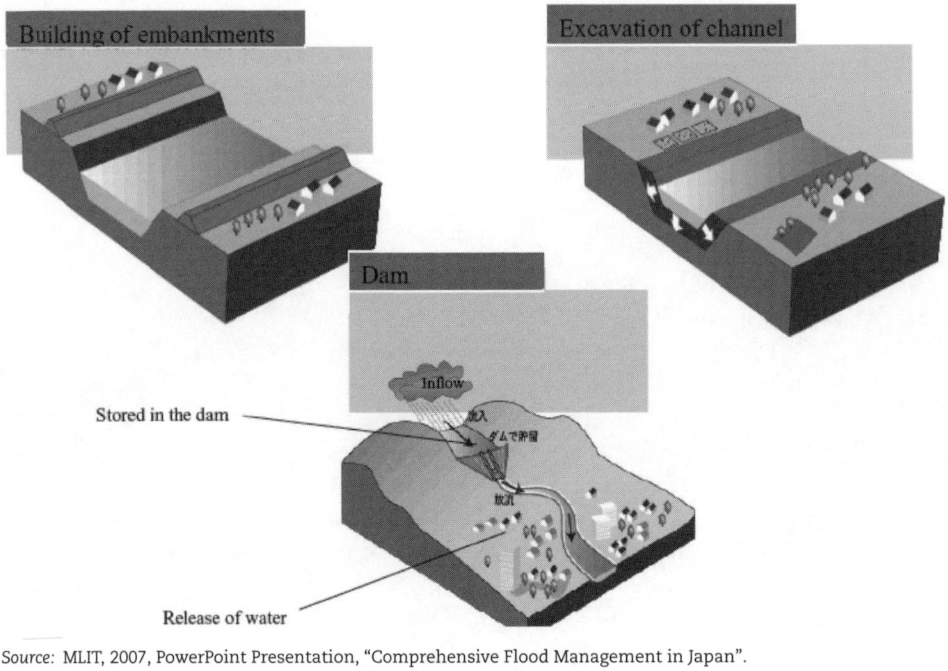

Source: MLIT, 2007, PowerPoint Presentation, "Comprehensive Flood Management in Japan".

in order to limit water flow downstream. The most appropriate way to restrain the urbanisation run off increase relate to urbanisation is to combine facilities that enhance the retention and detention capabilities of river basins. Some of the specific measures that can be enforced to achieve this goal are:

● Maintenance of urbanisation control zones.

● Conservation of natural areas such as parks.

● Construction of reservoirs, regulating basins and other storage facilities.

● Installation of permeable pavements and seepage sumps.

● Control of landfill.

● Development of interior drainage facilities.

The Prefecture of Saitama for example has systematically implemented standards so that the runoff from new constructions does not increase the actual runoff coming from existing land use. That means that every new construction has to build facilities to infiltrate or store rain water locally, in order to avoid increasing the downstream discharge released into the river.

Japan is world class in the construction of anti-inundation infrastructures even though much remains to be done to fully achieve flood protection goals.

The principal protective engineering structures that Japan has massively developed, and their respective flood-fighting actions, are the following:

Channels and embankments: River channel improvement includes channel widening, levee construction and reinforcement, and riverbed dredging so that flood waters below designated levels can be discharged without inundating lands along the river.

Detention basins: Water is diverted from an overflowing river in case of emergency, and the water is returned to the river after the threat of flooding has disappeared. Retarding basins and control basins mitigate flooding in the lower reaches. In the event of a flood, part or most of the floodwaters flow into the basins. The water stored in basins can also be used as water resources.

River floodways: A floodway is a canal constructed to lead flood waters from the middle and lower reaches of a river to another river or directly to the sea. A floodway is constructed when channel improvement is insufficient to carry the designated volume of flood waters.

Dams: The function of a dam is to regulate the downstream flood discharge by storing storm floodwater only when flood discharge is high. Thus, they prevent a sharp increase in streamflow in case of major rainfall events such as storms or typhoons. Besides their flood protection capacity, dams ensure stable water supply to downstream residents and help generate power through hydro-electricity.

Figure 4.2. **Examples of physical flood defences**
Underground floodways and underground regulating reservoirs in urban areas.

● Widening of channels and embankments   ● Detention basins

● Floodways   ● Dam

Source: MLIT, September 2006, *Rivers in Japan.*

High-standard levees / Super levees (see Figure 4.4): A "super levee" is a thick embankment created by applying a layer of fill material over a conventional embankment. Super levees are designed to prevent catastrophic flood damage which could result from urban levee breaks caused by overflowing of banks, seepage, and earthquakes. They also enhance urban spaces with water and greenery. Super levees are very costly so they are mostly constructed along rivers flowing through cities with high a density of population and property, where unexpected effects would have dramatic consequences (*e.g.* Tone, Edo, Ara, Tama, Yodo, and Yamato Rivers).

Other measures include the raising of residential land and the building of embankments such as ring levees.

To cope with increasing flood risk and achieve higher goals of safety against floods, construction of new facilities are complemented by improvement of existing protective devices. For example, the Kinu River

Figure 4.3. **Positive flood reduction thanks to underground floodways :
an example in Saitama Prefecture**

Floods in July 2000 (area around Midridai 2-chome, Satte City)

Headrace tunnel

Typhoon No.6 in 2002 (area around Midridai 2-chome, Satte City)

Source: MLIT, September 2006, *Rivers in Japan.*

Upstream Dam Group River project links two dams with a channel to achieve a better level of flood control together with promoting the improvement of the river environment. The principle is to reallocate the reservoir capacity efficiently between dams with high flood control functions and those with high water utilisation functions.

The benefits of these measures have been proved in some noteworthy cases. In Saitama Prefecture, the building of a 6.3 km long, 10 m wide channel between Kasukabe and Showa City has succeeded in eliminating flooding of homes in the surrounding area. During typhoon No. 6 in 2002, 141 mm of rainfall was recorded in 48 hours, which was similar to that of July 2000. Thanks to the construction of the headrace tunnel which drained the Naka river water, there was a complete elimination of the number of flooded houses, compared to 236 flooded houses in 2000.[1]

The focus above is on protection against river floods. When the risk of floods triggered by typhoons is considered, vulnerable areas are found not

Figure 4.4. **Effects of super levees**

Before Construction of Super Levee

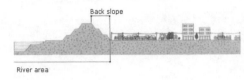

After Construction of Super Levee

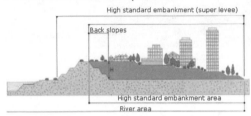

Source: MLIT, 2007, Power Point presentation, "Comprehensive Management in Japan".

only in the vicinity of rivers but also on the coastline. Specific structures need to be implemented to counteract sea water floods. In various parts of Japan, the seashore is protected mainly by steep seawalls and block mounds. To act more efficiently against erosion, scouring and wave overtopping, an Integrated Coastal Protection System was put into action recently. This system combines gently sloped embankments, artificially enhanced sand beaches and artificial reefs which will result in a higher level of resistance against high waves and erosion. Moreover, such measures give an added value to the coast's scenic and recreational aspects.

The efforts made by the government to implement a flood management strategy that integrates flood control, water use and environment protection is particularly interesting too. Japanese policies regarding flood protection development have gradually changed during the last ten years towards a more integrated environmental-friendly approach.

Since the amendment of the River Law in 1997, the central government has expressed a very strong ambition to integrate dams, reservoirs and retarding basins into the landscape and environment, in order to re-establish a close relationship between the rivers and local communities and also to promote a more sustainable development of rivers. A good example is the Tsurumi Multipurpose Retarding Basin which in addition to protecting people from floods, serves as the centre of a recreation area, which includes sport facilities and a natural park.

Findings

Japan has worked continuously towards better protection of its citizens through the use of structural defences. Many devices have been developed to cope with Japan's very vulnerable situation in relation to floods

For the major rivers, which are managed by the MLIT, the long-term goal is to improve each river so as to be capable of safely withstanding a 100 or 200-year flood. The short-term goal, for the beginning of the 21st century, is to improve the channels of major rivers in order to guarantee safety against 30-to-40-year floods. For smaller rivers, the objective is to safely withstand a 30-to-100-year flood, and the immediate goal is to cope with a 5- or 10-year flood. However, the accomplishments so far are falling far behind the targets, with a current prevention rate (or ratio of river lengths which can safely discharge floods at the target scale) of 59.1 %.[2] This general figure does take into account that there are significant local differences.

Another problematic question at present is how to set priorities in the building of flood defences when the budget is decreasing.

Besides the building of new flood defences, an important task for the government is to reinforce existing protection structures. An MLIT River Bureau study in September 2006 concluded that there is a need to reinforce 12 000 km of existing dykes.

An excellent example of local achievements can be found in the downstream part of the Arakawa River which flows right through downtown Tokyo. The effect in respect of flood protection is however limited due to budget reductions and new urbanisation development. The Arakawa Downstream River Office, which is one of three river offices of the MLIT managing the river, is in charge of the short downstream stretch where concentrations of population and assets are very high. The Arakawa River estuary is in downtown Tokyo. The budget of the office is JPY 10 billion, of which JPY 13 billion are spent on maintenance, and has been considerably reduced in recent years as the urgent investments in the lower part of the river are considered to have been completed and priority has therefore instead been given to upstream projects. Nevertheless, only 15% of the planned super dyke stretches in this area, which are strongly prioritised by the MLIT, have been constructed, and 85% of the super dyke program remains to be executed.[3]

The 200-year calculated return discharge of the river reaches 14 800 m^3/s. However, thanks to a recently completed new retarding pond that can take up to 39 million m^3 (construction started in 1970 and was finished in 2004 at a cost of JPY 40 billion), complete with an upstream dam, safety has been considerably improved. The master plan's target is to reduce the maximum discharge to 7 000 m^3/s by the construction of other flood control facilities, but the financing for this development has not yet been allocated.[4]

This indicates that even though Japan has probably worked harder than any other country to protect flood-prone areas, its current structural defences fall short of providing people and land with the level of protection deemed necessary. Another observation is that the reduction of flood risks through protection works has led to further concentration of city functions and buildings in the flood-prone areas protected by flood defences such as dykes, resulting in a higher damage potential. Also, the rising number of major rainfall events and typhoons due to climate change means that Japan is likely to have to face even greater vulnerabilities in the future. The financial needs to counteract these changes may multiply accordingly. Predictions of climate change made by the IPCC show the need to adapt protection measures, given that the degree of safety presently targeted and achieved would deteriorate with the future increase of precipitation. See Box 4.1.

Box 4.1. **The introduction in Japan of guidelines for the adaptation of mitigation strategies in response to climate change**

Following the conclusions of the IPCC on the increasing occurrence of large-scale floods with climate change, the central government issued basic guidelines for adaptation in March 2008. In face of the deterioration of flood safety, the proposal was put forward to reinforce structural measures and to go further in the implementation of non-structural measures. The strategy promoted specified that:

● Facilities-based adaptation measures would be taken, such as improving reliability and prolonging lives of existing devices and constructing new devices.

● Levels of protection would be redefined with respect to the projected and occurrences magnitude of precipitations.

● Damage mitigation measures would be promoted through:

  – Regional development adaptation including restrictions and review of land use, and guidance in planning of inundation-resistant communities (such as in pile houses).

  – Risk management improvement including measures on response, restoration and rehabilitation.

Such a strategy is a positive sign of the Japanese government's will to complement structural protection measures with non-structural mitigation measures. Still, implementation of such measures will require much effort.

Source: Japanese Ministry of Land, Infrastructure and Transport (MLIT), River Planning Division, March 11, 2008, PowerPoint Presentation, "Adaptation measures related to water-related disasters to reduce the impacts of climate change due to global warming".

Opportunities for action

With regard to the prevailing flood risks, Japan needs to continue reinforcing its structural flood protection, but the economic situation and the increasing probability of large-scale flood events mean that structural measures alone will not be able to solve the problems. There is a real necessity to keep on introducing new physical measures and to maintain the existing structural protection so that efficiency remains optimal. In order to make the best possible use of available resources, local cost-benefit analyses and risk communication with the public, organisations and enterprises including insurance could be strengthened as these are directly concerned by the rising costs of damage and the economic optimisation of prevention measures in relation to recovery costs. Cost-benefit analysis or multicriteria analysis should also be carried out more systematically in order to set priorities.

The comprehensive approach of integrating physical river improvements into the natural and social environment should be promoted further by the central government as it will increase citizen awareness about water and flood management. Some examples of water-related works undertaken with the development of leisure areas already exist in Japan. Cases such as the Kirigaoka regulating reservoir in Kanagawa Prefecture, which is normally used as a tennis court (see Figure 4.5), or the Tsurimi Multipurpose Retarding Basin,[5] should be used as models.

Figure 4.5. **The Kirigaoka Regulating Reservoir**

Outflow Control Facilities

The Kirigaoka Regulating Reservoir

The Kirigaoka during Flooding

Source: MLIT September 2006 *Rivers in Japan.*

Together with the promotion of structural measures, other flood-fighting actions and improved general risk communication with citizens to protect society and minimise the consequences should be promoted. This needs to be supplemented with the clear message that a zero risk situation does not exist even with flood control megaprojects in place. Flood risk management must be reinforced and encompass not only prevention, but minimise damage when floods occur.

Protective goals need to be redefined with respect to climate change projections, and adaptation measures enforced accordingly.

Recommendation 6. The highly vulnerable situation with respect to floods and increasing flood risks, not least due to climate change, requires a much higher level of investment in structural protection measures as well as continued comprehensive integration of physical flood defences into the natural and social environment.

2. Further development of mitigation measures

The limited resources available and the high level of investment necessary for structural measures in the flood defence strategy, lead to a need for improved damage mitigation measures as well as reduction in the vulnerability of people located in flood-prone areas. Such measures could apply to new constructions, involving land use, city planning and building requirements.

The legal framework for land use consists of the Basic Acts for Land and the Utilisation and Planning Acts. On the basis of the National Land Use Planning Law, prefectures prepare their basic land use plans (Land Use Master Plans) related to the use of all prefectural land in consultation with the national government. The Land Use Master Plans provide for the zoning of areas according to the way prefectural land is used, for urban areas, agricultural use, etc. From a legal viewpoint, Land Use Master Plans do not require citizens and NGOs to be consulted in their formulation process. Land use regulations are conducted in line with the Land Use Master Plans, based on individual statutes, and according to the purpose of each individual statute.[6]

With regard to city planning efforts related to the three largest urban zones, land for city planning is separated into "areas for the promotion of urbanisation" and "control areas" (where development is in principle forbidden) and zoning is implemented at a regional level in conformity with the City Planning Law. The setting of area zones is conducted by prefectures in principle, and subject to central government approval. Based on the City Planning Law, areas where disasters caused by overflow streams, floods, tsunamis or high tides could occur are not included in urbanisation areas (which are areas defined to be urbanised preferentially and systematically within 10 years).[7]

Construction standards are defined in the provisions of the Law on Building Standards. The law provides for minimum standards related to land plots, structures, facilities and usage of buildings. With regard to flood risks, Article 39, Paragraph 1 of the law allows local authorities to designate areas faced with the risk of tsunami, high tides or floods as "calamity danger districts."[8]

The number of such districts increased from 20 in March 1997 to 65 in March 2007.

Findings

Local measures concerning new facilities to mitigate medium size floods are apparently decided on by local authorities and are then presented to the public.

As far as city planning is concerned, some areas that are known as humid zones or flood-prone areas are protected from exploitation by local authorities, in order to maintain their capacity to reduce peak floods. Examples of such mitigation can be found in the prefecture of Saitama.

Some municipalities have also set up building requirements that will mitigate damage and increase the safety of persons. In some areas, for instance, where the highest water level of flooding of a river is known, the first floor of a new building must be higher than the maximum known water level. Such restrictions exist for instance in the city of Kawaguchi. To set up this requirement, a risk assessment is needed to inform investors about how high the water level will be in the event of floods.

Not only local authorities, but also some other important stakeholders seem to be quite involved in damage mitigation. As an example of a structural mitigation measure, the Tokyo Metro Company[9] has identified all entrances that could be flooded by local medium size floods, and has constructed defences to be able to shut some tunnels or subway entrances to avoid flood water intrusions. These defences are combined with an early warning system in order to be able to operate the system safely and in time. An example of voluntary non-structural measures is the case of a company interviewed during the review process. It was located beside a dyke where the Arakawa River and Nakagawa River flow in parallel, and decided to move away from Tokyo downtown to a safer area where other industries are already concentrated.

Nevertheless, even though the number of calamity danger districts is growing, non-structural measures such as land use, city planning or building requirements are not systematically implemented in zones which are protected by dykes but which could be affected by large-scale flood disasters. Moreover, it seems that far from limiting or controlling land use, government policies can sometimes encourage settlements and increase the concentration of assets in flood-prone areas protected by dykes, without apparently taking any vulnerability mitigation measures.[10]

Japan has developed probably the most rigorous standards in the world for buildings in order to ensure that security measures are taken to build fire-safe and earthquake-safe buildings. Thanks to strict legislation, the country has achieved the very high figure of 70% building safety regarding serious earthquakes. This means that the institutional and regulatory framework can play a leading role in promoting and implementing building requirements, even though most of the buildings belong to private companies or individuals. Moreover, such requirements are probably considered acceptable by the whole Japanese social community, thanks to the earthquake risk awareness promoted by the government and by the various catastrophes that have hit the country. Not respecting such requirements today would probably lead to denouncement and judgment by neighbourhoods.

Regarding flood risks, although construction standards for buildings have been elaborated by the MLIT, building standards are not always used for reducing flood vulnerability in areas protected by flood defences, nor is there mention of needs such as flood-proof or flood-resistant materials that could mitigate flood damage together with improving public safety.

Opportunities for action

In many OECD countries, land use restrictions as well as construction standards are likely to prove acceptable to citizens if risk communication and an open dialogue is introduced and if the restrictions aim at reducing vulnerability rather than simply and strictly forbidding constructions. Restrictions must then be integrated into an overall urban planning and development or exploitation approach.

Even when land use is allowed in flood-prone areas protected by dykes, the vulnerability of new constructions regarding very large-scale disasters should be evaluated and reduced as much as possible at both the planning and the design stage. Reducing vulnerability means the following: design buildings in such a way as to lower the material damage when a large-scale flood occurs; design in order to facilitate the management of an emergency response; move from the design stage to operational preparedness; and finally design to make recovery easier and faster.

For example, the Code for Sustainable Homes in the United Kingdom incorporates resilience standards. Such requirements may include construction materials that can resist and easily recover from being exposed to water immersion. Such requirements are being introduced in European countries. Some construction materials tolerate being under water for a while, whereas others (such as some types of wood, or insulating material) do not. Building requirements could also be encouraged with a view to gradually building cities and buildings that are less vulnerable to floods and recover easily after a flood, even when it is higher than 5 m.

Non-structural measures to restrict land use have to be thought through carefully and cannot simply take the form of "not allowing construction" in such areas with exposure to severe flood risks. Given the conditions in Japan, there seems to be essentially no alternative to having assets and population in flood-prone areas.

Measures to restrict land use need to be introduced at the city planning stage together with measures to reduce vulnerability in the event of large-scale floods. Very vulnerable buildings where peoples' safety and important assets are at stake, such as hospitals and hazardous installations, should be located in places where the flood risk is lower. This could avoid costly and risky evacuation, as well as mitigate damage. Other buildings might be located in more risky zones under stringent conditions, such as efficient early warning, limited evacuation needs and adequate building standards to ensure damage reduction.

Local government should have stronger support to make decisions establishing restrictions or setting requirements in building construction because of their negative impact on property values and on landowners' leadership. By raising hazard awareness at all decision levels and introducing vulnerability reduction methods through active risk communication that also involves the public, the authorities could encourage the ambition to ensure efficient implementation of mitigation measures, both structural and non-structural. However, communication on flood risks may be a real challenge for local government because of its likely negative impact on private investment for new constructions, on the development of economic activities, and on the satisfaction of established companies who may be reluctant to carry out new investment for mitigation purposes. Local authorities can experience significant political pressure linked to construction permits and to the requirement of extra spending from the private sector. On the other hand, ensuring people's safety is one of their main responsibilities, especially from the perspective of voters, and mitigation measures undertaken for more sustainable development and increased security are likely to enjoy a consensus in this regard. Consequently, there is definitely an appropriate way to communicate mitigation restrictions and regulations to citizens and private investors which counterbalances concerns by emphasising the benefits to people's security and the reduction of individual recovery costs.

In the United Kingdom, government policy aims to ensure that flood risk is taken into account at all stages in the planning process to avoid inappropriate development in areas at risk of flooding, and to direct development away from areas of highest risk. Where, exceptionally, new development is necessary in such areas, policy aims to make it safe, without increasing flood risk elsewhere, and, where possible, to reduce flood risk overall.

Recommendation 7. There is an urgent need for efficient non-structural measures to combat flood risks through a more holistic approach to prevention and damage mitigation.

3. The particular risks related to hazardous activities

An important challenge in the implementation of flood mitigation strategies is to limit the spread of polluting oil and other harmful substances with the flood waters. Rain is always a factor of dissemination of pollutants in the environment, but in the event of floods, the spread of oil and other harmful substances is likely both to geographically widen and qualitatively worsen the situation. This is for instance the case when water under pressure enters an industrial site and triggers an accidental release or spill of pollutants. During the 1999 flood in Bavaria, buildings and contents contaminated by oil suffered on average three times higher damage (in relation to total value) than buildings not contaminated by oil. In some cases, loss was even total. Protection of property and the environment is a central concern, but the safety of the population is at the top of the policy agenda.

In developed countries, including Japan, hazardous activities are obliged to take adequate preventive and preparedness measures based on risk assessments, in order to maintain safety and prevent or reduce environmental impacts. Legal requirements and control programs for hazardous activities are very far reaching. Hazardous activities are also subject to regular inspections by competent authorities. The establishment of new hazardous activities is as a rule subject to approval by planning and environmental authorities which will only be granted for suitable sites. Even for existing activities, safety requirements may be so burdensome that relocation may be the most appropriate and cost-effective solution.

Even though Japan is among the countries most threatened by natural disasters, formal measures are generally only required for hazardous activities in respect to earthquakes and not floods.

Since 1991, floods in the German *Land* of Baden-Württemberg have caused economic damage of around 1 billion Euros. It is estimated that catastrophic flooding in the Upper Rhine region on the same scale as the 2002 Elbe floods would cause damage in the order of EUR 6 billion. A large proportion of the costs would be due to hazardous substances leaking into the flood waters and damaging buildings and other structures (ranging from heating-fuel in the home to inadequately protected industrial installations). Indeed, the International Commission for the Protection of the Rhine has conducted studies which show that flood-proofing such potentially hazardous installations can reduce the scale of flood-related damage by between 50 and 75%.

In light of these events and findings, the government of the *Land* of Baden-Württemberg has recently tightened its legislation on flood protection. In addition to requiring the production and publication of detailed flood hazard maps for the whole of Baden-Württemberg (ready by 2010), the new reforms extend the legal requirement to protect potentially hazardous installations to all flood-prone built-up areas. The level of security required depends on the type and quantity of hazardous substances and the level of flood-risk to which the installation is exposed. For example, all installations have to be secured against 50-year flood events; particularly large and/or hazardous installations must be secured against 100-year events. Extensive provision is made to ensure that existing hazardous installations are retrofitted.[11]

The reforms are accompanied by comprehensive publicly available information material as well as guidelines on the practicalities of protecting hazardous installations against severe flooding.

Findings

Japanese legislation seems to take into account the potential impacts of hazardous activities on human health and safety and the environment when the installations receive their authorisation. Different laws apply to industrial activities, the City Planning Law and the Law Related to Rearrangement of Industrial and Business Facilities being the two most important. In the City Planning Law, the definition of the cross-sectoral decision-making process regarding industrialisation is illustrated by the mandatory tri-partite agreements between the MLIT, the Ministry of Economy, Trade and Industry and the Ministry of the Environment.

Three categories for the definition of industrial zones exist: exclusively industrial, industrial and quasi-industrial districts. According to the law, the "quasi-industrial districts are designated mainly for the promotion of industries which are not likely to deteriorate the environment". Allocation of land should involve "conservation of the residential environment, promotion of the convenience to commerce, industry, maintenance of the beauty of landscape, prevention of harm to the public". This demonstrates the concern devoted to industries' implementation requirements at the city planning stage. Moreover, the Japanese approach to consideration of safety and security of industries, especially chemical industries, is considered to be of a high standard. A review in November 1999 for the Science and Technology Service of the French Embassy in Japan underlined the very advanced level of industrial risk management in Japan, the focus being on managing earthquakes risks and the well-established Japanese industrial policies related to the limitation of available space.

Still, there are no particular obligations or restrictions imposed on land owners, including hazardous industries, for construction in flood-prone areas subject to large-scale disaster risks. Even without legislation, it is probable that most of the large Japanese companies have in their own interest voluntarily moved their production sites out of city centres and flood zones.

For example, one company interviewed during the review process has relocated two of its production lines, and is considering of moving its remaining line which has the least fragile equipment. The transfer cost between JPY 1 and 3 billion for each plant. Only small family businesses are still located in the area. One of the major reasons advocated by companies for leaving flood-prone areas is the inexistent insurance system against floods. Estimating costs of flood damages is an effective contraindication for companies in flood-prone areas. Nevertheless, the mitigation measures which have been introduced are not sufficiently effective and it seems that counting on industries' good will to ensure that enough is done even for such critical matters as the safety of persons and environment protection will not be sufficient. When seriously hazardous industrial activities are concerned, the legislation still needs to tackle flood risk reduction more systematically.

During severe flooding due to a typhoon breaking the dyke of the Tone River, an old copper mine area was flooded and caused considerable pollution problems. Such examples prove that current measures are not sufficient.

Opportunities for action

Chemical and nuclear industries and activities need to be obliged by law to take flood-related risks floods more specifically into account, especially large-scale ones, in their risk assessments and preventive and preparedness measures. The impact of floods should always be evaluated in the classical framework of security and safety assessment. To complement the individual relocation of hazardous industrial activities, more stringent and systematically implemented requirements in legislation should be introduced to avoid establishment of new activities in flood-prone areas. In order to achieve a satisfactory level of safety and environment protection in existing activities, there is a need for new legislation including requirements with respect to contingency planning and preparedness for emergency response. Such measures could be implemented in parallel to the existing framework for earthquakes.

Recommendation 8. Regulations applicable to hazardous industrial activities should include requirements for operators to assess and manage risks related to floods.

Notes

1. *Source:* MLIT, 2006, *Rivers in Japan.*

2. *Source:* MLIT, 2007, *Rivers Administration in Japan.*

3. *Source:* Interview of the OECD Review Team with the Arakawa downstream office, 15/05/07.

4. *Source:* Visit of the Arakawa facilities by the OECD Review Team, 17/05/07

5. MLIT, Kanto Regional Development Bureau, Tsurimi River Basin Water Council, 2004, *Life and Livelihood bound to the Earth : a vision for the regeneration of the Tsurimi River Basin.*

6. *Source:* Interviews of the OECD Review Team with the Land and Water Bureau (MLIT), 14/05/2007, and with the Saitama Prefecture, 16/05/2007.

7. *Source:* Interview of the OECD Review Team with the City and Regional Development Bureau (MLIT), 14/05/2007

8. *Source:* Interview of the OECD Review Team with the Housing Bureau (MLIT), 14/05/2007.

9. *Source:* Interview of the OECD Review Team with the Tokyo Metro Company, 18/05/2007.

10. *Source:* Interview of the OECD Review Team with the Saitama Prefecture, 16/05/2007.

11. *Source:* Baden-Württemberg Umweltministerium, January 2007, "Hochwasservorsorge in Baden-Württemberg: Anforderungen an Anlagen zum Umgang mit wassergefährdenden Stoffen" [Ministry for the Environment, Flood Protection in Baden-Württemberg: Requirements regarding installations concerned with the storage and treatment of water-hazardous substances].

ISBN 978-92-64-05639-8
OECD Reviews of Risk Management Policies
Japan: Large-Scale Floods and Earthquakes
© OECD 2009

Chapter 5

Emergency Response

Emergency response to floods in Japan has to be seen as a part of the Total Disaster Management System which has been developed through a seamless cycle of prevention, mitigation, preparedness, response, recovery and rehabilitation, *i.e.* protection against floods and river management on the one side and emergency management on the other. The system ensures strong national leadership and multi-sectoral coordination. According to the Disaster Countermeasures Basic Act, the central government, local government and public corporations are all responsible at their respective levels for protecting the land, the life and limb of people and property against natural disasters.[1]

1. Co-ordination during flood events

In view of the historical background against which flood-fighting has been conducted and developed by traditional autonomous organisations mainly at village level, the flood-fighting management entities are basically city, town and village authorities according to the Flood-fighting Act. Such entities organise flood-fighting teams and take part in flood-fighting activities supervised by fire-fighting agencies. The operational responsibility for emergency response thus falls mainly to the municipality.

In the event of large-scale floods which require more resources than those available at local level, the central government authorities become involved to provide general support and guidance to the local authorities, to ensure co-operation and co-ordination and to provide the additional resources required to manage the disaster.

An emergency team at national government level consisting of the directors-general of the various ministries and agencies gathers immediately at the Crisis Management Centre to take stock of and analyse the disaster situation. The Cabinet Office, under the authority of the Minister of State for Disaster Management, ensures the overall co-ordination of disaster reduction activities. Meanwhile, the Cabinet Secretariat provides situation awareness and incident information to the Cabinet based on the data collected 24 hours a day by the Cabinet Information Collection Centre.

The Red Cross Society may launch relief actions on its own judgement and initiative, or at the request of prefectural governments with whom it has agreements.[2] Any Red Cross Society chapter may send rescue teams to the scene of a disaster as soon as its members deem themselves ready. Red Cross actions are normally of a longer-term character. Co-ordination is thus established with the authorities involved in a relief action.

In an emergency, the MLIT River Bureau is responsible for river management and protection against floods and for the integration of the large number of volunteers in the flood-fighting teams integrated into the fire services. Numerous companies are under contract with river bureaus of MLIT for immediate repair of specific parts of a river dyke in the event of a breach. These contractors are selected from companies engaged in normal construction contracts with the river bureau. Because the companies need to respond urgently without knowing the scale of the disaster, they are obliged to act in accordance with a contract without pre-bidding immediately and must therefore have resources located close at hand in the area for which they have responsibility in an emergency. The companies will be prepared for emergency action but will also be able to get help from each other, if needed. Experience with a dyke breach that occurred nine years ago indicates that it was dealt with in the manner foreseen by the emergency plan.

Critical infrastructure providers such as the Tokyo Metro Co Ltd take action and measures against local torrential rain, but otherwise rely on the levees for protection. Station ventilation systems, tunnels and passages down to the tunnels can thus be shut down. For this purpose there is a control centre which can close the system by remote control. Information on the situation is passed on to each station which takes further measures, as needed, in the event of flooding. Still, in the event of a large-scale flood that could generate a dyke breach, no specific plan has been drawn up.

The river administration is in charge of organising annual drills and exercises. Every year before the flood season begins, residents and local government staff members are trained to develop levee-protection techniques during the early stage of overflow situations, such as shown in Figure 5.1 Such kinds of measure require very little money to obtain significant positive results.

The government has promoted business continuity planning as an important tool of risk management for organisations and industry. Starting from the private sector, this practice is now gradually extending to public organisations, also in a number of OECD countries, for instance in the UK British Standard on Business Continuity Management. Continuity planning raises the level of risk awareness and ensures that normal prevention and preparedness measures are actually in place, with a particular emphasis on critical infrastructures. In addition, it can minimise the direct or indirect economic and social impacts of disasters. In Japan, the Central Disaster Management Council has formulated business continuity guidelines.

In the event of a flood disaster, voluntary responders (almost 1 million part-time staff across the nation – these numbers are, however, decreasing which is seen as a major problem) can be mobilised under conditions defined

Figure 5.1. **Flood-fighting activities**

"Sandbag piling technique (Tsumidono ko)" (Torrential Rain in Niigata and Fukushima in 2004) The Ikarashi River in Niigata Prefecture

"Sandbag piling technique (Tsumidono ko)" (Typhoon No. 14 in 2005)
The Ooyodo River in Miyazaki Prefecture

Source: MLIT, May 2006, in Japan.

by the Flood-fighting Act. Local authority personnel are trained and informed about the large scale coordination needed. Agreements on mutual assistance are reached beforehand among the municipalities, and the prefectures can play a coordination role as needed in the form of assistance, as all the different levels of administration are considered to be equal. The provision of emergency response assistance from outside a municipality is governed by mutual help agreements between municipalities of the same prefecture (1940 existing agreements) or between prefectures (558 agreements).[3]

In addition, a parallel command and control structure at national and regional level to local level was created after the Great Hanshin-Awaji Earthquake in order to deal with large-scale disasters. Its role is to complement the municipal response by placing under its responsibility resources dispatched from the rest of the country. This large-scale rescue and evacuation framework has not yet been put to the test.

The central level will however only act when capacity is lacking, *i.e.* when the response capabilities of the affected local government are exceeded in a disaster. Various wide-area support mechanisms are then mobilised by MLIT, the National Police Agency, Fire and Disaster Management Agency and Japan Coast Guard. Furthermore, the Self-Defence Forces can be dispatched for emergency response activities upon request by the governor in the affected prefectural government. A wide-area medical transportation system for dispatching disaster medical assistance teams and ambulance parties for transporting seriously injured people to disaster management base hospitals outside of the disaster-stricken area is under development.

The Fire and Disaster Management Agency (FDMA) is the central government authority for fire and disaster management and performs its central role together with the prefectures and the municipalities. The personnel consist of full time and part time staff and to a certain degree volunteers, who form the large majority, but, as mentioned above, are becoming more difficult to recruit.

With regard to leadership and command of disaster management or incident response in Japan, the view is that most flood disasters are rather limited in extent, so that local-level organisation is considered advantageous for the initial response. As a disaster evolves into a more widespread, serious phase, responsibility shifts to a broader administrative organisation. As the inundation spills beyond the borders of the municipality, the command system changes drastically. While a powerful top-down system could be effective and even necessary for an extensive, large-scale disaster, it is not appropriate or efficient for daily emergencies and disasters. A new command-flow system is under consideration on the basis of a major disaster scenario in a low-lying metropolitan area. However, in general, local emergencies or disasters are frequent and municipalities need to be prepared for them. Disaster management organisation on the local level for preparedness and daily response operations can therefore provide a high level of capacity and mobilise resources efficiently for immediate use in a disaster.

Findings

The Disaster Management System in Central and Local Governments of Japan has developed progressively, making use of lessons learned from the many severe disasters from which the country has suffered. The organisational structure in general seems adequate in relation to prevailing natural disasters and in particular to flooding risks. The quantity and quality of resources that can be mobilised to respond to floods are impressive from an international perspective. This review contains findings that can serve as examples and best practice to many other OECD countries, and that can also be considered in the on-going development of Japanese organisation of emergency or disaster response. Needs identified for improvement of the disaster response in the system are mainly related to coordination, command and control and transparency.

Many different organisations are involved and play important roles in Japan, as in other countries, in emergency response to major flood disasters, mostly at the local or municipal level. In principle, the municipalities to which this responsibility has been delegated will to a great extent have the main practical responsibility for conducting necessary response or rescue operations. When needed, they will cooperate with each other in accordance with established agreements and under the coordination of the Prefectures.

In order to manage operations efficiently in the event of a major flood disaster, when all three layers of the administrative system in Japan are involved, there is a need for a clearer chain of command. This is particularly important as the central government at national level will in extreme situations be at the centre of mass media attention, have the overall political responsibility for management of the crisis and be held accountable by the general public.

Further, the division of tasks in the legislation between local and central government functions mainly exercised by the MLIT river administration and the JMA, the National Police Agency, the FDMA and the Japan Coast Guard as well as the Self-Defence Forces can be difficult to understand.

When Urgent Disaster Management Headquarters are established, the Prime Minister, as chief of headquarters, can give orders to the governors according to article 28 of the Disaster Countermeasures Basic Act. Completely changing the organisation of disaster management at the centre of government according to the size of events introduces complexities. Experience from different countries and sectors consistently indicates that changes to organisational structures during the management of a crisis should be avoided in order not to cause confusion and uncertainty.

The chain of command and the interfaces between the national and local government need to be made clearer to all involved in the crises management system, not least the personnel involved at the local government level. The personnel in the different bodies demonstrated during the interviews a strong commitment to their tasks and an excellent capability in their own area of responsibility. On the other hand, there seemed to be a lack of knowledge of the roles of other competent authorities and the Total Disaster Risk Management System in general. Examples of the Dutch organisation for emergency response and of the coordination of relief activities in Sweden are provided in Annexes I.6 and I.7.

Opportunities for action

Emergency response activities in Japan seem very well organised and adequate for small and medium size flood events and even for the initiation of the response to a major event. Generally, however, more focus needs to be put on improvements to the organisation and management of large-scale disasters even though the Japanese capacity for these disasters is greater than that of most other countries. In particular, more attention should be paid to the evolution of emergency response, when on the one hand more authorities at different levels and in different sectors become involved, and on the other hand, the command and control structure changes substantially, reflecting requirements for more complex coordination and collaboration. There is a need for clarification of the roles and responsibilities of the various public authorities and a reinforced and more transparent national chain of command.

Operational organisation at national level is modified in different respects during large-scale floods. Instead of changing the organisational structures during the operational management of a crisis, which is likely to provoke disturbance, mechanisms need to be established for effective and seamless reinforcement of organisational structures to meet the greater challenge.

There are indications of a need for systematic common education and training of officials in the different sectors and levels of bodies involved in the Disaster Management System. Such training could include joint scenario-based table-top exercises and command and control drills, supplemented by the very large-scale, and impressive, drills involving available resources against flooding which are held regularly. Examples of education and training can be found in other countries.

Such an ambitious drill, namely for the event of serious flooding on the Tone River, was observed in connection with the interviews. This drill illustrated the use in Japan of very large numbers of volunteer flood-fighting units conducting protection measures and cooperating with fire-fighting and other units. The main goals seemed to be to inspire and motivate the participants as well as create public awareness and demonstrate the services. The various actions to prevent and protect against floods and save lives were demonstrated, using different rescue boats, helicopters and other rescue equipment. Many participants from different services, including the Red Cross and the Self-Defence Army, took part in these training exercises.

The central government and the prefectures need to devise ways to consolidate disaster management capabilities in small municipalities. Providing increased training and education of their personnel, including on legal and administrative aspects of disaster risk management, would represent a minimal action in this regard. A bolder approach would consist of better concentration of local disaster management resources, by either enabling municipalities to engage in contractual arrangements for the provision of disaster management services (as in Switzerland), or by creating subregions where municipal resources would be pooled (as in the Netherlands).

Recommendation 9. The emergency chain of command needs to be streamlined, and the roles and responsibilities of organisations involved in emergency response at various levels to be clarified and made transparent.

2. Sheltering and evacuation for large-scale floods

Within the framework of comprehensive storm and flood countermeasures, warning and evacuation systems in possible inundation zones and landslide prone areas have been developed in accordance with legal requirements. Legislation was amended in 2005 to intensify measures, including through familiarisation with hazard maps and the identification of a method to disseminate disaster information to facilities caring for those requiring assistance at the time of a disaster, *e.g.* elderly people in the Municipal Disaster Management Plan. The designation and publication of possible inundation areas in the basins of 248 major rivers and 940 medium to small rivers across the country have been undertaken, and there are also requirements that municipalities promote the preparation and dissemination of flood hazard maps.

The evacuation of exposed populations is to a certain degree linked to improved flood risk information and communication. A low evacuation rate has been observed, but there is a need for a better understanding of the underlying reasons why persons choose not to evacuate. Studies in the United States show that there is a great difference in evacuation rates depending on the language used in the evacuation announcement – whether it is "mandatory" or "recommended" – and that "mandatory" evacuations are more respected. The chances of achieving a full evacuation are greater the earlier the announcement is made, but in that case it is subject to great uncertainty, and if it is inaccurate, it may lead to a higher degree of non-compliance at the next major incident.

Findings

To address the very complicated situation of evacuating large numbers of people in highly populated areas, hazard maps, early warning systems and measures for evacuation have been established. Before the flooding season, information and hazard maps are disseminated to the public.

Each river is assessed differently as to risks and vulnerabilities and information is provided by the river administration to the prefectures and municipalities.

When a certain water level is reached, a warning is issued, *i.e.* a flooding propagation or prediction is provided. The flood-fighting corps patrols the dykes from the time water levels reach the orange line (*i.e.* the alert line over which dyke break is likely to happen), and transmit information on the condition of the dykes to the relevant prefectures and municipalities, as a basis for decision making in respect to evacuation. The municipalities must assess the situation based on these warnings and consider evacuation.

The national government maintains close contact with the municipalities concerning flood warning. Exercises or drills are conducted each year before the rainy period in June-October. At high tide when there are risks of major flooding, three levels of warning are implemented, orange for a general alert, blue for preparation for evacuation and red for evacuation. Scenarios, risk maps etc. are established through the use of simulations, and possible flooded areas are indicated by the JMA in support of the municipalities. Information is provided to the public, including schools. Many residents in low level areas however, have not experienced floods for 30 to 40 years, and in many cases have moved in from other geographical areas, which creates a problem with respect to public risk awareness. Only long-term residents have this awareness.

Though the authorities in the Tokyo area have developed strong practical experience in disaster response, their preparation is still insufficient to deal with the consequences of large-scale disasters such as the evacuation of 3 million people when public transport is not available. Prevention has previously been emphasised, but recently it has been found necessary to enhance the capacity for disaster management. An expert group has been established to define objectives for technical measures and there is a trend towards prioritising preparedness even if large-scale preventive measures are more effective, but cannot be made available due to the extremely long time frames needed to introduce these, in particular with reduced budgets in recent years.

The interviews focused on the Saitama Prefecture, the City of Kawaguchi and the Sumida Ward of Tokyo. Considerable efforts are being made to provide shelters and facilitate evacuation through involving the general public in drills. When mobilised during a disaster, the flood-fighting force, which in Japan consists of 1 800 units and 900 000 people, is in principle the same as or integrated into the fire-fighting corps. Responsibility for airports and industry to maintain preparedness falls to the prefecture.

The City of Kawaguchi has 500 000 inhabitants. About half of the city's surface consists of high-lying land of more than 12 m elevation. In a major flood, this should provide enough evacuation and shelter possibilities for the city's population, but flows of people from neighbouring cities (including Tokyo) could be a problem. Discussions on this matter are starting with the relevant authorities.[4]

The Sumida Ward of Tokyo has 230 000 inhabitants. The Ward buys rainfall information from a private meteorological company (which provides more detailed data than the JMA), and sends it to the owners of underground facilities by fax. The Ward does not have any other preparedness activities. Its hazard map has not been completed, although the hazard information has been transmitted by the MLIT's Regional Bureau, because evacuation is a problem as there is no area available in the Ward for evacuation. A possible solution has been found, but needs to be approved by the Metropolitan Government and the MLIT. The law does not provide for systematic coordination procedures in such cases. The Ward's flood-fighting operations are managed by the civil engineering division for limited events, and by the disaster management division for disasters. But there is no clear definition of the threshold at which functions should be transferred.[5]

Opportunities for action

Due to the characteristics of rivers, the extreme weather events that are likely to increase with climate change and the very high concentration of assets and people in flood-prone areas, Japan is likely to face large-scale flood events that may require the rapid evacuation of a million or more people.

Under these conditions, the review findings, not least during the interviews with the Saitama Prefecture, the City of Kawaguchi and the Sumida Ward of Tokyo, indicate very clearly that there is a need for active co-ordination at both the national and the prefecture level of the conditions for large-scale evacuation. This disaster coordination measure should be supported by sufficient enforcement tools to allow for appropriate contingency planning by the municipalities. The legislation thus needs to provide for systematic coordination procedures in such cases.

The major problems are not only related to selecting areas for sheltering and evacuation, but also the evacuation of as many as 3 million people in the event of severe floods and when public transport is not available. In this respect there is a need for improved operational co-operation between municipalities, co-ordinated by prefectural and central government authorities with a more active role for the Cabinet Office in a necessary top-down approach.

Even if the prefectures have links with municipalities, these do not seem to involve the fire and rescue services. These services need to be more implicated in the various river, urban, and land use projects in order to mitigate rescue problems, to increase awareness of the other stakeholders involved and finally to better prepare themselves to cope with a flood disaster taking into account the specificity of the concerned area. Central government requirements in terms of best practices could promote and assist in achieving such co-operation. This would lead to growing risk awareness among the various organisations concerned.

Recommendation 10. There is an urgent need to make adequate provision for sheltering and evacuation of local populations that could be affected by large-scale flood events, including through enhanced co-operation between local governments.

OECD REVIEWS OF RISK MANAGEMENT POLICIES – ISBN 978-92-64-05639-8 – © OECD 2009

3. Emergency response regarding the most vulnerable groups of the population

Certain parts of the population are more vulnerable than others in disasters. This vulnerability may be geographical, i.e. the area in which people live is more exposed to the hazard than the surrounding areas; or it may be economic, i.e. a person may lack the necessary means for insurance, evacuation or recovery from a disaster. The New Orleans Katrina disaster demonstrated the significance of the economic aspects on vulnerability. Not only were low-income groups concentrated in the lower-lying areas which were geographically more exposed to flooding, but these groups also lacked the means to evacuate.

Vulnerability may also be physical, i.e. illness or incapacity may hinder a person's escape from anger, and cultural, social or cognitive, i.e. a person lacks the cultural capabilities including language skills to interpret danger signals and emergency information and to behave accordingly.

On all these fronts vulnerability is increasing, i.e. geographical vulnerability due to urbanisation opening up land for habitation in areas that are more exposed to floods than others; economic vulnerability is rising for some population groups in many OECD countries; and physical vulnerability as a result of the rising share of the elderly in the population. Finally, cultural vulnerability is growing with a rising share of immigration and tourism. It could also be argued that the increasing use of and dependency on ICT creates a cognitive vulnerability, i.e. creates barriers for those who are not used to handling modern technology.

The multiple vulnerabilities of elderly women illustrate some of these points. In Japan, the number of elderly households rose sharply between 1975 and 2003, from 3.3 % to 15.8 % of all households. Within these households, the number of one-person households increased five-fold, from 610 000 to 3.41 million, the majority of which consist of women. It should be noted that elderly persons living on their own, in particular women, are among the most economically vulnerable in the populations in OECD countries – especially in Japan.[6]

The elderly in general are also less resilient than others during disasters, for instance in the Great Hanshin-Awaji Earthquake, the population aged 65 and above had a much higher mortality rate than other groups, especially elderly women. This was partly explained by the fact that many elderly lived in traditional, low-cost residential areas consisting of wooden houses – constructions which performed very badly during the earthquake and which were ravaged by fire afterwards. In recent flood disasters in Japan, the majority of victims were elderly, and in Europe, the vulnerability of the elderly was underlined in the 2002 heat wave, which claimed the lives of more than 30 000 persons.[7]

Findings

The goal of legislative amendments in 2005 was to intensify measures such as the identification of a method to disseminate disaster information to facilities caring for those requiring assistance at the time of a disaster, like elderly persons in the Municipal Disaster Management Plan. Special measures must be taken to take care of groups such as certain elderly persons, the disabled and the poor, as they do not have the means to leave independently. Assistance and dedicated transport facilities must be provided for them.

Data are collected by municipalities on places where vulnerable people live (nursing homes, old peoples' homes, etc.). Such people can be helped within the framework of the municipal social welfare contact persons system. There is however a problem due to privacy protection rules in going further in registration of vulnerable persons, as people do not want to show their vulnerability and wish to hide their real needs in case an evacuation is required. Preparatory measures are however taken for extreme situations in respect to the capacity for providing early and accurate warning and evacuation.

In the discussion with the River Division, Disaster Management Division and Fire Department, of Kawaguchi City in Saitama Prefecture, information was provided that there are 200 000 inhabitants in the blue area where there can be 2 – 5 m flooding due to extremely heavy rain using the 200 years occurrence. Each household is informed and evacuation exercises are conducted. The city welfare system uses welfare commissioners for contacts with vulnerable groups. In the city of Kawaguchi which has 500 000 inhabitants, there are 187 voluntary flood prevention organisations and 600 welfare commissioners. The municipality has distributed 200 000 hazard maps and its communication policy is developed in cooperation with a network of 200 community organisations made up of dozens of citizen groups whose minimum unit is approximately 20 households. It has identified and reached out to 26 000 vulnerable persons, out of whom 58% have asked to be included in rescue plans – the rest relying on mutual help.[8]

Opportunities for action

There are clear indications that more attention needs to be given to the protection of vulnerable groups in all phases of the risk management cycle.

The challenge of dealing with vulnerable social groups seems to be a common issue for OECD countries, as shown by the 2005 New Orleans evacuation. In the European Union this is a normal task for the social welfare systems in the municipalities, as is the case in Japan. Under normal conditions the capacity will most probably be satisfactory, but the 2003 heat wave in France demonstrates that a severe disaster situation may not be handled in an acceptable way and that improvements are needed.

In Japan, risk management authorities need to be better prepared to address the issues related to vulnerability in specific parts of the population. Outreach to the most vulnerable groups calls for active cooperation between municipal services in charge of disaster response and health and social welfare. This could be done with the help of existing community associations. Municipal welfare services, with the help of local welfare commissioners, play the leading role in providing information about and to vulnerable persons in need of help and assist them in case of an evacuation.

Recommendation 11. Municipal services in charge of disaster response and health and welfare need to be better prepared to reach out to the most vulnerable groups of the population.

Notes

1. Cabinet Office, Government of Japan, 2007, *Disaster Management in Japan.*

2. Interview by the OECD Review Team of the Red Cross.

3. *Source:* Interview with the FDMA, 15/05/2007.

4. *Source:* Interview of the OECD Review Team with the Kawaguchi municipality, 16/05/2007.

5. *Source:* Interview of the OECD Review Team with the Arca Towers ltd and the Sumida ward, 17/05/2007.

6. *Source:* Japanese Statistics Bureau, 2005.

7. *Source:* *www.grid.unep.ch/activities/global_change/atlas/pdf/reagir_changements% 20climatiques.pdf*, accessed July 2008.

8. Interview of the OECD Review Team with the Kawaguchi municipality, 16/05/07/

ISBN 978-92-64-05639-8
OECD Reviews of Risk Management Policies
Japan: Large-Scale Floods and Earthquakes
© OECD 2009

Chapter 6

Recovery

1. The implementation of optimal reconstruction schemes

The last stage of the disaster management cycle deals with recovery. Basically, at that point, the major question is how to achieve the reconstruction in an economically and socially acceptable way, in respect to both the emergency of the situation and the need for a long-term vision encompassing the lessons learned from the disaster.

In Japan, the recovery and rehabilitation system focuses on providing support to help rebuild the normal livelihoods of the affected population as quickly and smoothly as possible, as well as on restoring public facilities.

For large-scale disasters, special Headquarters for Reconstruction are established, thereby integrating the efforts of concerned ministries and affected population committees.

The Act on Support for Livelihood Recovery of Disaster Victims, enacted in 1998 and revised in 2004, enforced the cooperation for natural disaster victims through the definition of local and central government responsibilities for reconstruction, provision of special low-interest loans to the affected population, and other economic measures such as tax reduction and exemptions.[1]

In 2005, the Central Disaster Management Council published the "Business Continuity Guidelines" to help companies in developing Business Continuity Plans (BCP). BCP are corporate management strategies aimed at resuming crucial business activities as quickly as possible in the recovery phase.

Despite these different actions which improved the recovery system significantly and helped define general strategies, the co-ordination of entities in charge of delimited actions such as response, planning and prevention against floods is currently not fully achieved at the reconstruction and recovery stage in Japan.

Administrations undertaking the recovery, namely the municipalities and prefectures with the financial help of the central government, mostly lack previous experience of the practical solutions to be implemented after the occurrence of floods.

Most of the time, the role of civil forces is confined to the implementation of response and remains limited regarding communication and integration into city planning of civil protection needs.

Findings

Though it is understandable that after a major disaster, given the stress put on the population and economy, the government focuses on emergency measures such as damage assessment, relocation of population in temporary shelters, quick rebuilding of disaster-stricken areas, medical help and economic revival incentives, these measures should be supplemented by long-term ones that include further cooperation of civil forces and city planning decision makers.

Regarding the intricate situation of the post-disaster event, decisions may be harder to take in a coordinated and participative manner at this stage due to individual preoccupations, time-consuming searches for funding and damaged communication and transport infrastructures. In order to cope with these difficulties, the bodies in charge could make use of pre-recovery schemes, whose role would be the global definition of city planning reorganisation strategies in floods.

The example of the Great Hanshin-Awaji Earthquake, after which the restoration works undertaken focused on overall city planning, proves that the Japanese government is able to work on long-term measures when reconstructing damaged zones, and to adapt its policies and actions at the recovery stage taking into account the lessons learnt from the past.[2] Still, concerning the difficulty of balancing immediate interests and long-term needs, the Kobe reconstruction process was not considered fully successful and is criticised for major shortcomings. This proves the complexity of post-disaster tasks, and the need to focus in advance on recovery organisation.

Reconstruction plans inspired by the wish to mitigate damage in case of a new disaster could be improved by the feedback of civil security forces. Their local experience can help better understand the real-time impacts of floods on populations. Moreover, if civil security forces were involved during the reconstruction process, they could explain what types of buildings or city planning facilitate or complicate rescue based on their experience. Indeed, some types of building architecture may make things easier for rescue during a flood (for example, outside staircases, or houses with heightened first floors) while others obviously worsen the situation (flats with no window on the street, etc.).

Opportunities for action

Civil protection services should be more involved in the various river, urban and land use projects to help design prevention measures, to mitigate rescue problems, to increase awareness of the other stakeholders involved and to better prepare themselves to cope with a flood disaster, taking into account the specificity of the concerned area.

Civil protection bodies with their practical experience of emergency management can give precious advice to avoid certain land uses or materials, or certain infrastructure designs, because experience tells them that they complicate or hinder the response or recovery phases.

If such collaboration was established, it would lead to growing risk awareness among the various organisations concerned and to an upgrading of flood control management regarding land use and building standards.

In order to match the required speed of economic reactivation and reconstruction, together with extending the short-term views that are subordinated to time-pressured city planning, the creation of pre-recovery schemes could be promoted. These schemes, as bases for the implementation of recovery measures, could be debated by citizen associations, NGOs and other stakeholders.

After the estimation of damages, detailed planning will be carried out through the double prism of the pre-recovery scheme and the collection of observations from civil security forces.

Under the United Kingdom's Civil Contingencies Act, local authorities play a key role in preparing for and responding to civil emergencies. Typically, local councils set-up an emergency planning unit to ensure that they have a robust and resilient major emergency plan, which enables prompt and appropriate response to any major incident occurring within or impacting upon the municipality. Emergency planning units work in collaboration with the emergency services, voluntary agencies and other agencies, to ensure there is a co-ordinated and effective emergency preparedness response. This includes co-ordinating the planning, training, exercise, activation and management of a council's response to emergencies.

The legislation on civil contingencies places a legal duty on local responders to co-operate not only in the delivery of emergency planning functions, but also to share information as part of a process of best practice. Information sharing is considered a crucial element of civil protection work, underpinning all forms of cooperation and developing a culture of cooperation. In this context, police, fire, ambulance, health and local authorities have a legal duty to undertake risk assessments and maintain them in a Community Risk Register.

Recommendation 12. In order to facilitate reconstruction, agreements need to be reached in advance. After the disaster, the detailed organisation of reconstruction should be discussed between civil protection and planning services.

2. The collection and communication of experiences

Flood risk management in Japan is certainly not based on an immutable system set up once and for all: the government has constantly updated laws and regulations on the basis of past disaster events. The enactment of the

River Law in 1964 five years after the deadly Ise-Wan Typhoon and its various amendments till its current 1997 version, the numerous changes brought to the Disaster Management Act after its elaboration in 1961, the restructuring of the central government in 2001 and the creation of the CDMC to cope with large-scale disasters such as the 1995 the Great Hanshin-Awaji Earthquake, are evidence of the highly adaptive capacity of Japan's strategy against disaster.[3]

The collection of past experiences or lessons learned is carried out by the central government and the need for further development in this field has been addressed through recent measures taken at the central level for the creation of information sharing platforms. In the MLIT subcommittee on rivers, a discussion group involving academic experts, governors, and people with knowledge of the localities and their culture discusses measures on policies for river equipment, based also on past experiences. The government and various administrations are thus already very well aware of the need to collect past experiences and learn lessons for policy improvement.

Findings

Various administrations, both central and local, have started working on the evaluation of their observed successes or failures towards better flood control policies. The collection of past experiences is carried out by central and local administrations with great care and helps strategies to be constantly updated. Tremendous effort is expended to disseminate the results of past experiences to the public. Still, communication towards citizens needs to be improved further, based on past flood experiences of affected persons, in order to advocate best practices that can be conducted by each individual.

Moreover, the tools used by various administrations to conduct post-disaster collection and communication are not clearly identified and systematically implemented. Post-event investigations, performance assessment, and risk/vulnerability scenario updating are powerful tools to draw lessons from experiences which could be promoted further in Japan.

Clarification of legal improvements that were undertaken upon analysis of past experiences requires enhanced communication to local decision makers.

Opportunities for action

There is a need to elaborate a systematic framework for learning and implementing lessons from flood events. The example of the lessons learned study that was conducted after floods occurred in England in 2007 is described in the 'Pitt Review'.[4] Other options that can be considered include:

- *Ad-hoc* post-event meetings between river managers, civil security services, land use and city planners, architects and general contractors.

- Policy guidelines.

- A national agency in charge of investigating the different aspects of the management of past events, collecting and harmonising data, establishing and disseminating best practices, and sharing experiences with international counterparts.

For that, obviously, the role of the central administration should be reinforced.

Another element that should be promoted at the post-disaster recovery stage is the enforcement of risk culture (see Annex I.9 for the development of risk culture benefits).

Finally, there is a need for an overall review of successive legislation related to disaster risk management, to make it more holistic and streamlined in order to facilitate understanding and implementation by all stakeholders.

Box 6.1. Collection of past experiences of floods in the United Kingdom

A "Lessons Learned Review" of the flooding that occurred in England during June and July 2007 is to be carried out by the Cabinet Office with support from the Department for Environment Food and rural affairs and the Department for Communities and Local Government. The review will examine both how to reduce the risk and impact of floods and the emergency response to the floods. The terms of reference for the review are:

a Flood risk management, including the risk posed by surface water flooding and the way in which the public and private sector might adapt to future risks.

b Vulnerability of critical infrastructure, including:

  i The ability of critical infrastructure to withstand flooding, and what improvements might be made.

  ii The resilience of dams and associated structures and what improvement might be made.

c The emergency response to the flooding, including social and welfare issues.

d Issues for wider emergency planning arising from the actual or potential loss of essential infrastructure.

e Issues arising during the transition period from the response to recovery phases.

> **Box 6.1. Collection of past experiences of floods
> in the United Kingdom** (cont.)
>
> As part of the review process, the Review team will seek the views of
> affected communities and local businesses as well as other key stakeholders
> such as the emergency services, professional associations, local authorities,
> voluntary organisations, industry associations, public and regulatory bodies,
> and will provide the opportunity to contribute and shape the direction of the
> review's recommendations. To this end the Review team has also established
> an online comments form to solicit ideas and suggestions from those
> affected by the floods in June and July 2007 or whose home or business is
> susceptible to the risk of flooding.
>
> Source: DEFRA news release, 8 August 2007, www.cabinetoffice.gov.uk.

**Recommendation 13. Risk management experiences should be
systematically collected, evaluated during the recovery phase and
disseminated widely to all stakeholders to enhance the development of an
overall risk culture. In addition, an overall review of successively developed
legislation should be conducted to improve transparency.**

3. Recovery costs and insurance

In Japan, municipalities have primary responsibilities for financing
recovery expenditures of public devices (roads or public buildings), while the
prefectures and the central government contribute financially in proportion to
the scale of an event. However, in regards to the repair and recovery of
residents' assets, the national government does not generally authorise
financial aid. Thus a considerable share of the repair and recovery costs for
residents' assets is usually borne by local residents. Regarding flood damage,
government policies and legislation in Japan aiming at supporting private
citizens and businesses financially are limited, and there are at present no
insurance or reinsurance schemes to reimburse assets damaged by floods.

Flood-related damage is covered through the householder's
comprehensive insurance (as are all natural hazards except earthquakes), as
an optional part of fire insurance. When a flood occurs, insurance covers a
maximum of 70% of the damage cost. In cases where there is no insurance,
only a fraction of losses is actually compensated.

Premiums are differentiated by a factor of 3 or 4 between locations, except in
Tokyo where risks are averaged, and the same rate is applied in the 23 wards.

To date, the insurance industry's record losses followed the Tokai flood in
Nagoya (JPY 700 billion), and a typhoon in 1991 (JPY 570 billion). [5]

Two floods in Japan figure among the ten highest insurance losses due to natural disaster calculated by Munich Re between 1989 and 1999. However, the ratio of the amount of insurance payment to economic losses for these floods was quite similar to floods in other developed countries. It is interesting to compare this fact to the Great Hanshin-Awaji Earthquake, which had an extremely low ratio of the amount of insurance payment to economic loss (0.03).

Today, the main request of the non life insurance industry is exemption from taxes for reserved funds for insurance payment.

Findings

The cost of disasters is shared by individuals, the government and the insurance industry. In accordance with the Disaster Relief Act, local public bodies are required to set aside a specific amount of money for a disaster relief fund managed by the prefecture. The Act Concerning Support for Reconstructing Livelihood of Disaster Victims stipulates the financial assistance available to disaster victims for reconstructing livelihoods. Private insurance that covers flood damage is called householders' comprehensive insurance: it is optional within the fire insurance policy. Its penetration rates are of approximately 70%, according to estimates by a major Japanese insurance company (although estimates do vary – the OECD estimates the rate is actually between 35-49%).[6] Such policies reflect the practice of many OECD countries.

Where several natural hazards together constitute a threat, a comprehensive package covering different types of hazards increases the

Table 6.1. **The 10 larger insurance losses between 1989 and 1999**

Year	Event	Area	Amount of insurance payment (USDM)	Economic losses (USDM)	Ratio of Insured/ Economic Losses
1992	Hurricane Andrew	USA	20 800	36 600	0.57
1994	Northridge earthquake	USA	17 600	50 600	0.35
1991	Typhoon Mireille	Japan	6 900	12 700	0.54
1990	Windstorm Daria	Europe	6 800	9 100	0.75
1989	Hurricane Hugo	Caribbean USA	6 300	12 700	0.50
1999	Winterstorm Lothar	Europe	5 900	11 100	0.53
1987	Winterstorm Lothar	Western Europe	4 700	5 600	0.84
1998	Hurricane Georges	Caribbean USA	3 500	10 300	0.34
1995	Earthquake	Japan	3 400	112 100	0.03
1999	Typhoon Bart	Japan	3 400	5 000	0.60

Source: Munich Re, 2000.

portfolio balance by reducing the adverse selection usually-related to flood risks. Still, Japan today lags far behind some countries using the same system, such as the United Kingdom and Israel which have market penetration rates close to 95%. This difference underscores the need for Japan to promote householders' comprehensive insurance and further develop existing systems of coverage.

Public transfers to victims are relatively modest compared to other countries and might help explain the high level of precautionary savings amongst Japanese households (40% of total saving). However, this might also imply higher exposure of economically vulnerable groups to hazards, which, in the context of rising flood risks, would call for the development of risk-sharing mechanisms. The government does not provide a reinsurance policy against floods. It is thus quite common in Japan that individuals carry an important part of the economic loss of disasters.

With climate change and further concentration of assets in flood-prone areas, it is necessary to prepare for increasing risks of flood disasters and higher recovery costs, shared by residents and insurance companies.

Moreover, in Japan, it is common to sign up for long-term insurance on purchasing a residence and securing back up bank loans. As typhoon and floods risks are covered through insurance policies paid as lump-sums in advance, insurance companies bear the risk associated with large-scale disasters for a long time and have very little room for manoeuvre to readjust their premiums when risks increase (except with climate change). Insurance companies also consider taxes on insurance reserves to be a heavy burden.[7]

Opportunities for action

In order to increase the proportion of insurance coverage, flood insurance could be made obligatory in disaster-related legislation. By making flood insurance compulsory, the government could stimulate the demand for insurance coverage by individuals and businesses through fiscal incentives. Policy premiums could be more reasonably differentiated to account for provisions made by households or companies to reduce their exposure and vulnerability to floods.

The National Flood Insurance Program in the United States, detailed in Annex I.10, illustrates one example of how the government can deal with the strategies of private insurance companies.

Risk sharing mechanisms such as CAT bonds, contingent debt facilities and pooling arrangements between direct insurers (e.g. Swiss Natural Hazards Pool) offer interesting opportunities for insurance companies to reduce the burden of a large-scale disaster. In the longer term, the government could study the advantages and costs of a compulsory insurance scheme and state-sponsored reinsurance for large-scale floods, already existent in several OECD countries.

Recommendation 14. In order to help citizens and private companies cope with the financial costs of major events, the system of flood insurance should be improved, with the aim to increase both population coverage and the capacity of insurance companies. This could be achieved through a stronger involvement of the national government as reinsurer.

Notes

1. *Source:* Cabinet Office, Government of Japan, 2007, *Disaster Management in Japan.*

2. *Source:* Cabinet Office, Government of Japan, 2007, *Disaster Management in Japan.*

3. Source for History of Flood-related Regulation: Cabinet Office, Government of Japan, 2007, *Disaster Management in Japan.*

4. *Source:* The Pitt Review: Learning Lessons from the 2007 Floods, 28/06/2008

5. *Source:* Interview of the OECD Review Team with the Tokyo Marine and Nichido Fire Insurance company, 18/05/2007

6. *Source:* OECD (2003), Flood Insurance.

7. *Source:* Interview of the OECD Review Team with the General Insurance Association of Japan, 18/05/2007.

ANNEX I.1

Basin Territory River Administration (EPTB) in France

In France, where developing flood protection measures falls under local governments' responsibility, various local administrations have federated at the river basin scale since the middle of the 1990's.

Indeed, in order to gather technical and economic resources, as well as to develop a coherent and integrated approach to river management, the national government has allowed and promoted through recent law the development of river basin institutions bringing together the local governments of a river basin.

Before 1992, the actions of such entities were generally limited to the construction of structures such as dykes or dams. With various growing concerns, such as protection of the environment, they have progressively incorporated the need for a more integrated basin management approach. Their very specific position is determined by both to the limits of their territory of action based on hydrographic qualities rather than administrative borders, and to their strong connection to both political and non-political local stakeholders. This advantageous situation allows their local activity to serve as a model for further environmental laws and central policies. Such a bottom-up approach, based on observed outcomes of local experiments, has proven very useful for innovation in both river and flood risk management.

Thanks to the river basin scale they have adopted, the EPTB has the power to provide advice in all phases of flood risk reduction, which covers prevention, protection, emergency response and vulnerability reduction - both at the local level through partnerships and through member communes. The approach they advocate includes environmental and social considerations.

Source: EPTB Loire and SEPIA Conseils, 2007, "Apprendre à vivre avec les inondations", "Les EPTB, un moteur d'innovation".

ANNEX I.2

The United Kingdom Administration of Flood Risk Management

In the United Kingdom the Cabinet Secretariat is non-departmental in function and purpose. It sits in the Cabinet Office, but serves the Prime Minister and Ministers who chair committees. It only serves Cabinet Office Ministers in their role as Committee Chairmen. The Cabinet Secretariat's overarching aim is to ensure that the business of government is conducted in a timely and efficient way and that proper collective consideration takes place when it is needed before policy decisions are taken. Through this work the Cabinet Secretariat contributes to two of the Cabinet Office's overarching aims: to support the Prime Minister in leading the government and to achieve coordination of policy and operations across government.

The Secretariat is composed of six individual secretariats one of which is the Civil Contingencies Secretariat (CCS), which guides and co-ordinates the activity taking place across government departments and wider stakeholders to ensure that the United Kingdom is resilient to any event which could pose a disruptive challenge to its welfare and day to day activities.[1] This could include the impacts of natural hazards such as flooding (in collaboration with the Department of Farm and the Environment Agency), as well as diseases, major accidents, and consequences of terrorist activity.

The main areas of this horizontal co-ordination activity are:

- Co-ordinating assessment of risks that could pose a disruptive challenge to the United Kingdom through Horizon Scanning and a periodic National Risk Assessment.

- Co-ordinating development of generic capabilities to deal with the consequences of disruptive challenges through a Cross-Government Capabilities Programme.

- Implementing legislation to support civil resilience in the United Kingdom.

- Providing a centre of excellence for training on emergency planning at the Emergency Planning College.
- During a crisis, coordinating consequence management to support the Government's response.

The Secretariat also provides the public with factual information about preparing for emergencies.

Notes

1. CCS website: *http://www.cabinetoffice.gov.uk/secretariats/civil_contingencies.aspx*

ANNEX I.3

Flood Protection and Climate Change – the Bavarian Adaptation Strategy

Climate change poses a growing challenge for spatial planning and local development, and in particular requires a higher level of concern regarding flood-prone areas and water management. In order to begin addressing the need for adapting to climate change, the European Cooperation project ESPACE was launched in 2003. This project advocates tackling three major aspects related to the increased danger of flooding: additional physical consequences, socio-economic and ecologic impact, and measures towards raising awareness and changing behaviours.

The Bavarian Environment Agency, as one of the partners, assessed the impact of climate change on the Catchment Area of the Fränkische Saale River in order to suggest appropriate countermeasures. A "Climate-Proof Planning Circle" was designed to illustrate the integrated approach required for the revision and adaptation of existing flood-fighting tools and planning processes.

An important stage of this circle is the prior assessment of the expected consequences of climate change on flood discharge and occurrences of flood events. For a designated return period, the Climate Change Factor is calculated to allow for the re-evaluation of dimensions for flood protection constructions. Decisions on whether to carry out the works are evaluated through the use of cost-benefit analysis. Together with this structural adaptation to climate change, the necessity for intensified mitigation actions and risk awareness is addressed through the publication of information on the Internet and running of surveys, conferences and meetings.

Source: Climate Change and River Catchment Planning, "Flood Protection for the River Fränkische Saale: A European Pilot Project", Edited by the Bayerisches Landesmat für Umwelt and Wasserwirtschaftsamt Bad Kissingen.

Figure I.3.1. **The "Climate-Proof Planning Circle"**

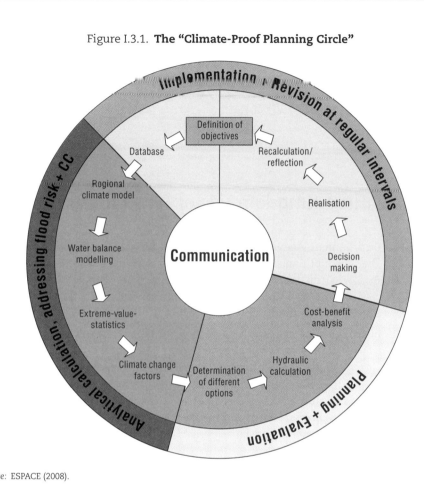

Source: ESPACE (2008).

ANNEX I.4

The United Kingdom use of Flood Risk Maps

The Environment Agency has been charged with preparing flood risk maps for the whole of England and Wales as part of its survey duties under Section 105 (2) of the Water Resources Act 1991. These maps show the boundaries of the "100 year flood" (also known as a 1% probability flood). Such a flood is expected to occur just once in 100 years.

The purpose of the maps is to inform planners and developers about flood risks so as to guide new development away from such flood risk areas and to build awareness of existing flood risk. While development within the boundary should be limited, it may be allowed in adjacent areas. In the context of climate change this is particularly relevant. Since more rainfall could result in more floods, new developments outside current flood risk areas may be at risk in the future. There is the possibility then that these maps could give a false sense of security.

Until very recently these maps were not in the public domain. Copies of the 1999 Indicative Flood Plain Maps are now available. The maps, at a scale of 1:10 000, each show an area of land 5 km x 5 km and are available at A1 plan size or A3 (reduced scale) plan size. A national set of these maps costs GBP 22 000 for the A1 Scale and GBP 8 000 for the A3 scale. The Agency also publishes leaflets that include local maps of areas at flood risk.

Source: United Kingdom National Press Office (2004).

ANNEX I.5

International Commission for the Protection of the Rhine (ICPR)

Since 1950, the four countries along the river Rhine have agreed to co-operate under the aegis of the International Commission for the Protection of the Rhine. The ICPR has adopted a policy Action Plan on Flood Defence encompassing integrated risk management, which is built around prevention, preparedness, rescue, rehabilitation and reconstruction. The plan has four objectives:

1. To reduce damage risks by up to 10% by 2005 and up to 25% by 2020.

2. To reduce flood stages: reduction downstream of the impounded part of the river by 30 cm until the year 2005 and up to 70 cm until 2020.

3. To increase awareness of flooding – increase the awareness of flooding by drafting risk maps for 50% of the flood plains and the areas facing flood risks by the year 2000 and for 100% by the year 2005.

4. To improve the system of flood forecasting, including short term improvements of flood forecasting systems through international co-operation. Prolong the forecasting period by 50% by the year 2000 and by 100% by the year 2005. With regard to increasing flood awareness, flood hazard maps are prepared to inform the public and are at the basis of measures of spatial planning. Inhabitants must be aware of being exposed to the risk of floods. If they themselves have not yet experienced flooding, knowledge about the risk must be passed on with the help of the flood hazard maps.

Relatively reliable flood forecasts can today be given for about 24 hours on the High Rhine, 36 hours on the Upper-, Middle-, and Lower Rhine, and 72 hours on the Rhine Delta. On the tributaries, the lead times of forecasts range between 6 and 24 hours. Against the year 1997, this is a prolongation of forecasting periods by 50%. Such improvement would not have been possible without the availability and the exchange of data from precipitation networks

Figure I.5.1. **ICPR flood hazard map**

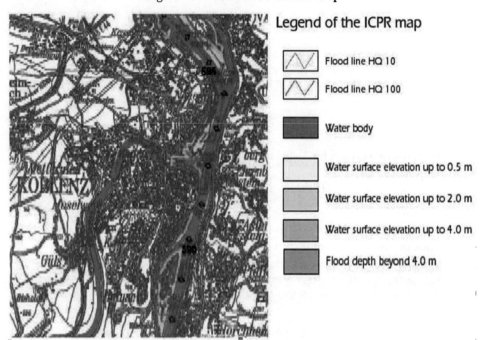

Source: Harm Oterdoom, 2001, *From use and protection to sustainable development: The river Rhine, a case study.*

in France, Luxembourg, and Germany, which have become denser and more automated over the past years and are thus able to provide the necessary data basis for rainfall-runoff modelling. The exchange of data between the forecasting centres is usually fast and easy via ftp and the Internet.

ANNEX I.6

The Dutch System for Emergency and Crisis Management

The organisation for emergency response in European countries such as the Netherlands, Sweden and the United Kingdom is characterised by a bottom-up approach with the main responsibility at the local government level even though a certain operational leadership can also be exercised at regional and central government levels. In a densely populated country such as the Netherlands, disasters and serious accidents can have far-reaching consequences. The Netherlands does not have a separate executive organisation for calamities. Putting fires out, caring for victims and maintaining public order are part of the daily tasks of such departments as the fire brigade, medical assistance services and the police. These organisations are at the core of disaster control. If necessary, other departments can be summoned to provide assistance and other organisations are also involved in disaster control, such as rescue teams, water boards, the Red Cross, environmental departments and other municipal and provincial services.

The responsibility for disaster control primarily lies with the mayor of the municipality where the disaster situation occurs.

Many disasters are not limited to one municipality, and can be so extensive that the capacity of the municipal services is inadequate. In that case, the operational emergency services must organise themselves in a larger context. This is called "*upscaling*". Such scaling-up can occur both at a regional and at a provincial or state level. If a disaster affects more than one municipality, then each mayor remains in charge of the administrative management of disaster control within his or her own municipality. The mayors can agree that one of them will act as co-ordinator for the disaster area. In the event of a large-scale disaster; The Royal Commissioner in the province or region can give instructions to the mayors regarding the administrative and operational management of disaster control.

Figure I.6.1. **The Dutch System for emergency management**

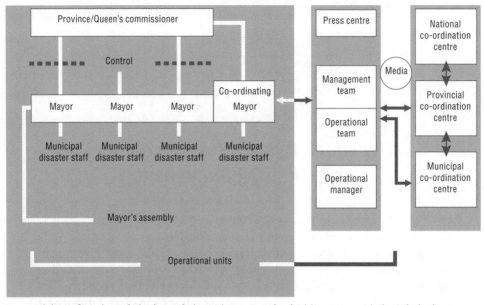

Source: Ministry of Interior and Kingdom Relations, *Disaster Control and Crisis management in the Netherlands.*

The operational management of disaster control is the responsibility of one official - in principle the commander of the fire brigade. The tasks of the fire brigade comprise a lot more than just putting fires out and rescuing people. The fire brigade is activated not only in disasters: together with other municipal services, it is an important partner in the prevention, limitation and control of risks. This is done according to the links in the "safety chain".

The national government, if possible together with the business community, prepares for internal and external threats by developing scenarios and adapting to them. In a serious crisis, the usual procedures and normal lines of decision-making may no longer be adequate. All departments must then switch to an adapted structure, involving a Departmental Coordination Centre (DCC). A DCC will become active if there is a crisis in the field of one ministry. If a crisis affects the policy fields of several departments, however, then stronger interdepartmental coordination is required, and a National Coordination Centre (NCC) must be activated (housed in the Ministry of the Interior). A National Public Information Centre (NVC) may also be activated. If the crisis is very complex, sweeping and far-reaching, the entire Council of Ministers will be involved in the decision-making. The Minister-President and the ministers concerned will then have joint responsibility.

The Ministry of the Interior and Kingdom Relations (Ministry of BZK) at the central government level has been charged with the system responsibility for disaster control and crisis management. This means that this ministry deals with the laws and regulations, and makes available additional facilities for the tasks at provincial, regional and municipal levels. Disaster control, fire services and medical assistance for disasters and accidents have been arranged by law. At both the administrative and the executive level, everyone involved in relief work must always be prepared for all possible situations. The national government puts a lot of work into these preparations, and makes additional facilities available. There are specific training courses for all officials involved in disaster control and crisis management at an administrative, public servant or operator level. The disaster control plans must also be continuously tested in actual practice by means of drills as well as multidisciplinary and administrative exercises.

ANNEX I.7

Administrative Organisation of Emergency Response in Sweden

The Swedish system for emergency and crisis management is quite similar to that of the Netherlands with the main operational responsibility on the local level fire and rescue chief. The county administrative boards and the central government can formally take over responsibility when necessary for regional or national coordination, but in practice they support local organisations and take necessary decisions for instance on the provision of extra resources. This requires capacity within ministries to monitor and make such decisions.

A recent report on the establishment of a crisis management centre within government offices concludes that such a centre should be based upon a cross-sector joint approach and coordinated by the Prime Minister's office. Planning and preparing for crises requires an efficient and professional organisation as well as an executive leadership that cuts across sectors and the responsibility of each individual ministry. A position of Director-General for Crisis Management will be established within the Prime Minister's office to oversee and ensure crisis management co-ordination and planning. The Office of the Director-General for Crisis Management will support the daily work of the Director-General. The office will enhance awareness, assemble and co-ordinate information and analyses, initiate inter-ministerial co-ordination and support decision-making during crises. Specifically, the office should identify and advise on relevant measures both within the government and in the interplay between ministries and authorities.

During crises, the State Secretaries of the Ministries play a key role in shaping the strategic direction of crisis management, and ensure co-ordinated measures and communication from government offices. The office of the Director-General for Crisis Management will support the work of the strategic group. An advisory committee consisting of senior representatives from agencies key to coping with crises will be appointed by the government. The committee should share information and ensure co-ordination between the government and the involved agencies during crises.

In normal situations the office will perform tasks to identify and benchmark crisis management capabilities and make sure that all ministries have a crisis management plan and capacity. The office will also provide advice on potential risks and threats to societal security, as well as plan and execute exercises and training activities. Furthermore, the office will be the point of contact for co-operation with similar offices or functions in other countries as well as within the joint European Union crisis management structures. A Government Offices Crisis Coordination Centre will be established with relevant technological support to be activated and used by the government during crises. The proposal is now being introduced for implementation.

Source: Government Offices of Sweden (2007).

ANNEX I.8

Post Disaster Experiences Collection and Communication in France

The major floods that France has experienced in the last ten years have led the government to systematically organise the collection of feedback using experts from different ministries. These meet with the various parties involved in the flooding event, including those managing the crisis as well as the victims. After consultation, the expert group produces a status report that includes recommendations for improvement and a brief proposal for short and mid-term action. In addition, the Inter-ministerial delegate to major risk publishes a yearly report on the damage-causing events of the past year, made available to the public. Comparable information updated by the government is available on the Internet at *www.prim.net* as a contribution to the prevention of major risks for the general public.

Source: Camphuis, Nicolas-Gérard: French Regulations for Urban Flood Management.

ANNEX I.9

The Post-disaster Recovery Stage: a Step Towards Enforcement of Risk Culture

Even though natural catastrophes such as floods cannot directly be avoided, their impact is definitely conditioned by human actions. The post-disaster event stage is characterised first by a massive focus of public media, second by a damage evaluation process, and third by the search for responsible entities. Less frequently, a collection of experiences is undertaken.

The escalation of damages is often related to neglect and omissions in protection, alarm, prevention or response, which could be avoided if memories of past actions were kept and communicated, or if people were properly warned of the likely consequences of floods. The development of risk culture, meaning the enforcement of the citizens' consciousness regarding risk occurrences and mitigation measures, should be pursued more systematically. The need for such measures is even stronger nowadays, as people are lulled by an increased confidence in protection techniques that give the illusion of "zero risk". This lack of attention to major protection structures is even more critical, for it is fully acknowledged by specialists that such measures, though essential, are designed for a defined threshold. Thus in unforeseen major events, they may be overtaken, and at worst, produce even greater damages. Such is the case when dikes or dams break because of exceeding flood discharge and release rapid, forceful water flows.

There is a need for an increased communication on flood hazards and a more systematic debate with local actors especially during the recovery process, in order to reverse the trend of excessive confidence in structural measures which leads to a false sense of total security, and to allow for the sharing of relevant feedback, While Institutional bodies involved in decision-making and in practical actions should be heard, risk culture cannot be set only as a top-down approach regulated by norms and legislative standards. There is also a very strong necessity for negotiations at the citizen level. Allowing victims to share their perceptions could both help them to recover personally and introduce calibration examples based on observed outcomes.

Source: French Ministry of Land Use Planning and Environment (2000).

ANNEX I.10

The National Flood Insurance Program in the United States

The National Flood Insurance Program (NFIP) administered by the Federal Emergency Management Agency (FEMA) is the principal means of delivering residential flood insurance in the United States. However, to encourage the marketing, purchase, and penetration of residential flood insurance where it is needed, there is a significant public-private partnership between the federal government and private home owners' insurers called the Write-Your-Own (WYO) program. While NFIP-FEMA underwrites flood insurance, private insurers and agents have assumed significant responsibility for marketing, administering policies and settling claims under the flood insurance program. This allows private insurers selling regular homeowners insurance covering most risks to provide flood insurance at the same time under the NFIP program. Because NFIP coverage is limited to a structure value of USD 250 000, there is some private market coverage available for values in excess of that amount for high-valued homes.

Although the NFIP writes some commercial flood insurance in vulnerable areas where private commercial coverage is difficult to obtain, much of the commercial or business property flood insurance in the U.S. is written by private insurers. In many cases, it takes the form of an endorsement to standard commercial property insurance policies or to a separate commercial flood policy. In recent years, commercial insurers have begun to pay much closer attention to the marketing, underwriting and pricing of flood coverage.

With increased awareness of the flood peril and more aggressive marketing by the NFIP and private insurers participating in the WYO program, the number of insured increased from about 1.4 million in 1978 to over 5.5 million in 2006. The Preferred Risk Program (PRP) is another major effort that has been successful in increasing the total number of insured, improving the spread of risk and reducing the problem of "adverse selection" in flood insurance. PRP is an effort that began in the late 1980s to market flood coverage to homeowners who may be outside the 100-year flood or high hazard areas, but still at some risk for flooding. The cost of coverage is generally much less expensive for PRP flood policyholders due to the lower risk.

Estimates of penetration rates are impacted by how one defines the market and need for flood insurance. As mentioned, the PRP program has expanded demand and penetration somewhat outside of the traditional, high hazard, high need areas most vulnerable to flooding. As a result of more aggressive marketing, the WYO partnership and the PRP program, penetration of the market for flood insurance has increased from approximately 13% in 1990 to an estimated 22-25% in 2002. This range in the estimate is based on FEMA studies of how many U.S. properties are in high hazard areas (100-year expected flood areas).

Source: Tsubokawa (2006).

ANNEX I.11

Self-Assessment Questionnaire

A. General Questionnaire

A.1. Risk assessment

Main actors: Ministry of Land, Infrastructure and Transport

A.1.a. Roles and responsibilities in flood risk and vulnerability assessment

- Please describe the role and responsibilities of your organisation with regard to the assessment of the following points:
  - Risk of different types of flood (flash flood, river flood, etc.).
  - Vulnerability of physical structures to floods (including structural flood defenses).
  - Vulnerability of industrial structures to flood.
  - Vulnerability of population groups to floods.
  - Secondary effects of floods and its ensuing risks and vulnerability.
  - Integrating the results of the identified risks and vulnerabilities in a central cost and damage assessment.
  - Other.

  Please describe the way in which your organisation is structured and the resources it devotes in order to fulfill this role. In support of your reply, please provide organisational charts, statistics, activity reports and any other information deemed useful.

- Which other actors cooperate with your organisation in assessing flood risk and vulnerability at the State level? At prefecture level? At municipality level? Private and non-government actors? Please describe the co-ordination and communication channels.

- Does the current legislation create any obligations to monitor the points identified above?

A.1.b. Risk assessment methods

- Please describe existing programs aimed at
  - Identifying, monitoring and evaluating the different types of flood risk.
  - Detecting physical vulnerabilities (installations, topographic particularities, etc.).
  - Detecting and monitoring new and existing vulnerable groups in the population.
  - Identifying secondary effects of floods, including business interruption costs.
  - Integrating different types of risk and vulnerability data.
- How is data collected for the above categories? (From where, how often, etc.)
- Are there any obstacles to the collection of data? (Confidentiality issues, privately-owned information, etc.)? If so, please elaborate your answer.
- Please describe ongoing or planned research programmed regarding flood risk and vulnerability assessment tools.
- Please describe any other method or tool used to assess flood risk and vulnerability.

A.1.c. Self-assessment

- How do you evaluate the Japanese population's exposure to floods, taking into consideration
  - Changing weather and precipitation patterns the last 20 years.
  - Increasing population density in flood plains.
  - Changes in land use (more use of underground space).
  - Societal developments in the last 10-20 years (ageing populations, changes in income, etc.).
  - Technological developments, with increasing interdependence of critical infrastructure, etc.).

A.2. Principles of strategic decision-making

Main actors: Ministry of Land, Infrastructure and Transport; other affected ministries; Cabinet Office; Central Disaster Management Council

A.2.a. Roles and responsibilities in decision-making

- Please describe the roles and responsibilities in designing and implementing national strategies for flood risk reduction and flood vulnerability reduction (of physical structures, the elderly population, etc.).
- What are the coordination and communication between the different decision-making organisations?

A.2.b. The decision-making process

- How are priorities defined and targets set at the national level?
- What are the programs and implementation plans related to these targets?
- What are the overall public resources devoted to flood risk and vulnerability reduction?
- What is the share of these resources of the overall spending on overall natural disaster risk and vulnerability reduction?
- Which stakeholders are consulted during the decision-making process, and how?
- At what stage, if any, are the costs, benefits and risks of alternative solutions considered?
- How are financial resources allocated to the measures in support of flood risk and vulnerability assessment? Please make a distinction between the various levels of government (State, prefecture and municipality) and between sources of funding (State or local taxes, earmarked funds, etc.).

A.3. Framework conditions

Main actors: Ministry of Land, Infrastructure and Transport; affected ministries

A.3.a. Land use policies and legislation

- Please describe the roles and responsibilities for formulating and implementing land use policies and legislation in Japan?
- Which are the land use criteria defined by the Ministry of Land, Infrastructure and Transport and others, in relation to flood risk?
- Please describe recent positive/negative evolutions in land use in Japan and possible measures taken by the State to support/discourage this development.
- How is the formulation of land use policies linked to flood risk assessment and lessons learnt from previous floods in and outside Japan? Please indicate co-ordination and communication channels.
- Which are the mechanisms for enforcing national land use policies in Japan (if existing)?

A.3.b. Building code

- Please describe the roles and responsibilities in designing and implementing building code in Japan?

- Does Japanese building code include provisions to protect against floods and flood damage in?
  - Private housing.
  - Public buildings.
  - Industrial facilities.
  - Underground facilities.
  - Critical infrastructures.
  - Other.
- Is the formulation of building code linked to flood risk assessment and lessons learnt from previous floods in and outside Japan?

A.4. Protection

Main actors: Ministry of Land, Infrastructure and Transport

- Please describe the roles and responsibilities in designing and implementing structural flood protection systems in Japan.
- Please describe the resources your organisation devotes in order to fulfill this role in this area. In support of your reply, please provide organisational charts, statistics, activity reports and any other information deemed useful.
- Please describe the major structural and non-structural protection systems and activities in Japan.
- Please describe the co-ordination of policies concerning structural and non-structural measures flood protection measures. Which share of the overall flood protection is devoted to structural measures? Which share is devoted to non-structural measures?
- Has the underlying policy of protection changed with the increasing frequency of floods and the increase in costs? Which effect, if any, has this had on the formulation and type of flood protection measures?

A.5. Information and early warning

Main actors: Ministry of Land, Infrastructure and Transport; Japan Meteorological Agency

A.5.a. Awareness-raising among public and private actors

- Please describe the resources and policies devoted to raising awareness of flood risk and vulnerability and possible mitigation measures among public and private actors (local and regional government, public and private infrastructure operators, etc.)

- Are there forums for information exchange among the different stakeholders concerning topics related to flood risk management (warning procedures, contingency planning, etc.)?

A.5.b. Warning

- Please describe your role and responsibilities with regard to flood risk warning, and your communication channels to:
  - Central government.

    Prefectures.
  - Municipalities.
  - Other actors (private, public).
- Please describe the warning routines.

A.6. *Evacuation and rescue*

Main actors: Defense Agency, Ministry of Health, Labor and Welfare

- Please describe your role and responsibilities with regard to evacuation and rescue of populations and structures in flood disasters?
- Please describe the main co-ordination and communication channels with other organisations participating in evacuation and rescue.

A.7. *Recovery enhancement*

Main actors: Ministries concerned

A.7.a. Damage compensation and insurance

- Please inform about government policies and legislation in Japan aimed at reimbursing flood damage to private citizens and businesses.
- What is the coverage of flood insurance in Japan?
  - Among private house owners.
  - Among small and medium-sized enterprises.
  - Among big firms.
- What is the coverage of business interruption insurance in Japan?
  - Among small and medium-sized enterprises.
  - Among big firms.

A.7.b. Contingency planning

- Is contingency planning promoted and encouraged by the central government towards local government and actors – if so, which are the tools employed, and to whom are they directed (municipalities, small- and medium-sized enterprises, critical infrastructure operators, etc.) (Legislation, campaigns, etc.)?

- Do the government and its ministries participate in forums with critical infrastructure operators and other actors where contingency planning is discussed and promoted?

A.8. Feedback and organisational change

Main actors: Ministry of Land, Infrastructure and Transport; affected ministries

- Please describe the existing routines for analysing past events and reporting the findings to other actors (in central government, local government and private organisations).

- Is there a mechanism for policy and legislative revision, taking into account past experiences (national and international), and technological and socio-economic changes?

B. Questionnaire to prefectures and municipalities

B.1. Risk and vulnerability assessment

- Please describe your role and responsibilities in assessing risks and vulnerabilities regarding flood disasters, and in communicating this information to other parties, including the population.

- Of these activities, which are implementation of decisions from the central administration and the prefecture and which draw from the municipality's sole responsibility in this area?

- What is the organisational structure in place to fulfil these responsibilities?

- Please provide available data on the municipality's specific resources corresponding to these functions (grants from the central government, taxes, etc.).

- Please describe the methods and tools you use to carry out risk and vulnerability analyses. Do you receive training in conducting such analyses?

- How do you evaluate the quality of the data used in the risk and vulnerability analyses? Who collects the data?

- How often are risk and vulnerability analyses updated?

B.2. *Policy decision-making*

B.2.a. Resource allocation

- Please indicate, as a percentage of total budgetary spending, the resources devoted to flood preparedness.

- Please indicate the funding sources of your spending on earthquake prevention. Is it mainly from your own local government budget, or via central government grants? Are the latter grants (if any) earmarked (attached to predetermined measures)?

- What is the balance between prevention and emergency response policies in your budget?

B.2.b. Strategic co-ordination and supervision

- Please describe your role and responsibilities when it comes to designing and implementing prevention and preparedness policies in the area of floods.

- Of these activities, which are implementation of decisions from the central administration and the prefecture and which draw from the municipality's sole responsibility in this area?

- What is the organisational structure in place to fulfil these responsibilities?

- How do the relevant services inside your municipality (rescue, buildings and infrastructures, education, social and health services, other) co-operate on flood disaster risk prevention and preparedness?

- Please describe the co-ordination and communication channels with other government actors when it comes to designing and implementing policy (other actors in local government, central government).

B.3. *Framework conditions*

B.3.a. Land use policies

- Please indicate the main principles and criteria (and existing legislation) for designing and implementing land use policies, in relation to flood preparedness.

- How do you assess your room for manoeuvre *vis-à-vis* central authorities when it comes to designing land use policies?

- If there are national principles and criteria of land use, how does the central government monitor their implementation at the local level (in your prefecture/municipality)?

B.3.b. Building codes

- Please indicate the main principles and criteria (and existing legislation) for designing and implementing building codes, in relation to flood preparedness?
- How does the central government encourage and monitor the implementation of building codes at the local level (in your prefecture/municipality)?

B.4. Protection

- Please describe the main policies of structural protection against floods in your prefecture/municipality. Please indicate whether these policies have been designed at the municipality, regional or state level.
- What is the organisational structure in place to fulfil these responsibilities?
- Please provide available data on the municipality's specific resources corresponding to these functions (grants from the central government, taxes, etc.).
- Who has the responsibility for the maintenance of flood defense structures?

B.5. Information and early warning

- How do you get your information concerning flood risks, methods of organising preparedness activities, necessary prevention measures, and so on?
- Do you exchange information with other government and/or private actors on these issues, and if yes, how?

B.6. Evacuation and rescue

- Please describe your role and responsibilities with regard to evacuation and rescue of populations and structures in flood disasters?
- What is the organisational structure in place to fulfil these responsibilities?
- Please describe the main co-ordination and communication channels with prefectural and governmental organisations participating in evacuation and rescue.

B.7. Self-assessment

B.7.a. The general situation

- What are the major challenges faced by your municipality in preventing and preparing for flood disasters? What are their causes?

- How has the physical and social vulnerability to floods evolved in the past 10 years?
- How do you expect these vulnerabilities to evolve in the next 10 years in your municipality?

B.7.b. Own capacity

- How do you evaluate your municipality's capacity to fulfil its responsibilities regarding flood disaster preparedness?

ANNEX I.12

List of Institutions Interviewed

Cabinet Office

Ministry of Land, Infrastructure, Transport and Tourism

- River Bureau.
- Road Bureau.
- City and Regional Development Bureau.
- Housing Bureau.
- Government Buildings Department.

Fire and Disaster Management Agency

Ministry of Land, Infrastructure, Transport and Tourism

- River Bureau.
- City and Regional Development Bureau.
- Housing Bureau.
- Land and Water Bureau.
- Kanto Regional Development Bureau.

Fire and Disaster Management Agency

Japan Meteorological Agency

Public Works Research Institute, The International Centre for Water Hazard Risk Management

Saitama Prefecture

Kawaguchi City

Sumida City

Japanese Red Cross Society

The General Insurance Association of Japan

Tokio Marine & Nichido Fire Insurance Co., Ltd

Tokyo Metro Co., Ltd

Hazkari Kougyou Co., Ltd

Taiseikako Co., Ltd

Arcatowers Co., Ltd

Kazo City Fire and Flood fighting group

Kitakawabe Town Fire and Flood fighting group

(Non-profit Organisation) Tsurumi River Basin Networking

Bibliography

Baden-Württemberg Umweltministerium (January 2007), "Hochwasservorsorge in Baden-Württemberg: Anforderungen an Anlagen zum Umgang mit wassergefährdenden Stoffen" [Ministry for the Environment, Flood Protection in Baden-Württemberg: Requirements regarding installations concerned with the storage and treatment of water-hazardous substances].

Bradbury, Andrew P. (2007), Channel Coastal Observatory, *Application of a large-scale, long term, regional coastal observation network to coastal management on the English-channel coast.*

Cabinet Office, Government of Japan (2007), *Disaster Management in Japan.*

Camphuis, Nicolas-Gérard: French Regulations for Urban Flood Management.

DEFRA news release (8 August 2007), *www.cabinetoffice.gov.uk.*

DHI Eau & Environnement, 7th International Conference on Hydroinformatics, HIC 2006, Nice, France, 2006, Flood Risk Management based on "*Méthode Inondabilité*".

EPTB Loire and SEPIA Conseils (2007), "Apprendre à vivre avec les inondations", "Les EPTB, un moteur d'innovation".

ESPACE (European spatial planning adapting to climate events) – Example Plans and Policies: Bavarian policies for integrating climate change in water management with a focus on flood protection, available at: *http://www.espace-project.org/part1/publications/pdf25.pdf.*

European Commission (23rd October 2007), Directive 2007/60/EC of the European Parliament and of the Council of 23 October 2007 on the assessment and management of flood risks (Text with EEA relevance).

French Ministry of Land Use Planning and Environment (2000), Major Risks Prevention Bureau (April 2000), Pierre A. Vidal-Naquet and Francis Calvet, "À l'epreuve d'une catastrophe : les inondations de novembre 1999 dans le midi de la France".

Government of Japan (2007). The City Planning Law (Law No. 100 of June 15, 1968), Final Revision: Law No. 61 of June 8, 2006.

Government Offices of Sweden (2007), *http://www.sweden.gov.se/sb/d/2174/nocache/true/a/89625/dictionary/true.*

Infrastructure Development Institute – Japan (7th December 2007), Power Point Presentation at the 7th Meeting of OECD Risk Management Steering Group, "The review of process of Floods and Earthquakes in Japan".

IDI Water Series No. 4, supervised by River Bureau, Ministry of Construction, Japan, compiled and commented by Toshikatsu Omachi (IDI), published by the Infrastructure Development Institute (February 1999), The River Law with commentary by article, Legal Framework for River and Water Management in Japan.

Japan Meteorological Agency (JMA) (2004), *Climate Change Monitoring Report 2003*, Tokyo.

Japanese Ministry of Land, Infrastructure and Transport (MLIT), Kanto Regional Development Bureau, Tsurimi River Basin Water Council (November 2004), "Life and Livelihood bound to the Earth : a vision for the regeneration of the Tsurimi River Basin".

Japanese Ministry of Land, Infrastructure and Transport (MLIT) and the Cabinet Office (2005), PowerPoint Presentation at 4th meeting of OECD Risk Management Project Steering Group, unpublished, Paris.

Japanese Ministry of Land, Infrastructure and Transport (MLIT) (May 2006), "Flood-fighting in Japan".

Japanese Ministry of Land, Infrastructure and Transport (MLIT) Arakawa – Karyu River Office (May 2006) "The Arakawa: River of the Metropolis: A Comprehensive Guide to the Lower Arakwa".

Japanese Ministry of Land, Infrastructure and Transport (MLIT) (September 2006), "Rivers in Japan".

Japanese Ministry of Land, Infrastructure and Transport (MLIT) (May 2007), Power Point Presentation, "Existing Conditions and Tasks of River Administration in terms of Flood Control".

Japanese Ministry of Land, Infrastructure and Transport (MLIT) (November 2007), Power Point Presentation, "River Administration in Japan".

Japanese Ministry of Land Infrastructure and Transport, River Planning Division (December 2007), Power Point Presentation at the 7th Meeting of OECD Risk Management Steering Group, "The Review of Floods in Japan".

Japanese Ministry of Land, Infrastructure and Transport (MLIT), River Planning Division (March 11, 2008), Power Point Presentation, "Adaptation measures related to water-related disasters to reduce the impacts of climate change due to global warming".

OECD (2003), *Flood Insurance*, Paris.

OECD (2003), A Methodological Framework for Evaluating Risk Management Policies, background document for the first meeting of the Project Steering Group, Paris.

OECD (2006a), *Information Security in Norway, OECD Risk Management Studies*, Paris.

OECD (2006b), *Risk Management Policies in Japan Concerning Large-Scale Floods, OECD Study in Risk Management*, Paris.

OECD (9th November 2007), Working Party on Global and Structural Policies, *Screening study: ranking Port Cities with high exposure and vulnerability to climate extremes, Interim analysis, Exposure Estimates*, Paris.

OECD (2008), *Environment Working Papers No. 1.*, "Ranking Port Cities with High Exposure and Vulnerability to Climate Extremes".

Tsubokawa, Hiroaki (2006), *Insurance Issues of Catastrophic Disasters in Japan: Lessons from the 2005 Hurricane Katrina Disaster. A better integrated management of disaster risks: Toward resilient society to emerging disaster risks in mega-cities*, pp.193-198.

The Netherlands Ministry of Interior and Kingdom Relations (2008), *Disaster Control and Crisis Management in the Netherlands*.

The Pitt Review: Learning Lessons from the 2007 Floods, 28/06/2008.

United Kingdom National Press Office (2004), Environment Agency, Press Release 198/04.

UN/WWAP (United Nations/World Water Assessment Programme) (2003), 1st UN World Water Development Report: Water for People, Water for Life, Paris, New York and Oxford, UNESCO (United Nations Educational, Scientific and Cultural Organization) and Berghahn Books, *Pilot Case Studies: A Focus on Real-Word Examples – Greater Tokyo Japan.*

Vidal-Naquet, Pierre A. and Francis Calvet, *À L'Épreuve d'une catastrophe: Les inondations de novembre 1999 dans le midi de la France.*

ISBN 978-92-64-05639-8
OECD Reviews of Risk Management Policies
Japan: Large-Scale Floods and Earthquakes
© OECD 2009

PART II

Earthquakes

Japan's risk management policies for earthquakes stand on the shoulders of lessons learned from previous disasters and investments that have led to the world's most concentrated seismic monitoring network. Its disaster risk management system includes excellent preparation and response capabilities which could be further enhanced by risk assessments that take account of societal trends such as Japan's ageing population.

ISBN 978-92-64-05639-8
OECD Reviews of Risk Management Policies
Japan: Large-Scale Floods and Earthquakes
© OECD 2009

Executive Summary

This executive summary presents the main findings and recommendations of the review of Japan's policies concerning the management of risks of large-scale earthquakes. It does not claim to do justice to Japan's remarkable performance in this area, but rather to bring together the principal conclusions of the review team regarding remaining weaknesses and areas where further improvement could be achieved at reasonable cost.

The general policy framework

National strategies and devolved responsibilities

All public entities in Japan, from central government to municipalities and public corporations, are responsible at their respective levels for protecting the land, and the life and limb of people and their property against natural disasters. Local government has substantial autonomy over disaster management decisions, and are encouraged to design plans adapted to their specific conditions. This autonomy is, in principle, bounded by the long-term principles and goals defined at central level. The review team identified four areas where the government could better support and coordinate local decisions in earthquake disaster management.

First, better sharing of scientific information; collection and dissemination of best practices; comparative studies; identification of problem areas; and provision of guidance adapted to the problems faced by local authorities are all flexible ways for central government to prepare the ground for, and positively influence, decision-making at the local level. Such "soft" tools should be used in a more forceful and systematic way.

Second, the central government and the prefectures should devise ways to consolidate disaster management capabilities in small municipalities. Providing increased training and education of their personnel, including on legal and administrative aspects of disaster risk management, would represent a minimal action in this regard. A bolder approach could consist of better concentration of local disaster management resources: one means is to enable municipalities to engage in contractual arrangements for the provision of disaster management services as in Switzerland's purchaser/provider relations between cantons (OECD 2002); another is to create regional groupings at an optimal scale for the pooling of municipal resources as in the Netherlands' safety regions. (Netherlands Directorate-General for Public Safety and Security 2004).

Third, there is a need to further clarify the sharing of responsibilities in operations, co-ordination and collaboration within the disaster management system both for the general public and for the authorities themselves, in particular at local level.

Fourth, the use of policy evaluation and monitoring needs to be enhanced. Disaster management should emphasise greater use of outcome indicators, and set measurable targets, with clear time frames for achievement. A central government organisation should receive a mandate (and adequate human and financial resources) to systematically evaluate local government policies in the area of disaster risk management, to identify inadequacies and co-ordination gaps, and to involve all relevant actors in addressing these issues.

Recommendation 1. Decentralised disaster management responsibilities should go hand in hand with a clarification of the roles and responsibilities and consolidation of resources of local government, increased exchange of information and co-ordination between all levels of government, and systematic evaluation and analysis of results by central authorities.

Sectoral competencies and co-ordination

The organisation of the government provides a comprehensive coverage of seismic risk management activities. The overarching role of the Central Disaster Management Council ensures that these activities are considered in an integrated manner, a feature that not many risk management systems in other OECD countries share. This is a crucial asset in an area where thousands of lives can be saved by quickly integrating progress in science and technology into warning and evacuation schemes, or co-ordinating risk prevention in transport infrastructures with disaster response.

It seems, however, that there is still some way to go in providing the centre of government with the ability to supervise and control the actions of ministerial departments in disaster risk management.

The Cabinet Office should be given effective responsibility for monitoring and coordinating disaster management activities from a whole-of-government perspective.

Its role in collecting data, analysing the strengths and weaknesses of governmental disaster management, drawing lessons, and suggesting improvements and priority areas of action should be enhanced.

The organisational structure of disaster management at the centre of government should be reconsidered with a view towards enhancing efficiencies and effectiveness. In the area of crisis management, the roles the Cabinet Office and the Cabinet Secretariat could be integrated further.

The Government might wish to consider creating an organ in charge of auditing and evaluating disaster management activities across sectors. This responsibility could be given to an existing government entity, providing organisational design ensures it be separated from the entity's operational responsibilities, if it has any. Various OECD governments have already developed such an internal evaluation capacity. Norway's Directorate for Civil Protection and Emergency Planning (DSB) is one example.

Recommendation 2. The monitoring and co-ordination of disaster management activities inside central government should be strengthened.

Policy evaluation and resource allocation

While Japan started the process of regulatory impact analysis (RIA) later than many OECD countries, its efforts have gained considerable momentum of late. In accordance with the new Three-year Plan and Programme for Regulatory Reform of March 2004, RIAs are to be conducted by Ministries and Administrative Agencies on planned and existing regulations as appropriate. The systematic use of RIA should be extended, as a priority, to earthquake risk management policies.

A more systematic evaluation of policy options could significantly improve disaster management. Both in the budgetary process and for organisational matters, there is significant scope for the application of results obtained through the Policy Evaluation System (PES) introduced in 2002, or other studies (*e.g.* the relative efficiency in terms of decreased probability of death of retrofitting houses, fixing home furniture, etc.). Ministers should be encouraged, if not required, to use the results of policy evaluations for regulatory measures pertaining to disaster management, from private and public building retrofitting and fireproofing to rescue preparedness and operations.

Strategic policy decision-making, which is already strongly grounded in scientific research and risk assessment, could also use cost and benefit considerations over a wider range of disaster risk management policies.

For this, existing methodologies should be reviewed and adapted to Japan's context.

In addition, individual policy evaluations should be reviewed, synthesised and gathered into a whole-of-government perspective of Japan's disaster management policies. Ideally, the Cabinet Office should perform this task. It could also be attributed to the Ministry of Internal Affairs and Communications, which is in charge of the design and implementation of the PES.

Recommendation 3. Policy decisions should be evaluated more carefully both before and after their application, and efficiency considerations should prevail in defining priorities within the complete spectrum of risk management measures.

Risk assessment and communication

Hazard and risk assessment

While Japanese scientific research on seismic hazards is of the highest quality, certain aspects of earthquake disaster risk assessment need to be strengthened. This is the case for vulnerability assessments. Attention to the use of scientific inputs in decision-making could also be enhanced, in particular at the local level where resources are often limited.

More emphasis should be placed on understanding individual and societal factors of vulnerability (or, on the contrary, of resilience) to earthquakes. The prevalence of vulnerability factors in the population, as well as general societal vulnerabilities linked, for instance, to critical infrastructures, should be gradually considered in damage evaluations, and used to calibrate preparedness and response measures.

Vulnerability assessment methodologies should be elaborated for the specific case of major earthquakes in Japan, based on the knowledge gained from past disasters. Vulnerability assessment would be a useful complement to the traditional risk-based approach to disaster management policies.

Epidemiological studies should be conducted in order to better understand the impact of major earthquakes on individuals and communities. This entails developing the resources and protocols for such studies *a priori*, since much relevant information is lost and consistent observations become difficult to make in the aftermath of a disaster.

The HERP's Policy Committee could have a broader mandate to investigate the use of scientific assessments in policy making and to reach out to decision-makers, in particular at local level.

Recommendation 4. The traditional focus on scientific risk assessment should be complemented with heightened attention to individual and societal factors of vulnerability.

Communication with the public

There seems to be a wide gap between the individual attitudes toward earthquake risks assumed in the design of public policies, and attitudes as they actually are. There is therefore a need for government entities in charge of earthquake disaster management to better understand how people act with regard to earthquake risks, and why.

Scientific research on the determinants of individual and social attitudes towards earthquake risks and on risk perception and acceptance should be encouraged.

Risk communication should not be designed and conducted as a one-way education of the public, but as a continuous dialogue in which it is equally important for risk managers to understand people's standpoints – and to adapt risk management procedures accordingly.

Efforts should be made continuously to maintain and reinforce the risk awareness and culture of the population, which increases in the aftermath of a major event but recedes thereafter – a pattern which can be observed in many other countries, but which has particular significance in Japan due to the exceptional prevalence of natural hazards.

Recommendation 5. Individual and collective attitudes with regard to earthquake risks have to be better understood. To this end, risk communication should be designed and implemented as a more regular and transparent dialogue between risk managers and the public.

Disaster prevention

Building structural defences against earthquakes

The Preparedness Strategy for the Tokyo Metropolitan Earthquake published by the Central Disaster Management Council in 2006, sets ambitious ten-year policy targets in terms of loss caused by a large-scale seismic event. This outcome-based approach has created momentum for the promotion of countermeasures against earthquakes. However, so far it seems to lack concrete methods and tools to achieve its goals. While all local authorities have adhered to the Policy's objectives, both municipalities and prefectures seem uncertain about their overall responsibilities.

Long-term policy objectives regarding structural defences should be accompanied by a better definition of roles and responsibilities, as well as criteria for resource allocation and the choice of instruments. A clarified national framework would certainly improve the coherence and efficiency of policy while preserving the autonomy of local government and public agencies in terms of implementation.

The systematic use of cost-benefit analyses should be encouraged in this area for both evaluating projects and defining priorities.

The OECD's guidelines on earthquake safety in schools recommend a systematic, risk-based and result-oriented approach, and the establishment of measurable objectives for seismic safety, design code and standards, and realisation plans (OECD 2005a).

Tangible measures should be taken to increase incentives for improving the earthquake resistance of buildings, such as requiring that information on earthquake hazards be systematically notified in real estate transactions.

Recommendation 6. Policy strategies in the area of structural protection should include a clear definition of implementation principles and responsibilities.

Land use and city planning

Although almost all of the national territory is exposed to seismic hazards, risks are highest in the country's major urban centres. In the Tokyo metropolitan area, 18 earthquakes of different types likely to occur were identified in order to raise public awareness and to provide possible contingencies for stakeholders. These come in addition to the Tokai Earthquake which, given its traditional cycle of recurrence, is considered very likely to occur at any moment with a magnitude approaching 8.

Authorities at central, prefectural and local levels indeed estimate that the concentration of people, constructions and assets is an extremely difficult challenge for disaster response (evacuation, sheltering, etc.). Still, land use and city planning policies do not include restrictive measures for land use in the vicinity of active faults, or provisions aimed at decreasing concentration in the areas where the overall magnitude of risk would be considered excessive. High population density in habitable places has probably helped preclude the idea that risk considerations could be integrated into land use policies.

The long-term decrease in the population will facilitate a gradual change in urbanisation patterns. But a business-as-usual scenario may not lead to substantial results in terms of risk exposure in the most earthquake-prone areas during the coming decades.

Long-term objectives in terms of altering the concentration of people and economic activities in earthquake-prone areas, partly established on a small zoning level under the current land use and city planning policies, should be extended in terms of geographical scope, and backed by more robust policy instruments.

Further work will be needed to make different levels of government and other stakeholders concerned with land use and urban development more aware of seismic risks. The legal instruments for land use and city planning policies may also need to be enhanced.

In the short term, it seems desirable to initiate a national debate on ageing, land use and natural hazards, bringing together all relevant stakeholders (t»he general public, civil society organisations, representatives of the private sector, critical infrastructure operators, academia, government agencies, etc.).

With regard to active-fault earthquakes, research on active faults and restrictions on land use should be considered in the short term at least for public buildings (schools, hospitals, etc.) and critical infrastructures.

Recommendation 7. In the context of a rapidly decreasing population over the coming decades, land use and urban planning could integrate more actively seismic risk factors, and aim at a gradual decrease in population density in the most hazard-prone areas. Prudent land use in the vicinity of fault strata should be considered in the short term.

Emergency preparedness and response

Mastering the secondary impacts of earthquakes

The government of Japan, despite its responsibilities in the overall management of societal risks related to earthquakes and its general instructions to the private providers of essential services and hazardous industries, does not have a precise knowledge of the state of some basic infrastructure elements such as hazardous product storage tanks, pipelines, power grids, etc. In the absence of precise information regarding secondary risks such as chemical spills, industrial accidents or power line disruptions, the government cannot control the development of indirect costs, which can be huge in the event of a major earthquake.

The CDMC has emphasised the need for a more stringent approach to the risks of industrial hazards triggered by earthquakes in the Tokyo area:

> "The national and local governments, and relevant businesses, will advance measures based on the Law on the Prevention of Disasters in Petroleum Industrial Complexes and Other Petroleum Facilities. They will also enhance evaluations of how a disaster at a petroleum complex would impact adjacent areas, and promote both high disaster preparedness through redevelopment of aged coastal industrial facilities and development of emergency earthquake bulletin applications and other technologies."

"To prevent disasters at coastal petroleum complexes from spreading to adjacent areas, the national and local governments, and relevant businesses, will promote comprehensive measures for preventing large-scale fires related to sloshing in petroleum tanks" (Central Disaster Management Council (2005), pp. 26 and 28).

It would be useful to apply these recommendations in a more systematic way to all critical infrastructure sectors and hazardous industry sectors.

Precise routines for collection of data and information-sharing procedures should be developed in each of these sectors, according to its specific regulatory and economic conditions. Information-exchange groups should be established.

Legal dispositions should be introduced to support the enforcement of necessary measures (as in the CalARP) and to create adequate safeguards in terms of information confidentiality.

As in other OECD countries, the control of risk management procedures in key industries could become part of the current operations of regulatory agencies and supervisory bodies.

Recommendation 8. Governmental regulatory agencies need to achieve a better knowledge of the management of earthquake risk in their areas of action and have clear responsibilities for supervising critical infrastructure sectors and hazardous industries in this regard.

Continuity planning in the public and private sectors

Business continuity plans have been developed in some of the country's large businesses. But the practice is not systematic and is almost non-existent among small- and medium-sized enterprises.

Turning to the government sector, interdependencies between public services create a strong need to co-ordinate continuity planning throughout the government, and the present organisation of disaster risk management seems to leave a gap in this regard.

Finally, there are important synergies between emergency preparedness, disaster prevention and business continuity planning, both inside organisations and within society at large. At present, interactions between these activities seem to be limited at both the local and the national levels.

Following the example of other OECD countries, the government and the public sector at large should include business continuity planning requirements in their procurement policies.

This should be backed by the development of a certification procedure based on a national standard adapted to Japan's specific situation with regard to earthquake risks.

In parallel, Japan should strongly contribute to the elaboration of an international standard of business continuity management, where its experience with the management of natural disasters would be of great value.

The role of the Cabinet Office in the adoption of continuity plans inside the government should be enhanced, and continuity plans should be considered a necessary element of disaster management during internal audits and evaluations.

Fire and rescue services should be better used in creating linkages between emergency preparedness and disaster prevention and in actively promoting business continuity planning. Municipality fire services could for instance take increased responsibilities in preparedness and continuity planning as an extension of their traditional fire prevention activities.

Recommendation 9. There is a need to further promote the implementation of continuity planning in both the private and the public sectors, in particular in SMEs.

Crisis management, from frequent events to large-scale disasters

---

Japan enjoys state-of-the-art warning systems for seismic risks, for both their extensive coverage of the national territory and their technological sophistication. The drawback is that, as the disaster response headquarters are each specific to a sector or level, they do not function as a holistic system for the management of crises at national level, neither in design nor in operation. As a consequence, the formal competence of the centre of government for exercising a national command and coordinating response might be hampered by the lack of effective tools.

Furthermore, decision-makers at local level do not always seem fully aware of the role of the centre of government in exercising command in the event of a major disaster.

The chain of command should appear more clearly to all actors involved in the crisis management system.

The division of roles and responsibilities at different levels has to account for the necessity to address overall national needs and interdependencies in an extremely efficient manner during emergencies.

When duties are delegated within a line of command, delegation should always be accompanied with clear objectives and tasks, and combined with clear reporting and evaluation requirements.

If changes in existing crisis management responsibilities according to the scale of the event are considered unavoidable, sophisticated organisational design with a simple structure should be sought. The need for exercise and training to compensate for the change should also be emphasised.

Recommendation 10. The competence and tools for exercising national co-ordination, and in extreme cases command, from the centre of government need to be reinforced.

Post-event issues

Disaster recovery and reconstruction

Recovering from a large-scale earthquake, especially in a metropolis, represents a huge challenge is terms of planning, co-ordination, financing, and decision-making. But the example of Kobe shows that it can also be an opportunity not only to reduce the vulnerability of urban structures, but more broadly to improve their sustainability, their economic attractiveness, and their suitability for residents.

For this, the objective should be to build consensus among local actors (citizens, non-government organisations, private companies, local government units) on the desired features of the reconstructed area in high-risk zones. External actors (regional or central government, neighbouring localities, etc.) would have to be involved whenever there would be consequences beyond the locality.

Such a broad consensus on the overall principle objectives of reconstruction would be used as a basis in the aftermath of a large earthquake, helping to avoid unnecessary conflicts, frame projects, and save time and resources. Obviously, such an overall framework would have to be adapted to the specific conditions, based on the needs engendered by the earthquake and the available resources.

Even in normal times, it would provide a needed long-term target for local land use and city planning policies.

The government should also try to smooth the reconstruction process and supervise its financial sustainability. The Disaster Aid Act and Disaster Relief Act should be utilised effectively to help those who are financially in need.

Recommendation 11. The government should encourage municipalities and prefectures to consult local actors and build consensus on the objectives of post-disaster recovery, and strengthen their tools for addressing the needs resulting from an earthquake.

Insurance: Sharing mega-risks

Japan's current earthquake insurance system was created in 1966, two years after the Niigata Earthquake, with the establishment of the "Act for Earthquake Insurance." The system is built on government-backed reinsurance, and has undergone several phases of improvement and refinement since its inception, including expanded coverage and revised premium rates, most recently in 2007. Still, in 2005, the rate of market penetration was 20% for household insurance, and limited to a few percentage points for commercial insurance.

Insurance products should have more detailed risk categories. The design of insurance products could better reflect the risk level within prefectures and large metropolitan areas. To achieve this, it is necessary to further improve risk assessment methods using both hazard maps and seismic motion prediction maps.

Public awareness of earthquake risks should be further improved. Policies to promote risk evaluation for each building and dissemination of the information in an easy-to-understand way should be pursued.

Risk prevention incentives should be strengthened by further differentiating insurance premiums on the basis of reasonable risk countermeasures taken by policyholders. As such differentiation for individual residents might make earthquake insurance unaffordable in some cases, it is crucial to consider measures for the high-risk group at the same time.

With better insurance coverage for individuals and enhanced incentives for damage prevention, an extension of government-backed reinsurance could be considered.

For the coverage of seismic risks affecting businesses, financial innovations such as CAT bonds and contingent debt facilities should be encouraged as alternatives to classic insurance.

Recommendation 12. The market penetration rate of insurance against earthquake risks should be improved through better premium differentiation and heightened public awareness.

ISBN 978-92-64-05639-8
OECD Reviews of Risk Management Policies
Japan: Large-Scale Floods and Earthquakes
© OECD 2009

Synthèse

Cette note de synthèse présente les principales conclusions et recommandations résultant de l'examen des politiques menées par le Japon pour gérer les risques sismiques majeurs. Elle n'a pas pour objet de faire état des remarquables performances du pays à cet égard, mais plutôt de rassembler les principales conclusions qu'a pu tirer l'équipe chargée de l'examen quant aux points faibles résiduels et aux domaines dans lesquels des améliorations seraient possibles pour un coût raisonnable.

Cadre généal de l'action publique

Stratégies nationales et dévolution
des responsabilités

Des autorités centrales aux municipalités et aux entreprises publiques, toutes les entités publiques du Japon sont chargées à leur niveau respectif d'assurer la protection du territoire, des habitants et de leurs biens contre les catastrophes naturelles. Les autorités locales disposent d'une large autonomie en matière de décision de gestion des catastrophes, et sont incitées à élaborer des plans adaptés aux conditions qui sont les leurs. Cette autonomie est en principe limitée par les principes et les objectifs de long terme définis au niveau central. L'équipe chargée de l'examen des politiques du Japon a identifié quatre domaines dans lesquels les pouvoirs publics pourraient mieux soutenir et coordonner les décisions locales pour la gestion des tremblements de terre catastrophiques.

Premièrement, un meilleur partage des informations scientifiques, la collecte et la diffusion de pratiques exemplaires, des études comparatives, l'identification des domaines posant des problèmes et la fourniture de conseils adaptés aux difficultés que rencontrent les autorités locales sont autant de moyens flexibles à la disposition des autorités centrales pour fonder et influencer de manière positive la prise locale de décisions. De tels outils "diffus" pourraient être utilisés d'une manière plus affirmée et systématique.

Deuxièmement, les autorités centrales et les préfectures devraient réfléchir à la manière de consolider les capacités de gestion des catastrophes des petites municipalités. Le minimum qu'elles pourraient faire à cet égard consisterait à renforcer les actions de formation de leur personnel, y compris sur les aspects juridiques et administratifs de la gestion des risques catastrophiques. Une approche plus audacieuse consisterait à mieux concentrer les ressources locales de gestion des catastrophes, soit en permettant aux municipalités de signer des contrats de prestations de services de gestion des catastrophes (sur le modèle des relations acheteurs/prestataires qui existent entre les cantons suisses) (voir OCDE 2002), soit en créant des regroupements régionaux d'une taille optimale pour mutualiser les ressources municipales (à l'instar des "régions sécurité" des Pays-Bas (Direction générale des Pays-Bas pour la sûreté et la sécurité publiques 2004).

Troisièmement, il apparaît nécessaire de préciser la répartition des responsabilités opérationnelles, de coordination et de collaboration au sein du système de gestion des catastrophes, et ce tant pour le grand public que pour les autorités elles-mêmes, notamment locales.

Quatrièmement, il convient de renforcer l'évaluation et le suivi des politiques. La gestion des catastrophes devrait mettre l'accent sur une plus grande utilisation des indicateurs de résultats, et fixer des objectifs mesurables assortis de calendriers précis de réalisation. Un organisme public central devrait recevoir un mandat (et les ressources humaines et financières adéquates) pour l'évaluation systématique des politiques publiques locales dans le domaine de la gestion des risques catastrophiques, afin de détecter les carences et les insuffisances en matière de coordination, et d'impliquer tous les acteurs concernés dans la résolution de ces problèmes.

Recommandation 1. Les responsabilités décentralisées de gestion des catastrophes devraient aller de pair avec un éclaircissement des rôles et des responsabilités des autorités locales et une consolidation de leurs ressources, davantage d'échanges d'informations et une coordination entre les instances de tous niveaux, ainsi que l'évaluation systématique et l'analyse des résultats par les autorités centrales.

Compétences sectorielles et coordination

L'État prend complètement en charge la gestion des risques sismiques. Le rôle prééminent du *Central Disaster Management Council* garantit que ces activités sont envisagées de manière intégrée – caractéristique rare parmi les dispositifs de gestion des risques des autres pays de l'OCDE. Il s'agit là d'un atout crucial dans un domaine où des milliers de vies humaines peuvent être sauvées grâce à l'intégration rapide des progrès scientifiques et technologiques aux systèmes d'alerte et d'évacuation, ou à la coordination de la prévention des risques dans les infrastructures de transport avec les opérations menées en cas de catastrophe naturelle.

Il semble toutefois qu'il reste un certain chemin à parcourir pour doter le gouvernement central d'une capacité de supervision et de contrôle des actions de gestion des risques catastrophiques des organes ministériels.

L'Office du Cabinet devrait se voir octroyer la responsabilité effective interministérielle du suivi et de la coordination des activités de gestion des catastrophes.

Il conviendra de renforcer son rôle en matière de collecte des données, d'analyse des forces et faiblesses de la gestion des catastrophes par les autorités, de réflexion sur les enseignements à tirer et de suggestion d'améliorations et de domaines prioritaires d'action.

La structure organisationnelle de la gestion centrale des catastrophes devrait être réétudiée dans l'optique d'en améliorer l'efficience et l'efficacité. S'agissant de gestion de crise, les rôles de l'Office du Cabinet et du Secrétariat du Cabinet pourraient être davantage intégrés.

Le gouvernement pourrait envisager de créer un organisme d'audit et d'évaluation intersectoriels des activités de gestion des catastrophes naturelles. Cette responsabilité pourrait incomber à une entité publique existante, à condition que son organisation garantisse la disjonction avec d'éventuelles responsabilités opérationnelles. Différents pays de l'OCDE ont déjà mis en place une capacité d'évaluation interne de ce type. La DSB norvégienne (Direction de la protection civile et de la planification d'urgence) en est un exemple.

Recommandation 2. Il conviendrait de renforcer le suivi et la coordination des activités de gestion des catastrophes au niveau des autorités centrales.

Évaluation des politiques et allocation des ressources

Alors même que le Japon a commencé plus tard que de nombreux autres pays de l'OCDE son processus d'AIR (Analyse de l'impact de la réglementation), ses efforts ont récemment connu un élan considérable. Conformément au nouveau plan triennal et au programme de réforme réglementaire de mars 2004, les AIR doivent être consacrées par les ministères et les agences administratives aux réglementations planifiées et existantes. Le recours systématique à l'AIR doit être étendu de manière prioritaire aux politiques de gestion des risques sismiques.

L'évaluation plus systématique des possibilités d'action pourrait améliorer de manière significative la gestion des catastrophes par la puissance publique. Que ce soit au niveau du processus budgétaire ou de l'organisation, il existe une belle marge de manœuvre pour l'application des résultats obtenus par le Système d'évaluation des politiques (PES) instauré en 2002, ou par d'autres études (par exemple, efficience relative que l'on peut attendre de la rénovation des logements ou de la fixation du mobilier en termes de probabilité inférieure de mortalité). À défaut d'y être tenus, les Ministres devraient être au moins encouragés à utiliser les résultats des évaluations des politiques dans les mesures de nature réglementaire concernant la gestion des catastrophes, qu'il s'agisse de rénovation et d'ignifugation de bâtiments privés et publics, ou de préparation et de conduite des opérations de secours.

Déjà solidement ancrée dans la recherche scientifique et l'évaluation des risques, la prise de décisions stratégiques d'action pourrait également prendre en compte des considérations de coûts et d'avantages au profit de politiques de gestion des risques catastrophiques plus nombreuses.

Il faudrait pour cela revoir les méthodologies existantes et les adapter au contexte japonais.

De surcroît, il conviendrait de revoir et de synthétiser les évaluations de toutes les politiques menées, et de les intégrer à une perspective interministérielle de l'action à mener au Japon en matière de gestion des catastrophes. Idéalement, c'est l'Office du Cabinet qui devrait se charger de cette tâche. Celle-ci pourrait également être attribuée au ministère des Affaires intérieures et des Communications, qui a la charge de la conception et de la mise en œuvre du PES.

Recommandation 3. Les décisions d'action devraient être évaluées plus soigneusement à la fois avant et après leur mise en œuvre, et les considérations d'efficience devraient prévaloir au moment de définir les priorités dans le spectre des mesures de gestion des risques.

Évaluation des risques et communication

Évaluation des aléas et des risques

Si la recherche scientifique japonaise sur les aléas sismiques est de premier ordre, certains aspects de l'évaluation des risques catastrophiques liés aux tremblements de terre méritent un approfondissement. C'est notamment le cas des évaluations de la vulnérabilité. On pourrait aussi prêter plus d'attention à l'intégration d'éléments scientifiques à la prise de décisions, notamment à l'échelon local, dont les ressources sont souvent limitées.

L'accent devrait être davantage mis sur l'appréhension des facteurs individuels et sociétaux de vulnérabilité (ou au contraire de résistance) aux séismes. Il faudrait progressivement prendre en compte dans les évaluations des dommages la prévalence des facteurs de vulnérabilité et de la population, ainsi que les vulnérabilités sociétales générales liées par exemple aux infrastructures essentielles, et les utiliser pour calibrer les mesures de préparation et d'intervention en cas de catastrophe.

Des méthodologies d'évaluation de la vulnérabilité devraient être élaborées pour le cas particulier des très grands tremblements de terre survenant au Japon, sur la base des connaissances accumulées lors des catastrophes passées. L'évaluation de la vulnérabilité viendrait utilement compléter la démarche classique fondée sur les risques qu'appliquent les politiques de gestion des catastrophes.

Il conviendra de mener des études épidémiologiques afin de mieux comprendre l'impact des grands séismes sur les individus et la collectivité. Il faudrait pour cela multiplier a priori les ressources et les protocoles destinés à des études de ce type puisque, à la suite d'une catastrophe, on note la déperdition de nombreuses informations utiles et une difficulté certaine à procéder à des observations cohérentes.

Le Policy Committee de l'HERP pourrait voir son mandat élargi afin d'étudier l'utilisation d'évaluations scientifiques pour formuler les politiques, et de pouvoir s'adresser aux décideurs – notamment locaux.

Recommandation 4. L'accent traditionnellement mis sur l'évaluation des risques scientifiques devrait être complété par une attention accrue aux facteurs individuels et sociétaux de vulnérabilité.

Communication avec le public

Il semble que les réactions réelles soient très différentes des attitudes individuelles face aux risques sismiques que les pouvoirs publics présupposent dans leurs politiques. Les entités gouvernementales chargées de la gestion des séismes catastrophiques se doivent donc de mieux comprendre comment la population réagit, et pourquoi, à ces risques.

Il faudrait encourager les recherches scientifiques sur les déterminants des attitudes individuelles et sociétales à l'égard des risques sismiques et sur la perception et l'acceptation de ces derniers.

La communication portant sur les risques ne doit pas être conçue et conduite comme une action unidirectionnelle d'éducation du public, mais comme un dialogue continu dans lequel il importe tout autant que les gestionnaires des risques comprennent les points de vue de la population et y adaptent les procédures de gestion des risques.

Des efforts continus devraient viser à maintenir et renforcer la sensibilisation aux risques et la culture du risque de la population, qui augmente lorsqu'une catastrophe majeure vient de se produire, mais décroît par la suite – schéma que l'on observe dans de nombreux autres pays, mais qui revêt une importance particulière au Japon en raison de la prévalence exceptionnelle des aléas naturels.

Recommandation 5. Les attitudes individuelles et collectives à l'égard des risques sismiques doivent être mieux comprises. À cette fin, la communication portant sur les risques doit être conçue et mise en œuvre comme un dialogue plus régulier et transparent entre les gestionnaires des risques et la population.

Prévention des catastrophes

Ériger des défenses structurelles contre les tremblements de terre

La "Stratégie de préparation au séisme métropolitain tokyoïte" publiée en 2006 par le *Central Disaster Management Council* fixe d'ambitieux objectifs publics décennaux à propos des dommages que provoquerait un événement sismique de grande ampleur. Cette démarche fondée sur les résultats a créé une impulsion favorable à la promotion de mesures de lutte contre les tremblements de terre. Néanmoins, il semble qu'aient manqué jusqu'ici des méthodes et des outils concrets permettant d'atteindre ces objectifs. Si toutes les autorités locales ont adhéré à ces derniers, les municipalités comme les préfectures ne semblent pas appréhender clairement leur responsabilité globale.

Les objectifs à long terme de l'action publique concernant les défenses structurelles devraient s'accompagner d'une meilleure définition des rôles et des responsabilités, ainsi que de critères d'allocation des ressources et de choix des instruments. Un cadre national plus précis améliorerait certainement la cohérence et l'efficience de l'action publique, tout en préservant l'autonomie de mise en œuvre des collectivités locales et des organes de l'État.

Le recours systématique aux analyses coûts-avantages devrait être encouragé dans ce domaine à la fois pour évaluer les projets et définir les priorités.

Les lignes directrices de l'OCDE relatives à la sûreté sismique des établissements scolaires recommandent une démarche systématique, fondée sur les risques et tournée vers les résultats, ainsi que la fixation d'objectifs mesurables en matière de sûreté sismique, de code et de normes de construction, et de plans de réalisation (OCDE 2005a).

Des mesures concrètes pourraient être prises pour renforcer les incitations à l'amélioration de la résistance sismique des bâtiments : on pourrait ainsi exiger que les renseignements relatifs aux aléas sismiques soient systématiquement mentionnés dans les transactions immobilières.

Recommandation 6. Les stratégies publiques en matière de protection structurelle devraient comporter une définition claire des principes et des responsabilités de mise en œuvre.

Occupation des sols et urbanisme

Bien que la presque totalité du territoire national soit exposée aux aléas sismiques, les risques sont maximaux dans les grands centres urbains du pays. Dans la région métropolitaine de Tokyo, 18 types de séismes potentiels ont été recensés afin de sensibiliser le public et d'informer les parties prenantes sur les aléas possibles. Cette typologie vient s'ajouter au séisme Tokai qui, compte tenu de son cycle historique de récurrence, présente une très forte probabilité d'occurrence à tout moment avec une magnitude voisine de 8.

Les autorités centrales, préfectorales et locales estiment de fait que la concentration des habitants, des constructions et des actifs représentent un défi extrêmement difficile à relever en matière d'opérations menées face à une catastrophe (évacuation, mise sous abri, etc.). Pourtant, les politiques d'occupation des sols et d'urbanisme ne comprennent aucune mesure restrictive d'occupation dans le voisinage des failles actives, et pas davantage de dispositions visant à déconcentrer les zones dans lesquelles l'ampleur globale des risques serait considérée comme excessive. La forte densité de population dans les zones habitables a probablement contribué à combattre l'idée que des considérations de risque pouvaient être intégrées aux politiques foncières.

Au cours des décennies à venir, la décrue à long terme de la population devrait cependant faciliter une évolution progressive des habitudes urbanistiques. Mais un scénario inchangé ne pourra aboutir à des résultats substantiels en termes d'exposition aux risques dans les zones les plus sujettes aux séismes.

Reposant en partie sur un faible coefficient d'occupation des sols lié aux politiques foncières et d'urbanisme en vigueur, les objectifs durables de déconcentration de la population et des activités économiques dans les zones sujettes aux séismes devraient être étendus géographiquement, et s'adosser à des moyens d'action publics plus forts.

D'autres travaux seront nécessaires pour mieux sensibiliser aux risques sismiques les différents échelons de la puissance publique et les autres parties prenantes concernées par l'aménagement foncier et urbain. Il faudra également renforcer les instruments juridiques des politiques d'aménagement du territoire et d'urbanisme.

À court terme, il semble souhaitable de lancer un débat national sur le vieillissement, l'aménagement du territoire et les aléas naturels, en y associant toutes les parties prenantes (grand public, organisations de la société civile, représentants du secteur privé, exploitants d'infrastructures essentielles, milieux universitaires, agences gouvernementales, etc.).

Il faudrait mener rapidement des recherches sur les failles actives et envisager dans ces zones des restrictions foncières applicables au moins aux bâtiments publics (écoles, hôpitaux, etc.) et aux infrastructures critiques.

Recommandation 7. Dans le contexte d'une population en décroissance rapide au cours des prochaines décennies, l'aménagement du territoire et l'urbanisme pourraient intégrer de manière plus active les facteurs de risques sismiques, et viser à réduire progressivement la densité de la population dans les zones les plus sujettes aux aléas. Une utilisation foncière prudente au voisinage des strates de failles devrait être envisagée à brève échéance.

Préparation et conduite d'opérations d'urgence

Maîtriser les répercussions secondaires des séismes

Malgré les responsabilités qu'il assume en matière de gestion globale des risques sociétaux liés aux tremblements de terre et en dépit des instructions générales qu'il transmet aux prestataires privés de services essentiels et exploitants d'activités dangereuses, le gouvernement du Japon ne connaît pas précisément l'état de certains éléments infrastructurels fondamentaux tels que les réservoirs de stockage de produits dangereux, les pipelines, les réseaux électriques, etc. En l'absence d'informations précises sur les risques secondaires que représentent les déversements de produits chimiques, les accidents industriels ou les ruptures d'alimentation électrique, les autorités ne sont pas en mesure de maîtriser l'ampleur des coûts indirects, qui peut être colossale en cas de séisme majeur.

Le *Central Disaster Management Council* a insisté sur la nécessité d'approcher de manière plus rigoureuse les risques d'aléas industriels que provoquerait un séisme dans la région de Tokyo :

> "Les administrations nationales et locales et les entreprises concernées proposeront des mesures sur la base de la loi sur la prévention des catastrophes dans les complexes industriels et autres installations d'hydrocarbures. Par ailleurs, elles renforceront les évaluations de l'impact éventuel d'une catastrophe survenue dans un tel complexe sur les zones adjacentes, et favoriseront à la fois un haut niveau de préparation aux catastrophes grâce au réaménagement des installations industrielles côtières âgées et la mise au point de bulletins sismiques d'urgence et d'autres technologies".

> "Afin d'empêcher la propagation aux zones adjacentes des catastrophes survenant dans des complexes pétroliers côtiers, les administrations nationales et locales et les entreprises concernées promouvront des mesures complètes de prévention des incendies de grande ampleur relatives au ballottement dans les citernes à hydrocarbures" (*Central Disaster Management Council* (2005), pp. 26 et 28.).

Il serait utile d'appliquer ces recommandations de manière plus systématique à tous les secteurs d'infrastructures critiques et d'activités dangereuses.

Il conviendrait d'élaborer pour chacun de ces secteurs, en fonction de leurs conditions réglementaires économiques particulières, des procédures précises de recueil des données et de partage de l'information. Des groupes d'échange d'informations devraient être établis.

Il faudrait instaurer des dispositions légales pour faciliter l'application des mesures nécessaires (comme dans le CalARP) et créer des garde-fous adéquats du point de vue de la confidentialité des informations.

Comme dans d'autres pays de l'OCDE, la maîtrise des procédures de gestion des risques dans les industries clés pourrait être intégrée aux activités normales des agences de réglementation et des organes de supervision.

Recommandation 8. Les agences gouvernementales chargées de la réglementation doivent se forger une meilleure connaissance de la gestion des risques sismiques dans leurs domaines d'action et assumer de manière claire la responsabilité de la supervision des secteurs d'infrastructures critiques et d'activités dangereuses à cet égard.

Plans de continuité opérationnelle dans les secteurs public et privé

Des plans de continuité opérationnelle ont été mis au point dans certaines grandes entreprises du pays. Mais cette pratique n'est pas systématique ; elle est même pratiquement inexistante parmi les PME.

Si l'on se tourne vers le secteur des administrations, les interdépendances entre services publics créent un besoin fort de coordonner les plans de continuité opérationnelle à tous les niveaux, et l'organisation actuelle de la gestion des risques catastrophiques semble quelque peu lacunaire à cet égard.

Enfin, il existe d'importantes synergies entre la préparation aux urgences, la prévention des catastrophes et les plans de continuité opérationnelle, tant au sein des organisations que dans la société en général. Aujourd'hui, les interactions entre ces activités semblent limitées au niveau aussi bien local que national.

À l'instar d'autres pays de l'OCDE, le gouvernement et le secteur public dans son ensemble devraient intégrer des exigences de planification de la continuité opérationnelle aux marchés publics.

Cette intégration devrait s'adosser à la mise au point d'une procédure de certification fondée sur une norme nationale adaptée à la situation spécifique du Japon en matière de risques sismiques.

Parallèlement, le Japon devrait contribuer fortement à l'élaboration d'une norme internationale de gestion de la continuité opérationnelle, pour laquelle son expérience en matière de gestion des catastrophes naturelles serait fort précieuse.

Le rôle de l'Office du Cabinet vis-à-vis de l'adoption de plans de continuité opérationnelle au niveau des administrations devrait être renforcé, et ces plans considérés comme un élément nécessaire de la gestion des catastrophes lors des audits internes et des évaluations (voir Chapter 1, section 2).

Il conviendrait de mieux utiliser les services d'incendie et de secours pour créer des liens entre la préparation aux urgences et la prévention des catastrophes, et pour promouvoir de façon active les plans de continuité opérationnelle. Les services municipaux d'incendie pourraient par exemple assumer à l'égard de la préparation et des plans de continuité des responsabilités accrues qui viendraient prolonger leurs activités traditionnelles de prévention des incendies.

Recommandation 9. Il est nécessaire de promouvoir davantage la mise en œuvre de plans de continuité opérationnelle dans le secteur public tout comme dans le secteur privé, et en particulier dans les PME.

La gestion de crise : des événements fréquents
aux catastrophes de grande ampleur

Le Japon bénéficie de systèmes d'alerte de pointe en matière de risques sismiques, tant du point de vue de la couverture – excellente – du territoire national que de leur niveau technologique. Le quartier général de la réaction aux catastrophes étant spécifique à chaque secteur ou niveau, le pays ne dispose toutefois pas, que ce soit au niveau conceptuel ou dans les faits, d'un système global de gestion des crises au niveau national. Dès lors, il se peut que la compétence formelle des autorités centrales pour exercer un commandement national et coordonner les interventions soit entravée par une insuffisance d'outils efficaces.

En outre, les décideurs locaux ne semblent pas toujours parfaitement conscients du rôle de commandement des autorités centrales en cas de catastrophe majeure.

La chaîne de commandement devrait être plus claire pour tous les acteurs concernés par le système de gestion de crise.

La répartition des rôles et des responsabilités aux différents niveaux doit prendre en compte la nécessité de traiter les besoins globaux nationaux et les interdépendances d'une manière extrêmement efficace pendant les phases d'urgence.

La délégation d'obligations le long d'une chaîne de commandement doit toujours s'accompagner d'objectifs et de tâches clairs, et d'exigences précises en matière d'information et d'évaluation.

Si une évolution des responsabilités actuelles de gestion de crise en fonction de l'ampleur d'une catastrophe est considérée comme inéluctable, il convient de viser une architecture organisationnelle élaborée, mais pourvue d'une structure simple. Il faut aussi mettre l'accent sur la nécessité de contrebalancer ces changements par des exercices et des formations.

Recommandation 10. La compétence des autorités centrales et les outils dont elle dispose pour la coordination nationale et, dans les cas extrêmes, pour le commandement, doivent être renforcés.

Questions à traiter après la survenue d'une catastrophe

Opérations de redressement et de reconstruction après une catastrophe

Les opérations de redressement après un séisme de grande ampleur, notamment lorsqu'il est survenu dans une métropole, représente un défi colossal en termes de planification, de coordination, de financement et de prise de décisions. Mais l'exemple de Kobe montre qu'un tremblement de terre peut aussi être l'occasion non seulement de diminuer la vulnérabilité des structures urbaines, mais aussi plus généralement d'améliorer leur pérennité, leur attrait économique et leur adéquation aux besoins des habitants.

L'objectif devrait être pour cela d'obtenir un consensus des acteurs locaux (citoyens, organisations non gouvernementales, entreprises privées et instances publiques locales) quant aux caractéristiques souhaitables de la zone reconstruite dans une région à fort risque. Il conviendrait d'impliquer des acteurs externes (administrations régionales ou centrales, localités voisines, etc.) chaque fois que les répercussions de ces travaux dépassent les frontières de la localité.

Un tel consensus large sur les grands objectifs de principe de la reconstruction servirait de base de départ dès lors que s'est produit un grand séisme, ce qui contribuerait à éviter des conflits inutiles, à cadrer les projets et à économiser du temps et des ressources. À l'évidence, un tel cadre général nécessiterait une adaptation aux conditions du moment, en fonction des besoins engendrés par le séisme et des ressources disponibles.

En dehors même de la survenue d'un tremblement de terre, ce consensus fournirait un objectif de long terme fort utile aux politiques locales d'aménagement du territoire et d'urbanisme.

L'État devrait également s'efforcer de faciliter le processus de reconstruction et d'en superviser la pérennité financière. Le *Disaster Aid Act* et le *Disaster Relief Act* devraient être utilisés efficacement pour apporter des ressources financières à ceux qui en ont besoin.

Recommandation 11. L'État devrait inciter les municipalités et les préfectures à consulter les acteurs locaux pour bâtir un consensus sur les objectifs des opérations de redressement après une catastrophe, et à renforcer leurs outils pour satisfaire les besoins nés d'un séisme.

Assurance : partager les méga-risques

Le système d'assurance des séismes actuellement en vigueur au Japon a été créé en 1966, deux années après le séisme de Niigata, avec la promulgation de l'*Act for Earthquake Insurance*. Ce système est fondé sur une réassurance adossée à l'État et a connu plusieurs phases d'amélioration et de perfectionnement depuis ses débuts, dont très récemment, en 2007, une extension de la prise en charge et une révision des taux des primes. Pourtant, en 2005, la pénétration du marché n'était que de 20 % pour les ménages et de quelques points de pourcentage pour les entreprises.

Les produits d'assurance devraient prendre en charge des catégories de risques plus détaillées. La conception de ces produits pourrait mieux refléter le niveau de risque au sein des préfectures et des grandes régions métropolitaines. Pour cela, il est nécessaire d'améliorer encore les méthodes d'évaluation des risques à l'aide à la fois de cartes d'aléas et de cartes de prédiction des mouvements sismiques.

Il conviendrait de renforcer encore la sensibilisation du grand public aux risques sismiques, et de mener des politiques visant à promouvoir l'évaluation des risques pour chaque bâtiment et à diffuser des informations de manière aisément compréhensible.

Il faudrait renforcer les incitations à la prévention des risques en différenciant davantage les primes d'assurance sur la base de mesures raisonnables de lutte contre les risques prises par les assurés. Une telle différenciation des primes individuelles étant susceptible de rendre l'assurance contre les séismes inabordables dans certains cas, il est essentiel d'envisager dans le même temps des dispositions adaptées aux assurés à haut risque.

Dès lors, les individus étant mieux couverts et les incitations à la prévention des dommages plus fortes, on pourrait envisager une extension de la réassurance adossée à l'État.

S'agissant de la prise en charge des risques sismiques courus par les entreprises, on devrait encourager le remplacement des polices d'assurance classiques par des innovations financières telles que les obligations-catastrophes et les dispositifs de créances conditionnelles.

Recommandation 12. Le taux de pénétration du marché de l'assurance des risques sismiques devrait être amélioré grâce à une meilleure différenciation des primes et une plus forte sensibilisation du public.

ISBN 978-92-64-05639-8
OECD Reviews of Risk Management Policies
Japan: Large-Scale Floods and Earthquakes
© OECD 2009

Chapter 7

Introduction – Seismic Risks in Japan

1. Japan's situation with regard to seismic events

Japan is located in one of the most earthquake-prone areas in the world. While the country only covers 0.25% of the globe's land area, it experienced about 18% of all earthquakes of magnitude 7 or more between 1997 and 2006.[1]

Japan's territory is almost entirely exposed to seismic risks, being located at the intersection of four tectonic plates.

Seismic activity is particularly high on the Pacific coast of the archipelago (the area running from Hokkaido in the north to the south-eastern tip of Honshu, and outside Kyushu in the south), where the oceanic plates (Pacific plate and Philippine Sea plate) sink into the continental plate (North American and/or Eurasian plate). This generates *subduction-zone earthquakes*, which can occur either in the plates (subducting or subducted) or at their boundary (interplate), and frequently reach a magnitude of 8. Their waves typically have a long period (one second or more), causing strong shaking on the surface. Tremors can last one to three minutes. These earthquakes very often cause tsunamis that can affect coastal areas far from the epicentre.

Large earthquakes of this type have occurred, for instance, every 90 to 150 years around the Nankai Trough, outside the Pacific coastline of Tokyo, Nagoya and Osaka. These earthquakes are given different names according to their source region – the Nankai and Tonankai earthquakes refer to those earthquakes originating in the area between Kyushu and the south-eastern tip of Honshu, whereas the Tokai earthquakes' source area is found further east, about 200 km southwest of Tokyo Bay.

Earthquakes can also happen away from these subduction zones, as the result of compression forces at work at relatively low depths (less than 20 km below the surface). Such *shallow inland earthquakes* happen along active fault lines, where seismic activity has occurred with recurrence periods of thousands, or even tens of thousands, of years. Their magnitude is usually smaller, and their tremors shorter, but they can cause considerable damage in limited areas. About 2 000 such active faults have been identified over Japan's territory, 110 of which are considered of major importance and studied with particular attention. However, shallow inland earthquakes can also happen along faults that are as yet unknown because of a very long recurrence period. The 1995 Great Hanshin-Awaji Earthquake (also known as Hyogoken Nanbu earthquake) was caused by a fault (the Nojima Fault) which was not considered particularly dangerous. The earthquakes that struck the Niigata and Fukuoka Prefectures, in 2004 and 2005 respectively, both happened on unknown faults. It is believed that a significant number of fault lines are yet to be discovered.

Finally, earthquakes also happen in the eastern margin of the Sea of Japan, according to some experts as the result of a nascent collision boundary between the North American and the Eurasian plates.

2. A history marked by devastating earthquakes

The history of Japan is marked by the experience of devastating earthquakes. The Kanto region, where Tokyo is located, has historically experienced magnitude 8 earthquakes every 200 to 300 years (with several magnitude 7 earthquakes in the interval). The last of these was the Great Kanto earthquake, which destroyed half of Tokyo and most of Yokohama on 1 September 1923 (see Figure 7.1). It caused firestorms and 12 meter-high

Figure 7.1. **Earthquakes of magnitude 7 or more in Japan and surrounding areas**
1885-1995, earthquakes with depth of 100 km or less

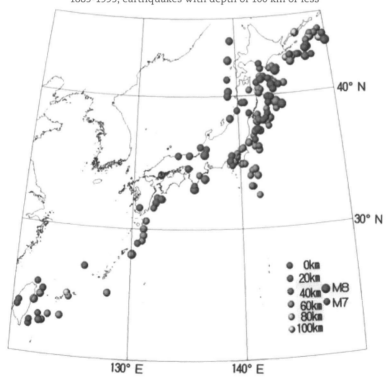

Source: Headquarters for Earthquake Research Promotion.

Figure 7.2. **The devastation caused by the 1923 Great Kanto earthquake in Tokyo**
Nihonbashi and Kanda seen from the roof of Dai-ichi Sogo Building, Kyobashi.

Source: Earthquake Pictorial Edition, Osaka Mainichi, 1923.

tsunamis, killed 105 000 people and made several million homeless (United States Geological Survey (2007) and Japan's Chronological Scientific Tables).

But the Great Kanto earthquake is also a landmark in the development of modern Japan, after which social change accelerated and urban landscapes were deeply modified (Reischauer 1953). The reconstruction of Tokyo was taken as an opportunity to develop modern transportation and public service infrastructures, and to build more resistant public buildings to serve as shelters in the event of a new disaster. In response to the state of confusion and social unrest that was caused by the earthquake throughout the country, more attention was devoted to better preparing people and organisations to face similar events, and improving disaster information. In 1960, 1 September was designated as the nation's Disaster Prevention Day.

The Great Hanshin-Awaji Earthquake was of the shallow inland type. It struck the city of Kobe at 5.46 a.m. on 17 January 1995, and led to the most costly disaster to strike Japan since the Second World War. The earthquake reached a magnitude of 7.3 and an intensity of 7 on the Japanese Meteorological Agency's scale – in other words the highest level of intensity, attributed to seismic events during which people are "thrown by the shaking and [it is] impossible to move at will", and where even highly earthquake resistant buildings may be severely damaged. It was the first time a major earthquake occurred directly underneath the centre of a modern city – Kobe had about 1.5 million inhabitants, and was the biggest port in Japan and sixth largest in the world.

The consequences of the earthquake were disastrous. More than 6 400 persons died and about 320 000 were evacuated. Fires started only minutes after the quake and spread rapidly. 400 000 buildings experienced damage, out of which 100 000 collapsed. At the end of January 1995, almost 230 000 people were using emergency shelters. A large share of the city's infrastructures was destroyed and 85% of its schools were heavily damaged. The port of Kobe, which was partly situated on artificial fill areas, was heavily affected by soil deformation (liquefaction). Main roads, railways, train and metro stations either collapsed or were seriously damaged. Gas services were disrupted for up to of 2.5 months, water and wastewater services for 4 months. The overall damage was estimated at close to JPY 10 trillion, or 2.5% of GDP.

The disaster triggered changes in every area of disaster risk management, from risk assessment to insurance, through building code enforcement and rescue operations.

The costliest earthquake in Japan since Kobe occurred in the area of Niigata on October 23, 2004. The earthquake (magnitude 6.8, JMA intensity 7) claimed 40 lives. Its overall economic impact, estimated to exceed JPY 3 trillion, makes it one of the costliest natural disasters in Japan's history. Around 100 000 persons had to seek temporary shelter, and thousand had to live in temporary housing for several years. The area of Niigata has experienced several earthquakes in the last 50 years, including the Niigata Earthquake in 1964, and there was relatively little shake-related damage to housing.

The particular features of this earthquake, which accounts for its high costs, were firstly the extremely high ground acceleration, which at 1.7 g was twice that of the Great Hanshin-Awaji Earthquake. This surpassed by far the existing building code, and led to extensive infrastructure damage on most roads, bridges, railway lines, etc. For the first time, the Shinkansen train was derailed during an earthquake. The second reason for high costs was a high number of earthquake-triggered landslides (442 landslides registered by Niigata Prefecture). The typhoon Tokage had recently crossed the area, and it is presumed that heavy rainfall had made the ground unstable.

3. Seismic risks today

This brief account shows the diversity of impacts that can be related to a major earthquake. There is, of course, the direct damage caused to individuals (fatalities, physical and psychological harm), to physical assets (buildings, plants and equipment, infrastructures, cultural assets, crops, etc.) and to the land itself (liquefaction on reclaimed ground). Earthquakes can also trigger a large number of other hazards, such as tsunamis, landslides, fires, oil spills or the release of hazardous materials, which in turn inflict damage on people, buildings and the environment. The indirect consequences of earthquakes include productivity losses due to the disruption of production in industry, service or utility sectors, and possibly the deterioration of a region's attractiveness or competitiveness.

The risks related to major earthquakes are continuously assessed in Japan. Among the most serious threats for the years to come are the Tokai, Tonankai and Nankai earthquakes, which are all generated along the same subduction-zone, among the most densely populated areas in the country.

The Headquarters for Earthquake Research Promotion[2] estimate that the Tokai earthquake has a probability of 87% to happen within the next 30 years with a magnitude of 8. The last Tokai earthquake occurred in 1854, and with a traditional cycle of recurrence of 100-150 years, it is considered by many as overdue. The Central Disaster Management Council evaluates the probable maximum consequences of the Tokai earthquake at 9200 fatalities, 260,000 completely destroyed buildings, and JPY 37 trillion in economic damages (7.2% of GDP).[3]

The Tonankai and Nankai earthquakes last occurred in 1944 and 1946 respectively, both with more than 1 000 fatalities. According to the HERP forecast, the Tonankai earthquake has a probability of 60-70% to happen within 30 years, and 90% within 50 years, with a magnitude of 8.1. The corresponding figures for the Nankai earthquake are 50%, 80-90% and magnitude 8.4. The maximum damage estimates of the CDMC for a joint Tonankai/Nankai earthquake are 17 800 fatalities and JPY 57 trillion (more than 11% of GDP).[4]

Such earthquakes represent, by any measure, a mega-risk, among the most serious that any OECD country is confronted with. If the CDMC's estimations are to be followed, a Tonankai/Nankai earthquake could be almost four times more costly than the most costly disaster to date, Hurricane Katrina. Its consequences would affect Japan for years, and would be very significant for the world economy.

Notes

1. According to calculations by the Japan Meteorological Agency.

2. The Headquarters for Earthquake Research Promotion evaluate the probability of occurrence of major subduction-zone and active-fault earthquakes in Japan, together with their probable magnitude and location, and publish comprehensive seismic hazard maps for the country (see Chapter 2, section 1).

3. Central Disaster Management Council, Damage estimates for a Tokai earthquake. Tokai Earthquake Countermeasure Expert Committee, March 2003.

4. Central Disaster Management Council, Damage estimates for a Tonankai/Nankai earthquake, Tonankai/Nankai Earthquake Countermeasure Expert Committee, September 2003.

ISBN 978-92-64-05639-8
OECD Reviews of Risk Management Policies
Japan: Large-Scale Floods and Earthquakes
© OECD 2009

Chapter 8

The General Policy Framework

1. National strategies and devolved responsibilities

The legal backbone of disaster risk management in Japan is the Disaster Countermeasures Basic Act of 1961. According to the Act, the central government, local government and public corporations are all responsible at their respective levels for protecting the land, the life and limb of people and their property against natural disasters.

At the highest level, decisions are taken by the Prime Minister, backed by the Central Disaster Management Council. The Council is chaired by the Prime Minister and comprised of the Minister of State for Disaster Management, the Cabinet Ministers, Presidents of major Japanese institutions (Japanese Red Cross Society, Bank of Japan, and public utility providers), experts from academia and others. Its main responsibilities include the definition of the nation's strategy against disasters (laid down in the Basic Disaster Management Plan) and the promotion of comprehensive measures to implement that strategy.

The administrative system is composed of three layers: central government and two levels of local government, namely prefectures and municipalities. Ministerial departments and prefectures are responsible for elaborating their own disaster management plans, provided these are in line with the Basic Disaster Management Plan. Likewise, municipalities develop their plans in line with the prefectural plans.

Operational responsibilities are borne by municipalities in areas as diverse as the protection of persons and assets, the regulation of land use, city planning, provision of information, early warning, emergency response, evacuation and sheltering.

Prefectures are made responsible by the Disaster Relief Act (1947) for the provision of relief services on an emergency basis: rescue, sheltering and temporary housing; health care; provision of basic supplies; emergency repairs. The role of national ministries and agencies is then essentially to secure the necessary resources, if needed by acquiring the support of other prefectures or private actors. The prefectural governor can delegate his missions to heads of municipalities. The costs of relief activities are borne by the prefecture below a certain amount, and shared between the prefecture and the central government above it.

This general framework is completed by more specific laws, which can be passed in reference to a particular event. For instance, the Large-Scale Earthquake Countermeasures Special Act, which was adopted in 1978 to prepare for a possible occurrence of the Tokai earthquake, enables the Prime Minister to designate areas at risk of a large-scale earthquake. In these areas, seismic observation and survey are enhanced, and all levels of government have to reinforce their disaster prevention and response plans.

The Earthquake Disaster Management Special Measures Act (1995) was elaborated after the Great Hanshin-Awaji Earthquake revealed deficiencies in the existing risk management system. In particular, the Act strengthened the definition of evacuation areas and routes and promoted the earthquake-proof retrofitting of schools.

In addition, a number of strategies and master plans define policy targets and options in the various fields of disaster risk management.

Findings

The policy framework for disaster management provides a positive example of how national policy objectives can be articulated with decentralised operational responsibilities. Local government has substantial autonomy over disaster management decisions, and is encouraged to design plans adapted to their specific conditions. This autonomy is, in principle, bound by the long-term principles and goals defined at central level. Prefectural governments have to report to the Prime Minister on their progress in developing disaster management plans and implementing national or regional objectives; within each region, municipalities make their own progress reports to the Prefecture.

International best practice indicates the importance of local government being able to develop its own capabilities in disaster management, on the basis of local knowledge, needs and possibilities.

At the same time, however, recent global disasters have highlighted the crucial importance of effective cooperation and coordination at regional and national level for prevention policies as well as management in emergencies. In spite of substantial changes and improvement in recent years, the Japanese earthquake disaster management system presents three weaknesses in this regard.

First, local government capabilities may not, as is also the case in other countries, be sufficient to respond adequately or flexibly to local needs or risks, in particular in a specific emergency and in the event of disaster. In many municipalities, the inadequacy of disaster management resources seems related to a broader problem of efficient delivery of public services (see Box 8.1). At present, the response to this issue consists in promoting mutual-

---

Box 8.1. **Some challenges of decentralisation in Japan**

Prefectures and municipalities are considered as two tiers of local government in Japan. The country's 47 prefectures and about 3 000 municipalities vary widely in population and size. The prefectures range in population from the Tokyo metropolitan area with more than 12 million to Tottori prefecture with 610 000. Their size varies from the Hokkaido region's 80 000 km^2 to 2 000 km^2 for the Kagawa prefecture. The municipalities range from Yokohama, with a population of about 3.5 m, to the village of Aogashima in Tokyo, with about 200 inhabitants. Ashoro town in Hokkaido covers about 1 400 km^2, and Takashima town, in the Nagasaki prefecture, only 1.3 km^2.

In addition to their responsibilities in disaster risk management, Japan's local government is in charge of important missions including education, healthcare, social services, infrastructures, waste management, and police. Their expenditures represent about half of total public spending, a high level by OECD standards.

Many municipalities are considered too small to fulfil their role efficiently, although the central government's support for municipality mergers has helped reduce their numbers by 70% since the Second World War. One study finds, for instance, that most municipalities do not have the critical size to exploit scale economies in the provision of public services (Hayashi, 2002). Unstable tax bases and volatile revenues are also an issue. A political agreement was reached in 2000 in order to further reduce the number of municipalities to 1000, but the exact conditions of such a reduction have not been clarified.

The fiscal situation of local government dramatically deteriorated during the years of economic slowdown. Local debt increased from 15% of the GDP in 1991 to 40% in 2003, a very high level compared to other OECD countries. Local government is faced with the imperative need to restore fiscal sustainability in the coming years. It is likely that efficiency gains in the provision of public services will be key to this aim (OECD, 2005).

---

help agreements between local governments. There are in fact a considerable amount of such agreements: 1940 between municipalities and 558 between prefectures. Although very positive in the event of a disaster, such arrangements can fall short of securing adequate disaster risk management capabilities at the local level. This could be due to neighbouring local governments suffering from the same disaster and therefore not being in a position to offer help. It also seems that municipal officials in charge of disaster management do not always have enough practical experience and the necessary knowledge of the administrative and legal context of this activity.

It may furthermore be argued that one of the governance problems affecting disaster management is that the devolution of functional responsibilities to local government has not been backed with an upgrading of their resources and the introduction of relevant management tools, *e.g.* inspection and evaluation requirements. In European countries such as the United Kingdom and the Nordic Countries, central government exercises its overall responsibility for national disaster management by monitoring functional implementation at local level through inspections and evaluations.

Second, the accumulation of laws and plans over the years, the result of a well-established and remarkable tradition of learning lessons from disaster experiences, seems to have created a fairly complex and not sufficiently transparent policy framework. Disaster countermeasures are taken based on the Disaster Countermeasures Basic Act and 6 other basic acts, 18 disaster prevention and preparedness acts, 3 disaster emergency response acts and 23 disaster recovery, reconstruction and financial measures acts. In particular, although the Local Autonomy Law has established some principles for the distribution of functions between prefectures and municipalities, the line of demarcation is not so clear and each tier shares responsibility with the others.

This can be compared with the recent development in the European Union and some of its Member States, where the policy has been directed towards more holistic framework legislation, supplemented by regulation through law and ordinance of particular issues. A single document, the European Flood Directive, tackles for instance all levels of flood risk management in order to facilitate the understanding of entrusted roles, responsibilities and objectives for all relevant stakeholders, including the public and local authorities. It is believed that such a structure of the legislation makes it easier for the public as well as the actors themselves to understand the roles, responsibilities and objectives of the competent authorities. Collaboration between administrative bodies could thus be facilitated and enhanced through similar, more coherent and consolidated legislation.

Although it can be argued that such complexity of the legislation is unavoidable with respect to the country's exposure to multiple natural hazards, it is nevertheless the case that, especially for small municipalities with limited resources, it can be a challenge to understand their exact duties in disaster risk management, and the way that they should share responsibilities with other levels of government.

Third, the central government does not seem to have the appropriate tools for effectively coordinating, and when necessary monitoring local decisions. The various master plans adopted in recent years were in part designed to address the lack of coordination and guidance from the central level. However, because of the inadequacy of instruments for promoting and implementing a coordinated approach, the problems seem to persist.

For instance, if gaps in the development or implementation of a local government's disaster management practices are identified, at present no governmental agency has a clear mandate to enforce corrective actions.

Issues of evacuation and sheltering in densely populated urban areas can pose very intricate co-ordination problems to municipalities, and there does not seem to be a clear and effective decision structure for addressing these problems.

There are some interesting cases of use of "soft tools" by the central government of Japan in order to influence regional and municipal disaster management decisions. For instance, in 2006, by publishing the list of 600 municipalities that would be affected by the Tohnankai-Nankai earthquake, the Central Disaster Management Council created strong incentives for municipal governments to take prevention and preparedness actions. Earthquake hazard, vulnerability and consequence maps published by the Cabinet Office and echoed by the mass media have also had a strong impact (see next section in this chapter).

On the whole, however, the use of such tools seems to be occasional and piecemeal.

As a consequence, while the architecture of disaster management plans ensures that policy objectives and principles are *formally* consistent from the local to the national level, there are limited instruments to bring about the same degree of consistency in *actual* policy measures.

Opportunities for action and recommendations

Japan's government could better support and coordinate local decisions in earthquake disaster management in four areas.

- First, better sharing of scientific information, collection and dissemination of best practices, comparative studies, identification of problem areas and provision of guidance adapted to the problems faced by local authorities are flexible ways for central government to prepare the ground for, and positively influence, decision-making at the local level. Such soft tools should be used in a more forceful and systematic way.

- Second, central government and the prefectures should devise ways to consolidate disaster management capabilities in small municipalities. Providing increased training and education of their personnel, including on legal and administrative aspects of disaster risk management, would represent a minimum in this regard. A bolder approach could consist of better concentration of local disaster management resources: either by enabling municipalities to engage in contractual arrangements for the provision of disaster management services – as in Switzerland's purchaser/provider relations between cantons (OECD 2002), or by creating regional groupings at an optimal scale for the pooling of municipal resources as in the Netherlands' Safety Regions (Netherlands Directorate-General for Public Safety and Security 2004).

- Third, there is a need to further clarify the sharing of responsibilities in operations, coordination and collaboration within the disaster management system both for the general public and for the authorities themselves, in particular at local level.

- Fourth, the use of policy evaluation and monitoring could be enhanced. Disaster management should emphasise greater use of outcome indicators and set measurable targets, with clear time frames, for achievement. A central government organisation should receive a mandate (and adequate human and financial resources) to systematically evaluate local government policies in the area of disaster risk management, to identify inadequacies and coordination gaps, and to involve all relevant actors in addressing these issues.

Recommendation 1. Decentralised disaster management responsibilities should go hand in hand with a clarification of the roles and responsibilities and consolidation of resources of local government, increased exchange of information and co-ordination between all levels of government, and systematic evaluation and analysis of results by central authorities.

2. Sectoral competencies and co-ordination

Japan's administrative system is characterised by decentralised and independent ministries armed with broad administrative discretion. In the area of disaster risk management, each ministry is responsible within its jurisdiction, which includes not only the ministry's staff, buildings and equipment and its affiliated organisations, but also public infrastructures, and outreach activities (awareness-raising, public-private partnerships, etc.).

The power of the civil service and the high independence of ministries necessitate a strong role for the prime minister, in order to ensure co-ordination and co-operation among powerful ministries. In the past decades, a number of prime ministers have taken a leading role in promoting various reforms, and their personal involvement has been a strength relative to many other OECD countries. However, given the fact that reforms depend on personal support from the prime minister also explains why progress is sometimes slow and selective.

The organisation of the government was substantially modified in January 2001, with the aim of (1) enhancing political leadership, (2) restructuring the national administrative bodies, (3) improving transparency in public administrations and (4) streamlining central government. Some of these changes had direct bearing on the government structure dealing with seismic risks.

The Cabinet Office was created with a specific support and inter-ministerial co-ordination role, and a number of prime ministerial panels and other advisory boards were introduced. One of these bodies was the Central Disaster Management Council, which was put in charge of promoting a comprehensive approach to disaster management inside the government and discussing important issues, under the authority of the Prime Minister. The Cabinet Office acts as the Council secretariat. A post of Minister of State for Disaster Management was established in the Cabinet, with responsibility for the coordination of disaster risk reduction activities.

Another important decision from January 2001 was the merger of four ministries into the Ministry of Land, Infrastructure and Transport (MLIT). As the ministry in charge of construction standards, transport infrastructures (roads, railways, bridges, ports, airports, etc.), water and river management facilities (dams, levees, etc.), the MLIT has a prominent role in the reduction of seismic risks.

Findings

The organisation of the government provides a comprehensive coverage of seismic risk management activities. The overarching role of the Central Disaster Management Council ensures that these activities are considered in an integrated manner, a feature that not many risk management systems in other OECD countries share. This is a crucial asset in an area where thousands of lives can be saved by quickly integrating progress in science and technology into warning and evacuation schemes, or coordinating risk prevention in transport infrastructures with disaster response.

In particular, there is a strong link between risk assessment and risk management decision-making. Some of the country's leading scientists and scientific organisations participate in the work of the Central Disaster Management Council, through its expert groups. It should also be mentioned that following recent organisational changes, scientific organisations dealing with seismic risks have made an effort to express their results in terms that are directly usable by policy-makers and the public.

The Cabinet Office also has a significant role in turning scientific data and studies into policy-relevant messages, such as the earthquake hazard maps produced in 2006 for the Chubu and Kinki regions. These maps enjoyed wide media coverage, and contributed to raising awareness among the region's inhabitants. In only a few years, the Cabinet Office has built a broad-based expertise on earthquake risk management in Japan and abroad, through its function as secretariat of the Central Disaster Management Council. It is gradually developing a detailed view of the country's exposure to seismic risks, the various elements of its risk management system and their potential weaknesses.

The most active parts of the Council are the Organisations for Technical Investigation. These collect and analyse experiences from past disasters, in order to obtain precise knowledge from earlier incidents and enhance awareness of disaster management issues. They also develop scenarios on the aftermath of earthquakes, which they use to elaborate countermeasures. For instance, a scenario regarding pedestrian jam in the aftermath of Tokyo Metropolitan area earthquakes was released by the Technical Investigation Committee on Evacuation Measures for the Tokyo Metropolitan Earthquakes in April 2008, and made the headlines of the country's major media.

The availability of such expertise at the centre of government should be considered as a major strength of Japan's government organisation.

It seems, however, that there is still some way to go in providing the centre of government with the ability to supervise and control the actions of ministerial departments in disaster risk management.

The Central Disaster Management Council, although ideally placed, has an operational role that is confined to planning countermeasures against the major seismic events. The Cabinet Office can only advise ministries and agencies on risk management matters, as it recently did with its Continuity of Operation Guidelines for National Government Offices. Other governmental entities provide technical guidance to ministries, for instance the MLIT's Government Building Department regarding the construction and retrofitting of government buildings. A number of entities have, as in other OECD countries, cross-sectoral control and auditing competencies, including the Evaluation Authority of the Ministry of Internal Affairs and Communications, the Accounting Office and the Ministry of Finance. But their actions do not encompass detailed aspects of disaster risk management.

In the absence of consistent checking and control mechanisms for disaster risk management inside the government, ministries are to a large extent responsible for defining their own roles for disaster management, financing and enacting the necessary measures, controlling their implementation, and evaluating the consequences.

This can potentially lead to large disparities in the achievements of different ministries, to inefficiencies in resource allocation and the definition of priorities (see also section 3 in this chapter), and to conflicts of interest inside ministries when it comes to identifying and addressing implementation gaps.

Opportunities for action and recommendations

The Cabinet Office should be given effective responsibility for monitoring and coordinating disaster management activities from a whole-of-government perspective.

Its role in collecting data, analysing the strengths and weaknesses of government disaster management, drawing lessons, and suggesting improvements and priority areas of action should be enhanced.

The organisational structure of disaster management at the Centre of Government should be reconsidered with a view to enhancing efficiencies and effectiveness. In the area of crisis management, the roles the Cabinet Office and the Cabinet Secretariat could be integrated further.

The Government might wish to consider creating an organ in charge of auditing and evaluating disaster management activities across sectors. This responsibility could be given to an existing government entity, providing organisational design ensures it be separated from the entity's operational responsibilities, if it has any. Various OECD governments have already developed such an internal evaluation capacity. Norway's Directorate for Civil Protection and Emergency Planning (DSB) is one example.

Recommendation 2. The monitoring and co-ordination of disaster management activities inside central government should be strengthened.

3. Policy evaluation and resource allocation

The share of disaster risk management expenditures in the government's total budget substantially decreased between the early 1960s and the early 1990s from around 9% of the total budget to nearly 4.5% (Cabinet Office 2002). This reduction was primarily due to a steady decline in the share of recovery and reconstruction spending. Disasters had a lower cost for the Japanese government, which seems to be due to both lower vulnerability of Japanese society (compared to the post-war period) and better damage prevention and mitigation. The irregular occurrence of natural disasters may however also have had some influence in this respect.

During the same period, the share of disaster preparedness expenditures (disaster prevention, awareness-raising and response) rose strongly, while land conservation measures (flood control, soil erosion control, prevention of landslides, etc.) have consistently absorbed about half of the budget of disaster risk management.

In the past few years, the downward trend of expenditures for recovery and reconstruction has stopped, and several factors indicate that it may be unlikely to resume.

The increasing frequency and severity of climate-related natural hazards (typhoons, floods, etc.) and the rising economic costs of all types of disasters will drive disaster recovery and reconstruction expenses. But they will also call for higher investments in some areas of prevention and preparedness.

In addition, Japan is engaged in a continuous process of improvement of its structural defences against earthquakes and other natural disasters, which entails a sustained effort of maintenance and upgrading of infrastructures and buildings, both private and public. For instance, approximately JPY 330 billion were devoted to the retrofitting of bridges on the country's major roads (excluding highways, which are managed by the private sector) between 2005 and 2007, based on the lessons from the Great Hanshin-Awaji Earthquake.

The ongoing campaigns for the retrofitting of private houses, public buildings and infrastructures show that even as regards disaster prevention, identified needs far outweigh the existing budgetary resources – even though all costs will not be covered by public expenditure. With the outlook for the government's budget seeming quite unfavourable over the medium term (see Box 8.2), this means that disaster management expenditures are likely to face stringent financial constraints, and that competition for government funding may become fierce.

The Ministry of Land, Infrastructure and Transport's spending projections give a clear idea of what the situation might look like in a few years: the MLIT calculated that if the current trend of reduction in public investment (–3% per year for national funding and –5% per year for local funding) was to continue until 2020, then its own infrastructure-related spending will be entirely devoted to reconstruction, renewal and maintenance of existing infrastructures by that time (see Figure 8.1).

Box 8.2. **The fiscal situation**

A decade of economic stagnation in the 1990s and the government's efforts to support economic activity brought about a dramatic deterioration of Japan's fiscal situation at the turn of the century. In 2002, the government's budget deficit peaked at 8.2% of GDP, and the public debt reached 150% of GDP.

The same year, the government adopted the *Reform and Perspectives* fiscal consolidation plan, which aimed at freezing public spending at 38% of GDP over 5 years, an objective which was attained thanks to a significant reduction in public investments.

Still, the fiscal outlook remains unfavourable for the years to come, notably because of the impact of an ageing population on social spending and the weight of the public debt in terms of interest payments. Other expenditures, in particular those related to disaster risk management, are therefore likely to experience downward pressures for several years.

Source: OECD (2006a).

Figure 8.1. **The Ministry of Land, Infrastructure and Transport's infrastructure spending if recent budgetary trends continue**

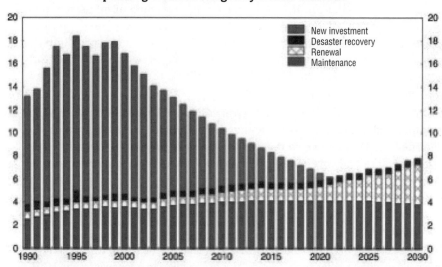

Source: Ministry of Land, Infrastructure and Transport (2005).

The scale of needs and the scarcity of resources together point to the relevance of policy evaluation and prioritisation based on costs and benefits. The comparison of the costs and benefits of alternative courses of action can be an efficient tool for directing resources towards the most productive uses in terms of saving lives and reducing economic and societal losses – although some aspects, such as the valuation of lives saved and of nonmarket goods, entail methodological difficulties and are debated continuously. [1]

In April 2002 the Japanese government introduced a new government-wide Policy Evaluation System (PES). The PES obliges each ministry and agency to conduct self-assessment-based evaluations of their policies, applying one or several of the following criteria: necessity, efficiency, effectiveness, equity and priority. The PES is linked to Japan's regulatory policies by providing an evaluation framework that can be used for *ex-ante* as well as *ex-post* evaluations of regulatory performance.

Findings

Since the introduction of the PES, evaluations have been conducted systematically for new public works, research and development and overseas development projects, and on a voluntary basis for existing projects (including regulations). So far, the item-by-item approach has made it difficult for observers to keep track of progress on the large number of reform projects and proposals.

On the whole, decisions to commit resources to risk management measures do not appear to rely on an assessment of the associated costs and benefits, but rather on the presumption that the decision making process led by the Diet and the ministries ensures appropriate allocation of resources. The problem is, of course, that a "social planner" is not always equipped with balanced information and knowledge. Moreover, in a decentralised system such as Japan's disaster management, it is important to ensure that decisions at all levels make the better use of public resources even if any social planners fail to recognise some key issues affecting costs and benefits. There could therefore be efficiency gains in making a greater use of decision support tools and stating more clearly the principles of budget allocation and priority definition.

The seismic retrofitting of river structures is a case in point. After inspecting a large share, but not all, of the country's river stretches, the services of the Ministry of Land, Infrastructure and Transport found that 2 400 km of dykes needed consolidation against seepage, at an overall cost of JPY 2.4 trillion (0.5% of GDP). The work has started based on a 3-year plan over 2005-08, and concerns 55 km of dykes which were given high priority.

Such projects are characterised both by the scale of the needs, which impose a very long time span, and by the considerable degree of uncertainty regarding the costs and benefits of the project over its duration – consider, for instance, the consequences of global warming for river structures; technological change; or the interest of private landowners in participating in safety-enhancing actions. It is therefore rational for decision-makers to adopt a stepwise approach, in order to preserve a high degree of flexibility and make irreversible choices only when uncertainties have receded. At the same time, however, decision-makers might be tempted, at each period, to postpone the necessary actions. In such a context, it is important to ensure that resources are allocated and priorities are defined based on a clear understanding of the expected costs and benefits and the relative urgency of the project compared to alternative courses of action. At present, such information often seems to be lacking.

In the absence of appropriate indicators, decentralised definition of priorities can clearly lead to efficiency losses in disaster risk reduction. The substantial variations in the retrofitting of schools from one municipality to the other is probably a relevant issue in this regard. Admittedly, municipalities have to weigh their expenditures in enhancing the resistance of school buildings against their relative exposure to seismic risks, as well as their other priorities. This explains that the municipality of Kanagawa, located in the Tokai earthquake area with a 26% chance of experiencing an earthquake of intensity 6 or more[2] within the next 30 years in its southern area, has retrofitted 89% of its primary and secondary schools, while the rate falls to 37% in Nagasaki, where the corresponding earthquake probability figure is below 3%.[3] However, school retrofitting rates can also differ widely among municipalities that have similar risk profiles, as between the wards of Tokyo (53% in Shinagawa, compared to 96% on average in the 3 adjacent wards).[4]

In this context, a strategic policy program evaluation for a broader range of disaster management policies can be an important step in establishing comprehensive and consistent assessments of government policies and activities.

Opportunities for action and recommendations

While Japan started the process of regulatory impact analysis (RIA) later than many OECD countries, its efforts have gained considerable momentum of late. In accordance with the new Three-year Plan and Programme for Regulatory Reform of March 2004, RIAs are to be conducted by Ministries and Administrative Agencies on planned and existing regulations as appropriate. The systematic use of RIA should be extended, as a priority, to earthquake risk management policies.

A more systematic evaluation of policy options could significantly improve disaster management. Both in the budgetary process and for organisational matters, there is significant scope for the application of results obtained through PES or other studies (e.g. relative efficiency in terms of decreased probability of death of retrofitting houses, fixing home furniture, etc.). Ministers should be encouraged, if not required, to use the results of policy evaluations for regulatory measures pertaining to disaster management, from private and public building retrofitting and fireproofing to rescue preparedness and operations.

Strategic policy decision-making, which is already strongly grounded in scientific research and risk assessment, can also use cost and benefit considerations over a wider range of disaster risk management policies.

For this, existing methodologies should be reviewed and adapted to Japan's context.

In addition, individual policy evaluations should be reviewed, synthesised and gathered into a whole-of-government perspective of Japan's disaster management policies. Ideally, the Cabinet Office should perform this task. It could also be attributed to the Ministry of Internal Affairs and Communications, which is in charge of the design and implementation of the PES.

Recommendation 3. Policy decisions should be evaluated more carefully both before and after their application, and efficiency considerations should prevail in defining priorities within the complete spectrum of risk management measures.

Notes

1. See, for instance, U.S. Office of Management and Budget (2003): Circular A-4 on Regulatory Analysis, pp. 29-30.

2. Japan Meteorological Agency intensity scale.

3. Estimations from the Headquarters for Earthquake Research Promotion (HERP).

4. Retrofitting rates drawn from a survey conducted by the Ministry of Education, Culture, Sport, Science and Technology (MEXT, 2007).

ISBN 978-92-64-05639-8
OECD Reviews of Risk Management Policies
Japan: Large-Scale Floods and Earthquakes
© OECD 2009

Chapter 9

Risk Assessment and Communication

1. Hazard and risk assessment

Japan has world-class seismological research, and probably the world's densest observation network of seismic tremors, crustal movements and geological conditions through sensors, GPS monitoring and surveys. A large number of organisations are involved in the observation of seismic phenomena and the collection of data.

The Japan Meteorological Agency possesses earthquake meters at about 200 locations nation-wide, analyses tremor data continuously and in real time, and disseminates earthquake early warnings and tsunami warnings through central and local government and mass media to citizens. In addition, the JMA has magnitude meters at 600 locations and provides the observed scale of earthquakes online within a few minutes. Furthermore, the JMA provides information related to Tokai earthquakes when it can detect earthquake precursors based on data from research institutes, local government and universities.

The Geographical Survey Institute (GSI, under the Ministry of Land, Infrastructure and Transport) is in charge of documenting crustal movements. The institute operates GEONET, a GPS Earth Observation Network System, designed to record plate movements through 1 231 GPS monitoring points within the national territory for earthquakes occurring along the land masses or sea trenches. The average distance between the monitoring points is 20 km and the network is the highest density GPS monitoring network in the world. The collected GPS data are transmitted to GSI, and through analysis, the co-ordinates of each monitoring point can be determined every three hours. The change in geographical co-ordinates is conducted with a precision of less than 1 cm of crust movement. In case of large-scale earthquakes, the crust movement is calculated within a few hours of its occurrence and is published.

The National Research Institute on Earth Science and Disaster Prevention (NIED, under the Ministry of Education, Culture, Sport, Science and Technology) operates three networks of seismographs disseminated throughout the country: K-NET, a network of strong-motion seismographs installed at approximately 1000 locations, able to record strong and destructive seismic motions; Hi-net, an observation network of high-sensitivity seismographs deployed at approximately 750 locations, to detect seismic motions that are too weak to be felt by humans (data transmitted in real time to the Japan Meteorological Agency for use in seismic warnings); and

F-net, a network of broadband seismographs deployed at approximately 70 locations nationwide, capable of accurately detecting slow ground motions originating from remote seismic sources (data used to research the development of earthquake faults and the interior structure of the Earth). The Institute has various activities in strong motion prediction and seismic hazard evaluation. It also produces seismic hazard maps.

The National Institute of Advanced Industrial Science and Technology (AIST, under the Ministry of Economy, Trade and Industry) carries out the national geological survey, and conducts emergency site surveys in the event of a geological disaster (earthquakes, landslides, volcanic eruptions), and provides scientific information on the natural phenomena at work to disaster management actors.

Several university centres also possess their own networks of earthquake meters.

Data is provided by diverse institutions to numerous research centres, and elaborated into hazard, consequence and vulnerability maps.

The Cabinet Office estimates the distribution of earthquake intensity and the heights of tsunami, especially for the predicted Tokai, Tonankai-Nankai, Japan Trench-Chishima Trench, and Tokyo Metropolitan shallow inland earthquakes.

In July 1995, in the wake of the Great Hanshin-Awaji earthquake, the Headquarters for Earthquake Research Promotion were established by the Special Measure Law on Earthquake Disaster Prevention, to co-ordinate efforts in seismic research and risk assessment. The HERP was placed under the authority of the Ministry of Education, Culture, Sport, Science and Technology. In 1999, the HERP issued the policy document "On the promotion of earthquake survey and research – integrated and basic measures for promoting observation, survey, and research on earthquakes". The document lists research topics that need to be promoted in the immediate term, one of which is the drawing up of a map of earthquake tremors for the entire national territory.

As a part of this effort, the HERP's Earthquake Research Committee has assessed the scale and long-term probability of occurrence of 98 major active-fault and subduction-zone earthquakes and has disclosed the results. In 2005, the Committee gathered these assessments in comprehensive earthquake hazard maps for Japan (Figure 9.1).

Findings

The observation and assessment of seismic phenomena is of the highest international standard, and the disaster management authorities are highly conscious of the need to maintain this excellence. For example, according to article 4 of the Special Law for Large Scale Earthquake Countermeasures, it is

Figure 9.1. **Earthquake hazard map**

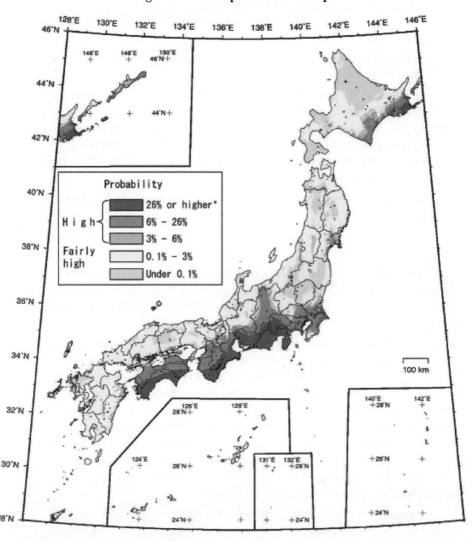

Source: Headquarters for Earthquake Research Promotion- HERP, website: *http://www.jishin.go.jp/main/index-e.html.*

stipulated that the central government should continuously monitor changes in land and water, and strengthen observation and monitoring by intensifying the density of survey points related to earthquakes on land and water masses for forecasting large-scale earthquakes in high risk areas, thereby preventing or mitigating earthquake-related disasters. The government is to put in place a system for observation, survey and research of earthquakes in other areas as well.

Table 9.1. **Governmental seismic observation facilities in March 2007**

Observation Stations [1] (as of March, 2007)

Headquarters for Earthquake Research Promotion

Observation / Organisation	High sensitivity seismographs		Broad-band seismographs		Strong-motion seismographs		Geodetic survey				Seabottom geodetic stations	Ground water observatories	Geo magnetic observatories	Gravity observatories	Tide and/or Tsunami observatories
	on land	ocean bottom [2]	TYPE1 [3]	TYPE1 [4]	on the ground	in the well	GPS	SLR	VLBI	Strain [5]					
Ministry of Education, Culture, Sports, Science and Technology							7								
National University Corporations	235	6(2)	12 [6]	34 [6]	126	17	73			93		19	36	3	4
National Research Institute for Earth Science and Disaster Prevention	777	6(1)	22	51	1707	681	4			56		5			5
Japan Agency for Marine-Earth Science and Technology		5(2)													4
Ministry of Land, Infrastructure and Transport					1332	105									74
Geographical Survey Institute							1337	1	4	5			16	2	27
Japan Meteorological Agency	183 [7]	8(2)			584					36			6		86 [10]
Hydrographic Department, Japan Coast Guard							30	1			16		1		28
The National Institute of Advanced Industrial Science and Technology	13			1	2	8	3			15		42			
Total	1208	25(7)	33 [10]	86	3751 [11]	811	1454	1	4	205	16	66	59	5	228 [9]

1. Temporary observation points are not counted.
2. Numerals in the parentheses show the number of cables.
3. Broadband seismographs covering the frequency range from small earthquakes to free oscillation of the earth.
4. Boradband seismographs covering the frequency range from microearthquakes to tsunami earthquakes which are relatively of short period.
5. Strain meters, volumetric strain meters, three-components strain meters, and extensometers.
6. The broadband seismographs of the National University Corporations are put by the side of high sensitivity seismographs.
7. Therefore, the number is included in the number of high sensitivity seismographs.
8. JMA high sensitivity seismographs include 20 seismographs corresponding to TYPE 2 broadband seismographs.
9. It includes 10 observation points operated by local governments et al, and 2 observation points that belong to other organisations.
10. The Nemuro observation facility is a co-operative facility of the National Research Institute or Earth Science and Disaster Prevention and National University Corporations.
11. In addition, there are approximately 2800 intensity meters of local public bodies.
Source: Headquarters for Earthquake Research Promotion: HERP (2007).

As a response to the Great Hanshin-Awaji earthquake of 1995, the GSI is to draw up detailed maps of large metropolitan areas with the locations of active faults. These are used in assessing the risks of earthquake occurrence and as basic information for formulating plans for disaster prevention by regional government. The fault surveys were extended after the Niigata-Chuetsu earthquake of 2004, where damages in the mountainous areas were also large.

While scientific research on seismic hazards is of the highest quality, certain aspects of earthquake disaster risk assessment need to be strengthened. This is the case for vulnerability assessments. Factors of human vulnerability to natural disasters have started to be identified, and can help better understand and predict the consequences of an event (see Box 9.1).

Research conducted by Wisner and Uitto in the framework of a United Nations University Project in the late 1990s, showed that Tokyo earthquake damage models did not take into account gender and age in their calculations, only day-time and night-time populations. Equally, these factors were not accounted for in the assessment of "evacuation risk", i.e. time used and dangers encountered on the way to the dedicated "open spaces". In 1996, only one of Tokyo's 23 "special wards" (Setagaya) had incorporated social data of any kind (identifying the share the population aged 65+) in their preparedness planning. However, this information was used only in preparedness exercises, and not in the GIS-based vulnerability assessment. These observations still seem to be valid to a large extent.

In addition, there is a lack of knowledge regarding the long-term impacts of major earthquakes on the physical and mental health of exposed populations, as well as the long-term socio-economic consequences.

The link between scientific risk assessment and policy-making is one of the strengths of Japan's earthquake risk management system, notably thanks to the work of the Central Disaster Management Council's expert groups and of the Cabinet Office. The country's leading scientists and scientific institutions are consulted during the decision-making process, both in normal times and in crisis situations. The government's strategies regarding the major earthquake risks faced by the country (the Tokai, Tohnankai-Nankai, Chishima crust and the Tokyo shallow inland earthquakes) are all based on sound scientific inputs.

One aspect that could be further enhanced in this regard is attention to the use of scientific inputs in decision-making, in particular at the local level where, as noted earlier, resources are often limited.

Opportunities for action and recommendations

More emphasis should be placed on understanding individual and societal factors of vulnerability (or, on the contrary, of resilience) to earthquakes. The prevalence of vulnerability factors in the population, as well

Box 9.1. **Factors of human vulnerability to natural disasters**

Three factors of vulnerability have traditionally been identified in emergency situations: gender, age and disability. In spite of high awareness of emergency preparedness officials, children, the elderly, women and the disabled are recurrently the principal victims of disasters.

This was tragically illustrated during the Kobe disaster: about 50% of the fatalities were aged 60 and more; the death rate of people aged 80 and more was six times that of people aged 50 and under; and in the 60+ age group, the number of female fatalities was almost the double that of male fatalities.

The excess deaths of the elderly have been explained by the fact that many of the wooden houses which collapsed were inhabited by elderly people. Furthermore, many of the elderly slept on the ground floor, which was more susceptible to collapse, whereas the rest of the construction remained intact. There are indications that the suffering of certain groups of elderly continued well after the disaster, and that the elderly were subject to a higher mortality and morbidity in the shelters and later in the temporary housing. Rises in deaths in the shelters were attributed among other things to the occurrence of pneumonia among the older age groups. There was also anecdotal evidence of suicides among the elderly in temporary housing in the months following the earthquake.

This is an important lesson to draw in a society where the share of older persons in the population is already high, and bound to rise further in the coming decades. Within this group, however, which is admittedly highly diverse, some persons are more vulnerable than others. Elderly women living on their own, for instance, are among the lowest-earning groups in the OECD area. In Kobe, mortality was especially high in the low-cost areas with traditional, non-earthquake proof housing, and inhabited by many elderly persons.

Gender, age and disability are not the only factors of vulnerability. Foreign temporary residents, immigrants and tourists are groups which may not have the cultural and linguistic tools to act rapidly and correctly in an emergency situation. This was the case in the 2004 Indian Ocean tsunami where thousands of tourists and poor, often immigrant inhabitants on exposed coastal strips were equally helpless when faced with the deadly threat.

as general societal vulnerabilities linked for instance to critical infrastructures should be gradually considered in damage evaluations, and used to calibrate preparedness and response measures.

Vulnerability assessment methodologies should be elaborated for the specific case of major earthquakes in Japan, based on the knowledge gained in past disasters. Vulnerability assessment would be a useful complement to the traditional risk-based approach to disaster management policies.

Epidemiological studies should be conducted in order to better understand the impact of major earthquakes on individuals and communities. This entails developing the resources and protocols for such studies *a priori*, since much relevant information is lost and consistent observations become difficult to make in the aftermath of a disaster.

The HERP's Policy Committee could have a broader mandate to investigate the use of scientific assessments in policy making and to reach out to decision-makers, in particular at local level.

Recommendation 4. The traditional focus on scientific risk assessment should be complemented with heightened attention to individual and societal factors of vulnerability.

2. Communication with the public

Correct reactions and behaviour of inhabitants may save many lives during and after the occurrence of a harmful event. Time is always crucial in rescue operations, and the local community should learn to help themselves as much as possible in the immediate phase after the event, before they can be reached and helped by trained rescue personnel. In an urban setting where telecommunications and transport systems may have broken down, it is an almost impossible task for relief workers to reach all the affected population in time. Experiences from the 1985 Mexico City earthquake and Kobe and similar disasters shows that the majority of victims trapped in buildings are rescued by neighbours and people in the community. Tragically, it was recorded in the Mexico quake that there were deaths among these volunteer rescue workers due to lack of training.

In Japan, government agencies and municipalities devote important resources to developing a culture of risk among the public, through information campaigns, distribution of hazard maps, use of pictograms, simulations, etc. The most notable example is "Disaster Prevention Day", 1 September, a yearly event which takes place within the framework of "Disaster Prevention Week", and which has been organised since 1982. "Disaster Prevention Week" consists of exhibitions, drills, dissemination of information material, and aims to raise citizen awareness about disaster preparedness. On "Disaster Prevention Day" the government carries out a comprehensive emergency drill, each time in a different location in Japan. The drill can involve several hundred thousand participants, interventions of regional and local authorities, as well as participation of the major disaster management actors in the central government.

Numerous local initiatives are also taken to prepare the population for a disaster. For instance, the Ward of Chiyoda, in central Tokyo, organises public drills in six locations every six months, involving each time 500 persons (1% of the Ward's night-time residents).

OECD REVIEWS OF RISK MANAGEMENT POLICIES – ISBN 978-92-64-05639-8 – © OECD 2009

In addition, the establishment of small citizen groups with basic skills in life-saving and rescue operations has been encouraged after the Great Hanshin-Awaji earthquake, as a complement (and not substitute) to government rescue activities. The same model has been used in Los Angeles in the United States, with the establishment of the Community Emergency Response Teams.

Findings

The Japanese population enjoys an exceptionally high level of risk culture compared to other developed countries, related to the country's exceptional exposure to natural hazards. The existence of numerous resident discussion groups, community organisations and the like dealing with disaster issues bears witness to its high degree of self-organisation in this area.

However, surveys and studies indicate that the awareness of earthquake risks among the Japanese population is still incomplete in certain respects. A survey conducted by the Cabinet Office in 1991 showed that only 8.4% of the population in Western Japan, where Kobe is situated, believed that a big earthquake could occur in their area, compared to 22.9% nationwide. This perception was in no way justified by the actual probabilities of occurrence of earthquakes. In line with this, commercial installations in Kobe had been erected on soil susceptible of liquefaction, and a high proportion of residential and commercial buildings had a low level of earthquake resistance.

Although the general level of knowledge regarding earthquakes is unquestionably higher than in many other countries, there seems to be sometimes confusion among the public between the earthquake intensity figures, which indicate tremor strengths, and magnitude figures measuring the scale of the earthquake.

The Cabinet Office's Survey on disaster preparedness also shows that risk awareness, as measured by the actions undertaken by individuals to protect themselves and their relatives from harm, increases in the aftermath of a major event, but recedes thereafter (see Figure 9.2).

As a result, there seems to be a wide gap between the individual attitudes towards earthquake risks assumed in the design of public policies, and what these attitudes actually are. For instance, individual decisions to retrofit houses do not always seem to match the government's objectives in this area. Likewise, the government and the industry's efforts to promote insurance coverage against earthquake risks have been only moderately successful in the past.

There is therefore a need for government entities in charge of earthquake disaster management to better understand how people act with regard to earthquake risks, and why.

Figure 9.2. **Measures taken in preparation for a major earthquake**

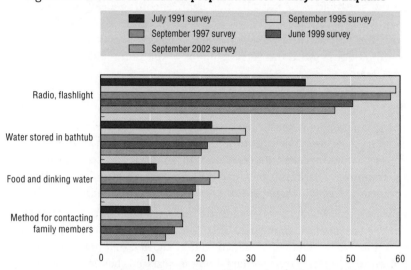

Source: Suganuma (2006), based on data from the Cabinet Office's *Survey on Disaster Preparedness.*

Opportunities for action and recommendations

Scientific research on the determinants of individual and social attitudes towards earthquake risks and on risk perception and acceptance should be encouraged.

Risk communication should not be designed and conducted as a one-way education of the public, but as a continuous dialogue in which it is equally important for risk managers to understand people's standpoints – and to adapt risk management procedures accordingly.

Efforts should be made continuously to maintain and reinforce the risk awareness and culture of the population, which increases in the aftermath of a major event but recedes thereafter – a pattern which can be observed in many other countries, but which has particular significance in Japan due to the exceptional prevalence of natural hazards.

Recommendation 5. Individual and collective attitudes with regard to earthquake risks have to be better understood. To this end, risk communication should be designed and implemented as a more regular and transparent dialogue between risk managers and the public.

OECD REVIEWS OF RISK MANAGEMENT POLICIES – ISBN 978-92-64-05639-8 – © OECD 2009

ISBN 978-92-64-05639-8
OECD Reviews of Risk Management Policies
Japan: Large-Scale Floods and Earthquakes
© OECD 2009

Chapter 10

Disaster Prevention

1. Building structural defences against earthquakes

The Kobe disaster emphasised the importance of earthquake-resistant design and seismic retrofit of buildings. Many deaths were caused by the collapse of one- or two-floor wooden houses, erected directly after the Second World War. There was also damage to newer, multiple-floor buildings in reinforced concrete, whereas buildings constructed according to the revised building code of 1981, which introduced requirements of flexibility, fared generally very well.

The government has tried to promote the retrofitting of private and public buildings, in particular in the aftermath of the Great Hanshin-Awaji earthquake. In 1995, the Japanese Parliament (Diet) adopted the Earthquake Retrofitting Promotion Act, which introduced relaxation of the restrictions on existing disqualified buildings and a lending programme with reduced interest from the Housing Loan Corporation. The Law mainly targeted buildings where a large number of people gather such as schools, hospitals, office buildings, etc. It excluded single-family houses. In 1998, however, the government introduced a new measure to subsidise the earthquake-related inspection of single-family houses.

However, about ten years after the passing of the Act, only 12 000 buildings in which many people gather have been retrofitted according to local government figures, leaving 90 000 buildings in which many people gather with inadequate resistance (25% of the existing buildings in which many people gather). The Ministry of Education, Culture, Sport, Science and Technology estimated, for instance, that more than 40% of school buildings (public primary and secondary school) are seismically unsafe (see Table 10.1).

Table 10.1. **Seismic grades of school buildings (public primary and secondary schools)**

Building code	Grade	Numbers	% of total
Post 1982	Assumed safe	48 797	37.7
Pre 1981	Evaluated safe or retrofitted	27 126	20.9
Total of safe buildings		75 923	58.6
Pre 1981	Evaluated unsafe, not retrofitted	45 041	34.8
	Not evaluated, assumed safe	8 595	6.6
Total of unsafe buildings		53 636	41.4

Source: MEXT (2007).

Regarding private homes, the second half of the 1990s witnessed a substantial decrease in the share of buildings with inadequate earthquake resistance (Yamamoto 2005). But the improvement was already underway when the 1998 government support was introduced, and there are indications that it was primarily linked to the impact of the Kobe disaster on people's awareness of earthquake risks, which gradually faded away. Only about half of the budget allocated by the government to support measures for the retrofitting of wooden houses in densely populated areas was actually spent between 2001 and 2005 (for a total of JPY 917 billion, versus JPY 1 432 trillion between 1996 and 2000).[1]

As of 2003, it was estimated that 25% of all houses in which households dwelled had not been built according to the 1981 standards or retrofitted in order to provide the same level of safety. In other words, 11.5 million private homes in Japan are still estimated not to provide adequate resistance to earthquakes.

This has led the government to re-emphasise the importance of building retrofitting. In 2002, the government subsidy for earthquake retrofitting was extended to stand-alone houses. In 2005, parts of the Act for Promotion of the Earthquake Proof Retrofit of Buildings were revised, introducing systematic promotion of seismic retrofit based on the earthquake-proof retrofit promotion plan, guidance and/or advice for owners, extension of the range of buildings for which the government can order retrofitting, and provisions for public announcements in case of non compliance. The support menu related to the inspection and the retrofitting of houses and buildings, which existed for individual businesses, was unified, and the business of earthquake retrofit of houses and buildings, etc. was created.

In 2006, the Basic Policy for the Promotion of the Earthquake-proof Inspection and Retrofit of Buildings established the target of raising the share

Figure 10.1. **Percentage of houses having insufficient earthquake resistance**

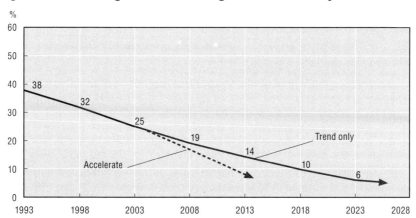

Source: Yamamoto (2005).

of seismically safe buildings to over 90% by 2015, for buildings used by individuals and many people. Prefectures make plans to promote seismic retrofitting based on national policies, and municipalities make similar plans in view of national policies and prefectural plans.

For privately owned non-residential buildings, public subsidies may not be sufficient to encourage seismic retrofit. For seismic retrofit of buildings, it is established that central and local government generally supports about 15% of the necessary funds. In the case of stand-alone houses, the average cost of seismic retrofit is considered to be around JPY 1.5 million.

Regarding schools, hospitals and other public buildings, there are indications that retrofitting costs can sometimes represent a significant fraction of the overall value of the building (Spence 2004, RAND Corporation 2002). This does not even account for costs associated with disruption of activity and loss of productivity during the works, which can be higher than the direct costs of retrofitting according to an evaluation by the California Seismic Safety Commission (California Seismic Safety Commission 2001).

Findings

Japan's current construction standards for earthquake resistance were adopted in 1981 and have proven adequate during the most severe events of the past two decades, including the Great Hanshin-Awaji Earthquake. It must be emphasised that the general level of earthquake-resistance of Japan's constructions is high by international standards (Whittaker *et al.*, 1998), and that the government's current policy sets very high-profile targets. The question is not whether these objectives are sufficient – they certainly are – but how to attain them in the stipulated timeframe.

Under the Basic Policy for the Promotion of the Earthquake-proof Inspection and Retrofit of Buildings, it is considered desirable for prefectures to review their earthquake-proof retrofit promotion plans in accordance with the progress of seismic retrofit and the implementation of new measures. Such a trial-and-error approach seems well adapted to a challenging long-term issue for protection policy.

However, as explained above, the current incentive schemes do not seem sufficient to bring about the scale of improvement that the government is aiming for.

The Central Disaster Management Council has adopted seismic retrofit of buildings as the most highly prioritised measure in the preparedness plan against the Tokai earthquake. To this end, the Council's General Principles of Measures for Dealing with Major Earthquakes Centered in Tokyo are quite directive, stating that the government should give instructions for the improvement of homes in areas with high concentrations of wooden structures, and make public announcements when its instructions are not adequately followed. The Council adds:

"It is especially important for the national government to take the lead and for relevant ministries and agencies to work in close co-operation to systematically advance the effective implementation of measures to improve the earthquake resistance of structures, and other measures to mitigate the effects of a major earthquake. Therefore, the national government will establish quantitative disaster mitigation objectives and deadlines and will create a "Preparedness Strategy for a Major Earthquake Centered in Tokyo" setting forth quantitative objectives, concrete implementation methods, etc. for achieving disaster mitigation objectives. Local governments will work to create local objectives based on this earthquake preparedness strategy" (Central Disaster Management Council (2005), p. 47).

The Preparedness Strategy for the Tokyo Metropolitan Earthquake, which was published in 2006, sets ten-year policy targets such as halving the 11 000 death toll expected from the North Tokyo Bay Area earthquake (M 7.3) under strong wind conditions (15 m/s). For this, the Strategy set intermediary targets regarding the share of seismically safe buildings (from 75% to 90%), the fixation of furniture (from 30% to 60%), the extension of the fire resilience zone (to more than 40%) and so on. This outcome-based approach, advocated by the Council, has created momentum for the promotion of countermeasures against earthquakes. However, it seems to lack concrete methods and tools to achieve its goals so far. While all local authorities have adhered to the Policy's objectives, both municipalities and prefectures seem uncertain about their overall responsibilities.

Opportunities for action and recommendations

Long-term policy objectives regarding structural defences should be accompanied by a better definition of roles and responsibilities, and criteria for resource allocation and the choice of instruments. A clarified national framework would certainly improve the coherence and efficiency of policy while preserving the autonomy of local governments and public agencies in terms of implementation.

The systematic use of cost-benefit analyses should be encouraged in this area for both evaluating projects and defining priorities.

The OECD's guidelines on earthquake safety in schools recommend a systematic, risk-based and result-oriented approach to earthquake safety in schools, and the establishment of measurable objectives for seismic safety, design code and standards, and realisation plans (OECD 2005a).

Tangible measures should be taken to increase incentives for improving the earthquake resistance of buildings, such as requiring that information on earthquake hazards be systematically notified in real estate transactions.

Recommendation 6. Policy strategies in the area of structural protection should include a clear definition of implementation principles and responsibilities.

2. Land use and city planning

Japan has a total population of 128 million (2005 census), about half of whom live in the country's three major urban areas of Tokyo (Tokyo Metropolis, and Kanagawa, Saitama and Chiba Prefectures), Kansai (Osaka, Kyoto, Hyogo and Nara Prefectures) and Chukyo (Aichi, Gifu and Mie Prefectures). With an average of 340 inhabitants per km^2, it is one of the most densely populated countries in the world, but with large geographic discrepancies. Habitation is predominantly in lowland or coastal areas. Density can be low inland and on the northern island of Hokkaido, while it reaches 13 000 persons per km^2 in certain parts of Tokyo.

The process of urbanisation in large metropolitan centres has been continuous in the past half-century – a unique case among OECD countries. The Japanese people commonly refer to Tokyo as a case of "unipolar concentration": all of the country's main political and economic decision centres and sources of information are located in the capital.

The principal instruments for urban planning in Japan are the Comprehensive National Development Plan (CND Plan), which has provided a comprehensive spatial articulation of priorities, and the National Land Use

Figure 10.2. **The concentration of population in the three major urban areas**

	Other area	Tokyo area	Nagoya area	Osaka area
2005	50.3	26.8	8.7	14.2
2000	50.5	26.3	8.7	14.5
1990	51.1	25.7	8.5	14.7
1980	52.3	24.5	8.4	14.8
1970	53.4	23.3	8.4	14.9
1960	60.0	19.1	7.9	13.0

Population (%)

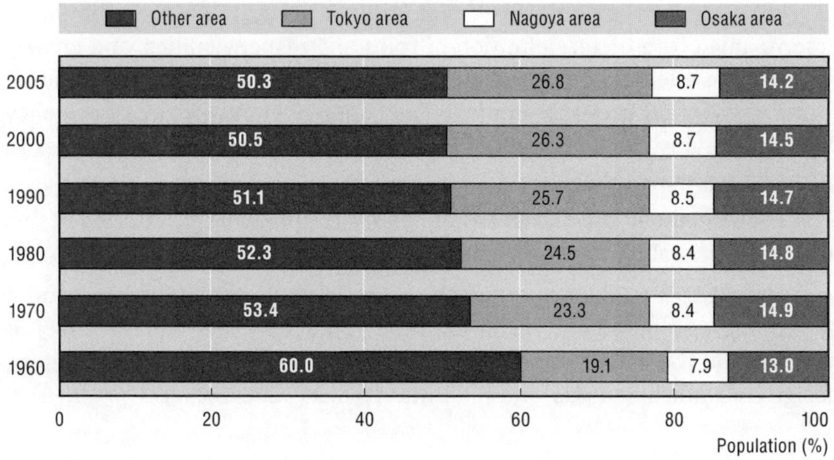

Source: Council of Local Authorities for International Relations (2004).

Plan, which has been formulated to promote well-balanced and effective land use by each level of government. The CND Plans and the National Land Use Plans are formulated by the Ministry of Land, Infrastructure and Transport on the basis of deliberations with all the relevant ministries and sub-national authorities. Dispositions regarding earthquake risks concern the prioritisation of building retrofits alongside major transport routes, emphasis on the renewal of areas with high concentrations of wooden structures, and when possible the creation of open spaces.

At the national level, strict restrictions regarding site selection related to the risk of earthquakes can be found for nuclear power plants and dams, where specific legislation imposes conducting preliminary research on active faults. Geological considerations, regarding for instance the upper layer of land, which can be a factor of tremor acceleration as well as liquefaction, are not explicitly included in the land use regulations.

Findings

Although almost all of the national territory is exposed to seismic hazards, it is in the country's major urban centres that risks are highest. In the Tokyo metropolitan area, 18 earthquakes of different types likely to occur were identified in order to raise public awareness and to provide possible contingencies for stakeholders. These come in addition to the Tokai earthquake which, given its traditional cycle of recurrence, is considered very likely to occur at any moment with a magnitude approaching 8 (see Chapter 7: Introduction).

The concentration of people, assets and activities in these areas therefore creates the possibility of a mega-risk, with specific challenges in terms of risk management: the need to secure and efficiently use huge resources for response and recovery, varieties of possible knock-on effects, and repercussions for the rest of the country, the region and the world. According to the CDMC:

"If a major earthquake were to occur in this area, ensuring the continuation of political and governmental functions necessary for responding to a disaster (…) as well as the continuation of economic functions critical for the nation (…) would be a key concern."

"Damage to the core functions of the nation's capital could magnify the massive damage to life and property that would accompany a major earthquake centered in metropolitan Tokyo and prolongs confusion in the aftermath of an earthquake. The types of damage that could result from such an earthquake would be seen nowhere else" (Central Disaster Management Council (2005), pp. 7 and 8).

Authorities at central, prefectural and local levels indeed estimate that the concentration of people, constructions and assets is an extremely difficult challenge for disaster response (evacuation, sheltering, etc.).

Still, land use and city planning policies do not include restrictive measures for land use in the vicinity of active faults, or provisions aimed at decreasing concentration in the areas where the overall magnitude of risk would be considered excessive. Admittedly, almost all of Japan's territory is exposed to seismic risks, and fault strata are particularly difficult to identify, especially where sediment densely covers them. In addition, high population density in habitable places has probably helped preclude the idea that risk considerations could be integrated into land use policies. International illustrations show that it may be possible to adopt a more active stance in this area (see Box 10.1). But it should also be mentioned that these examples concern restrictions in the vicinity of fault strata, and that a broader consideration of seismic risk factors in land use and city planning remains a challenge in all exposed countries.

Opportunities for action and recommendations

The long-term decrease in the population will facilitate a gradual change in urbanisation patterns. But a business-as-usual scenario may not lead to substantial results in terms of risk exposure in the most earthquake-prone areas during the coming decades.

Long-term objectives in terms of concentration of people and economic activities in earthquake-prone areas, partly established on small zoning levels

---

Box 10.1. **International examples of land use restrictions with regard to earthquake risks**

In the United States, the State of California, where many earthquakes occur, established the Alquisito-Priolo Special Studies Zone Act in 1972, which can be called "active fault law". According to the law, the State defined active fault strata and made an official map that shows a 1 000 foot-wide earthquake fault zone around an active fault. When building confirmation applications are submitted, cities and counties make sure that there is no active fault and give permission to develop the land and construct buildings. If active fault strata are found through geological research, buildings have to be built 50 feet away from the fault.

In New Zealand, some cities and towns have acts that limit the development of land on active fault strata. The Wellington government has a provision stating that buildings have to be built more than 20m away from the Wellington Fault, which lies in the south of the northern island.

---

under the current land use and city planning policies, should be extended in terms of geographical scope, and backed by more robust policy instruments.

Further work will be needed to make different levels of government and other stakeholders concerned with land use and urban development more aware of seismic risks. The legal instruments for land use and city planning policies may also need to be enhanced.

In the short term, it seems desirable to engage a national debate on ageing, land use and natural hazards, bringing together all relevant stakeholders (the general public, civil society organisations, representatives of the private sector, critical infrastructure operators, academia, government agencies, etc.).

With regard to active-fault earthquakes, research on active faults and restrictions on land use should be considered in the short term at least for public buildings (schools, hospitals, etc.) and critical infrastructures.

Recommendation 7. In the context of a rapidly decreasing population over the coming decades, land use and urban planning could integrate seismic risk factors more actively, and aim at a gradual decrease in population density in the most hazard-prone areas. Prudent land use in the vicinity of fault strata should be considered in the short term.

Note

1. *Source:* Government of Japan, Budget for the Five-Year Term Plans of Urgent Earthquake Countermeasures.

ISBN 978-92-64-05639-8
OECD Reviews of Risk Management Policies
Japan: Large-Scale Floods and Earthquakes
© OECD 2009

Chapter 11

Emergency Preparedness and Response

1. Mastering the secondary impacts of earthquakes

Large-scale natural disasters such as major earthquakes often have, in addition to their devastating direct impact, considerable indirect impacts in terms of disruption of lifelines and secondary accidents.

Among the hazards that can be triggered by an earthquake, the most common is fires. In Kobe, a total of 175 fires started in the hours following the earthquake, and damaged about 82 hectares of urban land. To address this risk, city gas networks are being equipped with automated sensors that shut off flow when an earthquake tremor is detected. In some cases, people have also been advised to activate electrical circuit breakers before evacuating their homes.

Another source of accidents caused by natural disasters is the release of hazardous materials such as oil products, chemicals, or radioactive material: the December 2004 Indian Ocean tsunami caused the leakage of 8 000 m^3 of oil from an oil facility in Banda Aceh, Indonesia (UNEP, 2005). In 2005, hurricanes Rita and Katrina caused oil spills of more than 30 000 m^3 from production facilities in the Gulf of Mexico.

A recent example was given in Japan by the Niigata-ken Chuetsu-oki earthquake, which affected the Kashiwazaki-Kariwa nuclear power station of the Tokyo Electric Power Company on 16 July 2007. The earthquake reached maximum seismic accelerations exceeding the values assumed in the design. The impacts included a fire in the Unit 3 transformer, and a release of spilled water containing small amounts of radioactive material. Preliminary investigations led by Nuclear Safety Commission and the International Atomic Energy Agency showed that the automatic shutdown had worked for all the units in operation or in power ascension, that the impact for the outside environment had been negligible, and that the accident had been well handled with, however, one important exception: the notifications from the operator to central and local government had been delayed, and communication with the public had not been adequate.

In Japan, critical infrastructures in areas such as transport, energy, water and gas supply, communications and finance are principally operated by private companies, which are responsible for assuring adequate security of supply. A large body of evidence from various OECD countries shows that disaster prevention and mitigation crucially relies on mutual trust and intense cooperation between operators of critical infrastructures and the government, for instance through well-established procedures for information-sharing, as well as on the existence of adequate incentives for safety.

Findings

Generally, private companies in Japan are strongly committed to assuring a high level of safety and continuity of operations with regard to earthquake risks. Many private firms, in particular utility providers like the Tokyo Electric Power Company, have diversified their production sites and created distant backup sites. In the event of a major earthquake in Tokyo, the communication system is expected to remain operational and power supply is expected to be completely restored in less than three days.

Cooperation between critical infrastructure operators and local government is effective, although often informal, in large urban areas on issues such as contingency and business continuity planning or emergency response.

However, there has traditionally been little exchange of specific information regarding earthquake risk prevention and mitigation with central government. Private sector companies tended to be reluctant to disclose potentially sensitive information to public agencies, and uncertain about how that information would be used and how well it would be protected. For example, several private hospitals in Tokyo have in the past been unwilling to share information to be used in risk assessments conducted by the Tokyo Metropolitan Government (Uitto, 1998). When some data is provided to public authorities, it is often deemed inaccurate.

The experience of the Great Hanshin-Awaji Earthquake, and more recently of the Niigata accident, also show that co-operation between critical infrastructure operators and government entities at central and local level is not always sufficient.[1]

In this area, the situation might be improving, as witnessed by the dialogue between key infrastructure operators and the government regarding recovery time in critical infrastructures. Although the locations of the core critical facilities have usually not been communicated by the operators, the Central Disaster Management Council has been able to establish a broad picture of the expected situation and to publish (in 2005) estimated recovery times for energy, water and gas supply, and communications in the event of the Tokyo Metropolitan Area Earthquake.

In addition, there is probably room for strengthening the legal framework to oblige operators of critical infrastructures or hazardous industries to systematically make safety provisions for earthquake risks and report to government agencies, both in normal times and during emergencies. The Large-Scale Earthquake Countermeasures Special Act has introduced amendments to sector-specific laws such as the High-Pressure Gas Control Law, the Fire Fighting Act or the Law on the Prevention of Disasters in Petroleum Industrial Complexes and Other Petroleum Facilities. For industrial installations located in areas considered at risk of a major earthquake, the Special Act calls for additional measures to ensure seismic safety. But it creates fairly limited obligations for the operators compared to equivalent regulations in other countries (Cruz and Okada, 2007).

In the State of California, for instance, hazardous industries are submitted to the California Accidental Release Prevention (CalARP) Program, which since 1998 has required operators to produce a seismic assessment study. The aim is to obtain "reasonable assurance" that a release of regulated substances having offsite consequences would not occur as a result of an earthquake. Furthermore, the assessment studies have to be based on a geotechnical report analysing the underlying soil conditions at the facility (CalARP Program Seismic Guidance Committee, 2004). Various seismic guidelines provide specific recommendations for the elaboration of such studies, and for seismic design and safety measures at chemical facilities.

The government of Japan, despite its responsibilities in the overall management of societal risks related to earthquakes and its general instructions to the private providers of essential services and hazardous industries, does not have a precise knowledge of the state of some basic infrastructure elements such as hazardous product storage tanks, pipelines, power grids, etc. In the absence of precise information regarding secondary risks such as chemical spills, industrial accidents or power line disruptions, the government cannot control the development of indirect costs, which can be huge in the event of a major earthquake.

Opportunities for action and recommendations

The CDMC has emphasised the need for a more stringent approach to the risks of industrial hazards triggered by earthquakes in the Tokyo area:

"The national and local governments, and relevant businesses, will advance measures based on the Law on the Prevention of Disasters in Petroleum Industrial Complexes and Other Petroleum Facilities. They will also enhance evaluations of how a disaster at a petroleum complex would impact adjacent areas, and promote both high disaster preparedness through redevelopment of aged coastal industrial facilities and development of earthquake early warning applications and other technologies."

"To prevent disasters at coastal petroleum complexes from spreading to adjacent areas, the national and local governments, and relevant businesses, will promote comprehensive measures for preventing large-scale fires related to sloshing in petroleum tanks" (Central Disaster Management Council (2005), pp. 26 and 28.)

It would be useful to apply these recommendations in a more systematic way to all critical infrastructure sectors and hazardous industry sectors.

Precise routines for collection of data and information-sharing procedures should be developed in each of these sectors, according to its specific regulatory and economic conditions. Information exchange groups should be established.

Legal dispositions should be introduced to support the enforcement of necessary measures (as in the CalARP) and to create adequate safeguards in terms of information confidentiality.

As in other OECD countries, the control of risk management procedures in key industries could become part of the current operations of regulatory agencies and supervisory bodies.

Recommendation 8. Government regulatory agencies need to achieve a better knowledge of the management of earthquake risk in their areas of action and have clear responsibilities for supervising critical infrastructure sectors and hazardous industries in this regard.

2. Continuity planning in the public and private sectors

Business continuity plans have become an important tool of risk management for organisations. In a globalised, networked economy, it has become crucial for commercial enterprises to avoid serious disruptions to their activity. Business interruption has become an important category of damage caused by natural disasters in OECD countries, in particular because of its consequences for smaller companies. For instance, 80% of Kobe's 2000 small- and medium-sized companies are reported to have failed in the aftermath of the Great Hanshin-Awaji Earthquake (RMS, 2005). Starting from the private sector, the practice of business continuity planning is now gradually extending to public organisations in some OECD countries.

The benefits of business continuity plans are not limited to the organisations that adopt them – they also have an impact on society's resilience to shocks such as disasters. Continuity planning raises the level of risk awareness, and ensures that normal prevention and preparedness measures are actually in place. It thereby improves personnel safety at work and to some extent outside of the work environment, and reduces the economic and social impacts of disasters. These "external" benefits justify that governments promote the adoption of continuity plans by both private and public organisations, with a particular emphasis on critical infrastructures at one end of the spectrum, and on small- and medium-sized enterprises at the other.

In countries with the longest experience with business continuity planning, governments have usually adopted a gradual approach: establishing guidelines in partnership with the private sector; gradually refining these guidelines, and in parallel making them more binding; establishing a national standard; and enforcing the adoption of the standard through various means, including public procurement policy (see Box 11.1).

In Japan, the Central Disaster Management Council formulated business continuity guidelines for commercial firms through one of its Technical Committees in 2005. The Council's guidelines explicitly recommend using a major earthquake as a reference scenario. The Council's aim is to establish a good practice, which could then be disseminated by the private sector.

The website of the Ministry of Economy, Trade and Industry also provides guidance on continuity planning.

The Cabinet Office issued business continuity guidelines for ministries in 2007, and each ministry is preparing the first edition of its business continuity plan, all scheduled to be issued in mid-2008.

Box 11.1. **National standards of business continuity management**

Australia's HB 221 is considered as the first national standard specifically targeting business continuity management. The HB 221 was adopted by Standards Australia in 1994.

The American National Standard for Disaster/Emergency Management and Business Continuity Programs (ANSI/NFPA 1600) was developed by the National Fire Protection Association (NFPA) in 1995, and approved as a national standard in 2000. The standard defines a common set of criteria for preparedness, disaster management, emergency management, and business continuity programs for both public and private sectors. The standard was specifically endorsed by the 9/11 Commission in its 2004 report to Congress and the President.

The British standard BS 25999 was issued first issued as a code of practice consisting of guidance and recommendations, in 2006 (BS 25999 part 1). It establishes the process, principles and terminology of business continuity management. The second part of the standard, launched in 2007, specifies the process for achieving the certification that business continuity capabilities are adapted to the size and conditions of an organisation.

Sources: Standards Australia (www.standards.org.au), American National Standards Institute (www.ansi.org), British Standards Institution (http://www.bsi-global.com/).

Findings

Business continuity plans have been developed in some of the country's large businesses. But the practice is not introduced systematically and almost non-existent among small- and medium-sized enterprises.

The experience of companies, both small and large, that have adopted business continuity plans confirms the theoretical arguments in favour of it. These companies report that it has substantially improved their level of preparedness, and consider that the government should play a more active role in the promotion of continuity planning.

The CDMC has made a number of proposals to this end in its General Principles of Measures for Dealing with Major Earthquakes Centered in Tokyo, including: "to achieve broad understanding of the BCP guidelines" among businesses, to work with the private sector in order to elaborate a system "for publicly releasing disaster preparedness reports" and "certifications of participating disaster preparedness facilities" (Central Disaster Management Council (2005), p. 34.). To date, although understanding of the BCP guidelines has spread to some extent, other proposals seem to have recorded limited progress.

Turning to the government sector, decentralisation of responsibilities for developing and implementing continuity plans enables each ministry to adapt its plan to its precise needs and constraints. However, interdependencies between public services create a strong need to coordinate continuity planning throughout the government, and the present organisation of disaster risk management seems to leave a gap in this regard. The Cabinet Office does not have a defined role in coordinating continuity plans, beyond supervising the first edition of each ministry's plan.

Finally, there are important synergies between emergency preparedness, disaster prevention and business continuity planning, both inside organisations and within society at large. At present, interactions between these activities seem to be limited at both the local and the national levels.

Opportunities for action

Following the example of other OECD countries, the government and the public sector at large should include business continuity planning requirements in their procurement policies.

This should be backed by the development of a certification procedure based on a national standard adapted to Japan's specific situation with regard to earthquake risks.

In parallel, Japan should strongly contribute to the elaboration of an international standard of business continuity management, where its experience with the management of natural disasters would be of great value.

The role of the Cabinet Office in the adoption of continuity plans inside the government should be enhanced, and continuity plans should be considered a necessary element of disaster management during internal audits and evaluations.

Fire and rescue services should be better used in creating linkages between emergency preparedness and disaster prevention and in actively promoting business continuity planning. Fire services at municipal level could for instance take increased responsibilities in preparedness and continuity planning as an extension of their traditional fire prevention activities.

Recommendation 9. There is a need to further promote the implementation of continuity planning in both the private and the public sectors, in particular in SMEs.

3. Crisis management, from frequent events to large-scale disasters

Recently, failures in the management of response to disasters have led to intense political controversies in several OECD countries, showing that even where operational responsibilities are decentralised, the central leadership of the Total Disaster Risk Management System is often held responsible in crises.

In Kobe, both central and local government were widely criticised for their handling of the emergency after the Great Hanshin-Awaji Earthquake. Many observers estimated that the authorities had been too slow in realising the extent of the disaster, and that cooperation between government agencies had been inadequate. It should be mentioned, however, that the conditions were extremely difficult. The emergency response staff were quite often themselves affected by the earthquake, and response management and coordination were significantly impeded by the breakdown in transport and communications infrastructures. Furthermore, the rubble and debris from the collapsed buildings accumulated in the narrow streets of the older areas of Kobe city, and the prevalence of fires made it impossible to reach some of the most damaged areas for several days.

The difficulties in assessing the impact at the local level delayed response from central authorities. Authorities at the national level were criticised for having rejected international offers of assistance, notably professional search and rescue teams. The military was also deployed at a relatively late stage. In the meantime, local resources were stretched in conducting search and rescue operations, inspecting remaining buildings, and trying to cover the basic needs of more than 300,000 homeless persons gathered in overcrowded shelters.

Numerous aspects of emergency management were reformed in the aftermath of the disaster. In particular, the Disaster Countermeasures Basic

Act was amended in order to strengthen the authority of the emergency headquarters and to systematically establish field headquarters.

In emergency situations, the Cabinet Office is competent for the overall coordination of disaster reduction activities, under the authority of the Minister of State for Disaster Management, while the Cabinet Secretariat Office is in charge of collecting incident information for the top officials in the Cabinet. In severe situations (earthquake of intensity 5 or more in the Tokyo Metropolitan area and 6 or more in other areas), the two organisations merge, forming a body directed by the Emergency Management Chief Officer in the Cabinet Secretariat Office.

In both cases, the central government ministries or authorities continue to exercise roles within their areas of competence at central, regional and local level. However, when Urgent Disaster Management Headquarters are established, the Prime Minister, as chief of headquarters, has authority over the prefectural governors, in conformity with the Disaster Relief Act (article 28).

Findings

Japan enjoys state-of-the-art warning systems for seismic risks, for both their extensive coverage of the national territory and their technological sophistication. The Japan Meteorological Agency monitors seismic activity and provides information on tsunamis and earthquakes in real time. The JMA disseminates earthquake early warnings regarding tremors within a few seconds after detecting the first seismic waves, to announce earthquake source, magnitude, expected scale and tremor impact time. It also issues tsunami warnings within 2 minutes, with forecasts of tsunami height and impact time. This information triggers emergency response in central and local government. Prefectures have also installed magnitude meters in municipalities, and make the data available to the Japan Meteorological Agency through an information network.

Data from these magnitude meters, together with information from the Ministry of Land, Infrastructure and Transport regarding the state of infrastructures, and from other sources converge towards a number of disaster response headquarters. Different ministerial departments and central agencies, prefectures and municipalities (or wards) have such dedicated command and control centres, adapted to their jurisdictions and missions, from which they can manage their response activities.

The drawback is that, as the disaster response headquarters are each specific to a sector or level, they are not designed to function as a holistic system for the management of crises at national level. According to the Disaster Countermeasures Basic Act, a national emergency centre is to be established in a disaster situation, and each ministerial/local headquarters should obey the command from the national centre. Gaps seem to remain between the autonomous design/operation of each emergency management organisation and the central command and control system authorised by the Act.

In particular, the integration of information into a coherent crisis management system, where risk analyses and mapping and all other relevant data would be used for a real-time monitoring of the situation, has not been fully achieved yet at the national level. The present systems give access to information sources, but are to a great extent only adapted to different sector needs and do not form a common information and decision support system for exercising command and control.

As a consequence, the formal competence of the centre of government for exercising a national command and coordinating response might be hampered by the lack of effective tools.

Furthermore, decision-makers at local level do not always seem fully aware of the role the centre of government in exercising command in the event of a major disaster.

Changing the organisation of disaster management at the centre of government according to the importance of events might be a source of complexity. Admittedly, both the Cabinet Office and the Prime Minister's Secretariat have a role to play, the former as a centre of expertise and oversight on Japan's disaster risk management system, and the latter as the decision centre for the management of national emergencies. However, experiences from different OECD countries and risk sectors consistently indicate that changes of organisational structure for the management of crises should be avoided as far as possible.

Opportunities for action

The chain of command should appear more clearly to all actors involved in the crisis management system.

The division of roles and responsibilities at different levels has to account for the necessity to address overall national needs and interdependencies in an extremely efficient manner during emergencies.

When duties are delegated within a line of command, delegation should always be accompanied with clear objectives and tasks, and combined with clear reporting and evaluation requirements.

If existing changes in crisis management responsibilities according to the scale of the event are considered unavoidable, sophisticated organisational design with a simple structure should be sought. The need for exercise and training to compensate for the change should also be emphasised.

Recommendation 10. The competence and tools for exercising national co-ordination, and in extreme cases command, from the centre of government need to be reinforced.

Note

1. While the overall management of the Niigata accident was deemed effective by an IAEA investigation mission, communication and reporting delays between plant operators and the authorities were considered as a matter of concern (IAEA, 2007).

ISBN 978-92-64-05639-8
OECD Reviews of Risk Management Policies
Japan: Large-Scale Floods and Earthquakes
© OECD 2009

Chapter 12

Post-Event Issues

1. Disaster recovery and reconstruction

The recovery needs after a major earthquake are huge and extremely diverse. Public services need to be restored as swiftly as possible. Long-term housing solutions have to be found for thousands of people living in temporary shelters. Dangerous buildings and infrastructures have to be demolished and replaced. The persistent effects of the disaster on physical and mental health, on social relations and on the local economy need to be addressed.

Correctly assessing the needs and efficiently allocating resources to recovery and reconstruction projects is, in itself, a considerable challenge. In this area as well as in others, the Kobe disaster has provided some precious lessons.

The Hanshin-Awaji earthquake confronted Japanese authorities with a reconstruction task that few OECD countries have faced since the Second World War. In Japan, municipalities have primary responsibilities for financing recovery expenditures, while the prefectures and the central government contribute in proportion to the scale of the event. The Building Standards Law imposes restrictions on reconstruction in disaster-stricken areas, in particular in order to leave enough time for planning and coordination (article 84).

In March 1995, at the end of the reconstruction freeze, the City of Kobe and the Hyogo Prefecture had developed complementary plans, with a common aim not only to rebuild what had been destroyed by the earthquake, but also to draw lessons in terms of urban planning and land use, and to rehabilitate the city and promote future economic growth. A total of 16 priority restoration districts were identified, with development projects ranging from the creation of open spaces, parks and new streets and the widening of roads to the construction of new public facilities. In these areas, the rebuilding freeze was extended for another two years, in order to allow for negotiations. In some cases, public funds were used to purchase all properties in an area in order to run large-scale redevelopment projects.

In April, the Municipality of Kobe and the Hyogo Prefecture together established the Great Hanshin-Awaji Earthquake Reconstruction Fund in order to offer support to victims and to finance recovery projects. The Fund, which is still active, has gathered a total of JPY 900 bn, and provided interest-free loans to more than 100 000 businesses and households.

The planning, financing and decision-making tools proved inadequate for addressing the consequences of a disaster of such magnitude. In the three months following the earthquake, the government passed more than fifteen laws in order to define the framework, develop the institutions and organise financial transfers for disaster recovery.

Still, a number of issues were experienced in the effort to rehabilitate the city's building stock. Homeless inhabitants were accommodated in more than 49 000 temporary housing units, in some cases for several years. Central government funds were principally dedicated to the reconstruction and repair of basic infrastructure and public facilities. Local government support to households and businesses focused on totally destroyed properties, leaving a gap for those inhabitants who had endured lesser damage. Partly as a consequence, a considerable share of the repair and recovery costs was eventually borne by local residents.[1] In order to support private reconstruction, the government eventually decided to provide rent subsidies and allow homeowners to increase the pre-earthquake surface area of their houses. The delayed effect of these measures, together with extensive public building programs, led to a surge in the number of constructions, and the city's housing market shifted from shortage to a large surplus that still persists twelve years after the earthquake. The commercial real estate market experienced a similar imbalance.

Although the central government allocated a total of JPY 5 trillion to the recovery effort between 1995 and 1997, the reconstruction had a significant impact on local public finances. The municipality of Kobe largely relied on bond issuance to finance its reconstruction projects, resulting in a heavy municipal debt that overshadows its long-term financial situation. In some areas, the local economy did not fully recover from the disaster, in particular the port of Kobe which lost part of its activity to Japanese and other Asian competitors. The decline in the city's population and economy further undermined the local tax base.

Some of the city's neighbourhoods were dramatically modified, and there were criticisms regarding the consultation and involvement of stakeholders, in particular residents, in the projects. A number of *ad hoc* structures were created to consult members of civil society and other stakeholders, such as the Kobe City Restoration Promotion Council dealing with recovery issues, the Kobe City Restoration and Rejuvenation Promotion Council discussing the long term structural agenda of reconstruction, or the Housing Restoration Council dealing with health and welfare issues related to life in temporary housing and the transition to permanent housing. But some estimated that their action was tardy, and their influence limited. (Hyogo Research Centre for Quake Restoration 2005.)

Findings

Recovering from a large-scale earthquake, especially in a metropolis, represents a huge challenge is terms of planning, coordination, financing, and decision-making. But the example of Kobe shows that it can also be an opportunity not only to reduce the vulnerability of urban structures, but more broadly to improve their sustainability, their economic attractiveness, and their suitability for the residents.

The Central Disaster Management Council recently stated the type of strategic and co-operative approach that should prevail in the recovery phase after a disaster:

"The national and local governments will create an image of what Tokyo should be by establishing recovery principles and objectives (...). The national and local governments will consider ways for promoting agreement among relevant parties in the aftermath of a major earthquake, and other measures for realising the planned image of what Tokyo should be. They will also consider measures for implementing urban development plans guided by recovery principles, before a major earthquake strikes." (Central Disaster Management Council (2005), p. 46, emphasis added.)

It can be argued that such strategic principles and goals should be pre-established. Naturally, the detailed recovery measures cannot be planned in advance, since they will to a large extent depend on the situation at hand. However, creating a general framework for recovery measures ex ante can have important advantages. Experience shows that in the aftermath of a large disaster, reconstruction can be very urgent and the context usually does not allow time to build a social consensus around such long-term issues.

The considerable financial needs – and sometimes conflicting interests – engendered by a disaster make it all the more useful to investigate a priori where the use of public funds would be most productive, and to establish priorities for public recovery and reconstruction spending accordingly.

Partial initiatives have been taken in recent years in this direction. In particular, the Tokyo Metropolitan Government adopted a recovery plan in 2001 entitled "Grand Design for Recovery after an Earthquake", which consists of a set of strategic objectives and principles to guide reconstruction efforts after the occurrence of a major earthquake. As of today, however, the government does not have any particular planning tools for post-disaster reconstruction.

Past disasters have also shed light on some specific challenges in the financing of recovery and reconstruction measures. The aim should be to immediately assess and respond to the needs after the emergency situation is over, and thereafter to continuously adapt to the situation in the field, for instance in terms of providing financial support and housing solutions. These conditions make administrative tools and financing procedures developed for normal situations inadequate.

While an important share of recovery costs would fall on the municipalities and prefectures, it is clear that no local government, including the Tokyo Metropolitan Government, has the means to cope with the financial burden resulting from a large earthquake.

Opportunities for action

In high-risk zones, the objective should be to build consensus among local actors (citizens, non-government organisations, private companies, local government units) on the desired features of the reconstructed area. External actors (regional or central government, neighbouring localities, etc.) would have to be involved whenever there would be consequences beyond the locality.

Such a broad consensus on the overall principle objectives of reconstruction would be used as a basis in the aftermath of a large earthquake, helping to avoid unnecessary conflicts, provide a framework for projects, and save time and resources. Obviously, such an overall framework would have to be adapted to the specific conditions, based on the needs engendered by the earthquake and the available resources.

Even in normal times, it would provide a needed long-term target for local land use and city planning policies.

The government should aim at smoothing the reconstruction process and supervising its financial sustainability. The Disaster Aid Act and Disaster Relief Act should be utilised effectively to help those who are financially in need.

Recommendation 11. The government should encourage municipalities and prefectures to consult local actors and build consensus on the objectives of post-disaster recovery, and strengthen their tools for addressing the needs resulting from an earthquake.

2. Insurance: Sharing mega-risks

In addition to the traditional challenges posed by natural hazards to the insurance industry, catastrophic risks such as major earthquakes pose a clear problem of capacity. Although the chances of an earthquake are small compared with the possibility of fires or automobile accidents, a single occurrence of a large earthquake could lead to tremendous claims for the incurred damage costs.

As exposed earlier, the costs of disasters increased rapidly in the 1990s and there are reasons to believe that the trend will continue. The public sector is not alone in struggling with the financial consequences of this trend. Two thirds of the losses caused by the Northridge Earthquake were borne by insurance companies (Petak, William J., 2000, p. 10). In a single event, California insurers lost three times the total earthquake premiums that they had collected in the previous 25 years (Ibid). The financial difficulties experienced by the insurance/reinsurance industry in recent years, especially after the New York terrorist attacks in 2001, have raised questions about the insurability of such "mega-risks". A major earthquake hitting Tokyo would be an extreme event in that regard.

The household earthquake insurance system covers residential buildings and household goods. It has several characteristics:

1. Earthquake insurance is contracted with the fire insurance policy for the same property, and cannot be contracted alone.

2. It covers various disasters related to earthquakes including volcanic eruptions, tsunami and – importantly – fires following earthquakes.

3. Earthquake insurance amount is limited, with policyholders choosing within a range of 30% to 50% of fire insurance coverage and a cap of up to JPY 50 m for a building and JPY 10 m for household goods.

4. Benefits are paid according to three levels of damage assessment classified as a total, half, or partial loss, after being multiplied by a designated rate for each earthquake insurance amount.

5. Premiums include discounts according to the type of structure (wooden or otherwise), the location, the seismic capacity of the building and the year of construction.

6. The earthquake insurance system is operated subject to reinsurance by both the Japanese Earthquake Reinsurance Co. and the Japanese Government.

7. The insurance settlement for a given event is limited to a JPY 5.5 trn. If insurance liability following a disaster exceeds this amount, there are cases in which the settlements to all claimants are proportionately reduced.

Earthquake insurance for businesses does not benefit from government-backed reinsurance. Each company can contract earthquake insurance policies with insurance companies, but underwriting conditions are stringent.

Findings

Japan's current earthquake insurance system was created in 1966, two years after the Niigata Earthquake, with the establishment of the "Act for Earthquake Insurance." The system is built on government-backed reinsurance, and has undergone several phases of improvement and refinement since its inception, including expanded coverage and revised premium rates. Premium rates were revised in 2007 on the basis of the most recent seismic motion prediction maps issued by the HERP. Following this amendment, premium rates decreased by 7.7% on average in the country. In addition, earthquake insurance premium deductions were established. The same year, the government introduced income tax deductions for earthquake insurance premiums as a way to promote earthquake insurance and improve loss coverage. Finally, the total payment limit of the earthquake insurance system was reduced to JPY 5.5 trn in April 2008.

With the occurrence of several important earthquakes in the prefectures of Niigata, Fukuoka and Ishikawa, insurance purchase has increased steadily. As of December 2007, the number of household earthquake insurance contracts was more than 11 m.

In spite of these improvements, insurance penetration in Japan is low with regard to the magnitude of seismic risks. In 2005, the rate of market penetration was 20% for household insurance, and limited to a few percentage points for commercial insurance.

Inadequate insurance coverage signifies that households and corporations cannot protect their income from large fluctuations caused by disasters. Recent studies based on the Family Income and Expenditure Survey find that the economic shock of the Great Hanshin-Awaji Earthquake was not shared between the Kobe area and the rest of the country (Kohara *et al.*, 2006). This indicates not only that earthquake insurance, but also that financial assistance from the central government, were not sufficient to spread out the costs of the disaster.

Some businesses have developed alternatives to classic insurance, such as self- and mutual-insurance, as a way to cover earthquake risks. Recently, innovative financial solutions have started to emerge.

In 2004, four financial institutions arranged a contingent debt facility (CDF) and syndicate loan for the Tomoegawa Paper firm, in the event of a large-scale Tokai earthquake. The arrangement provides a portion of the funds that Tomoegawa Paper would need to recover from the earthquake. It strongly relies on the company's measures to prevent and mitigate damage, notably through a business continuity plan.

Building on this experience, three financial institutions together launched a credit line in 2006 for use in the event of a catastrophic earthquake. After an earthquake exceeding a certain magnitude, companies will be able to draw on the line in order to finance their recovery needs. Eligible companies have been selected on a case-by-case basis, with a view both to their degree of exposure and their prevention and business continuity measures.

Opportunities for action and recommendations

Insurance products should have more detailed risk categories. The design of insurance products could better reflect the risk level within prefectures and large metropolitan areas. To achieve this, it is necessary to further improve risk assessment methods using both hazard maps and seismic motion prediction maps.

Public awareness of earthquake risks should be further improved. Policies to promote risk evaluation for each building and dissemination of the information in an easy-to-understand way should be pursued.

Risk prevention incentives should be strengthened by further differentiating insurance premiums on the basis of reasonable risk countermeasures taken by policyholders. As such differentiation for individual residents might make earthquake insurance unaffordable in some cases, it is crucial to consider measures for the high-risk group at the same time.

With better insurance cover for individuals and enhanced incentives for damage prevention, an extension of government-backed reinsurance could be considered.

For the cover of seismic risks affecting businesses, financial innovations such as CAT bonds and contingent debt facilities should be encouraged as alternatives to classic insurance.

Recommendation 12. The market penetration rate of insurance against earthquake risks should be improved through better premium differentiation and heightened public awareness.

Note

1. According to one evaluation, 70% of the restoration costs over the five-year period following the earthquake were borne by households and private companies (Tenth Year Restoration Committee, 2005). See also next section regarding insurance and risk-sharing mechanisms.

OECD REVIEWS OF RISK MANAGEMENT POLICIES – ISBN 978-92-64-05639-8 – © OECD 2009

ANNEX II.1

Methodology

The review process

As a result of the first phase of the OECD Futures Project on Risk Management Policies, the OECD Secretariat delivered a study on disaster mitigation policies for large-scale earthquakes to the Japanese authorities in January 2006 (OECD, 2006). The study analysed the architecture of earthquake disaster management in Japan, as well as the principal lessons learned from past large-scale events, and derived some key policy challenges for the coming years. Japan's government then decided to mandate the OECD Secretariat to further investigate these issues in the second phase of the Project, based on a self-assessment of earthquake disaster management procedures by Japanese institutions. To conduct the self-assessment, two questionnaires were developed for public administrations to self-assess and take stock of their disaster management policies related to seismic risks (see Annex II.2). Together with the initial study, the information collected through the questionnaires provided the basis for an in-depth review of policies concerning the risks of large-scale earthquakes in Japan.

In order to introduce the self-assessment questionnaires to the respondents (representatives of the sample of stakeholders) a "kick off" meeting was organised in Tokyo on 22 February 2007. Relevant authorities from the Cabinet Office, IDI and the OECD/IFP Secretariat gave a presentation about the background and answered questions from the floor.

The review mission took place in the Tokyo Metropolis, from 21 to 25 May 2007, and included interviews of central government authorities, local government at prefectural and municipal level, public agencies, research institutes, private companies and organisations, as well as site visits and inspections. The review's geographic basis of observation was therefore principally the Greater Tokyo area. However, using complementary sources of information such as the Project's Phase 1 study, replies to the questionnaires sent out to a selection of actors, public evaluation reports, academic studies and legal texts, the review team has extrapolated its findings and recommendations to the whole nation to the extent that this seemed possible.

The team submitted an interim report of its findings and recommendations to the Japanese authorities in July 2007 and requested their comments. In November 2007, the team delivered the first draft of this final report.

Overview of the methodology followed to evaluate risk management policies

Risk management is a complex process involving many different phases, from the evaluation of threats and the creation of protection strategies, to understanding liability issues and investigations after a disaster. Failure to complete the entire risk management process can lead to important linkages among these activities being overlooked, thereby undermining the overall effectiveness of a policy. This is the case, for instance, when the assessment of risk is not closely associated with the identification of affordable means of avoidance, or when risk prevention measures are designed with little attention to the actual incentives provided by insurance policies.

- In order to address the need for a holistic approach, the OECD Project on Risk Management Policies has developed a methodology (OECD, 2003) which considers risk management as a multi-layered system, where each layer performs a particular function with regard to risk, and provides inputs to some of the other layers:

- Risk or vulnerability assessment.

- Policy decision-making, based on risk assessment and acceptability, and on available options for treating or transferring risk.

- Framework conditions, i.e., laws, norms, and all regulations and public actions that create obligations and incentives with regard to risk.

- Protection, i.e., devices, constructions and procedures to protect exposed populations and systems: dams, shields, shelters, displacement of threatened persons, quarantines, etc.

- Information, i.e., awareness-raising, information-sharing.

- Alert and rescue, to mitigate the immediate impact of hazard.

- Recovery enhancement, to mitigate the longer-term impact of hazard.

- Experience feedback and organisational change.

When elaborating the self-assessment questionnaires, all relevant actors, institutions and rules are considered in each layer. The layer's performance is evaluated against a set of criteria falling under three major headings: coherence of organisation, effectiveness in achieving objectives, and openness to external sources of information. To evaluate the performance of the overall system, the linkages between layers are also investigated through questions such as the management of past crises; the quality of experience-feedback and the capacity to trigger organisational change; the ability to detect changes and to adapt to new conditions; the management of uncertainties and the consistency of precautionary measures; and the existence and pertinence of a risk management strategy.

This approach was applied to the Review of Policies concerning Large-Scale Earthquakes in Japan, and followed to a large extent in the structure of this report. However, a number of adaptations have been made

Policy decision-making and framework conditions are addressed in Chapter 8 of the report.

Risk assessment, R&D, awareness-raising and experience feedback questions have been grouped in Chapter 9.

The prevention and protection layer is the topic of Chapter 10.

Information-sharing, alert and rescue are dealt with in Chapter 11.

Chapter 12 comprises items of both recovery enhancement and insurance.

ANNEX II.2

Self-Assessment Questionnaires

In order to conduct a self-assessment of earthquake disaster management procedures by Japanese authorities, the two following questionnaires were developed and sent to relevant administrations:

- A general questionnaire on the institutional organisation of earthquake preparedness policies at State level, focusing on the clarity and consistency of the legal framework in defining roles and responsibilities, and on coordination with other administrative and private actors.

- A questionnaire to the prefectures and municipalities, with particular focus on existing resources and capabilities of elaborating and maintaining a viable earthquake preparedness policy.

In these questionnaires, risk management is understood in a broad sense, including risk and vulnerability assessment, risk prevention and damage mitigation, early warning, preparedness, emergency management, business continuity management, insurance and reconstruction. Any policy measure relating to one of these areas should therefore be considered as relevant.

A. General Questionnaire

A.1. Risk assessment

Main actors: Cabinet Office; Central Disaster Management Council; Affected Ministries.

A.1.a. Roles and responsibilities in earthquake risk and vulnerability assessment

- Please describe the role and responsibilities of your organisation with regard to the assessment of the following points:
  - Earthquake risk.
  - Vulnerability of physical structures to earthquakes.

- Vulnerability of population groups to earthquakes.
- Secondary effects of earthquakes and its ensuing risks and vulnerabilities.
- Integrating the results of the identified risks and vulnerabilities in a central cost and damage assessment.
- Other.

● Please describe the way in which your organisation is structured and the resources it devotes in order to fulfil this role. In support of your reply, please provide organisational charts, statistics, activity reports and any other information deemed useful.

● Which other actors cooperate with your organisation in assessing earthquake risk and vulnerability at the State level? At prefecture level? At municipal level? Private and non-government actors? Please describe the coordination and communication channels.

● Does the current legislation create any obligations to monitor the points identified above (earthquake risk, etc.)?

A.1.b. Risk assessment methods

● Please describe existing programmes aimed at:
- Identifying, monitoring and evaluating earthquake risks.
- Detecting vulnerabilities in physical structures.
- Detecting and monitoring new and existing vulnerable groups in the population.
- Identifying secondary effects of earthquakes, including business interruption costs.
- Integrating different types of risk and vulnerability data.

● How is data collected for the above categories? (From where, how often, etc.)

● Are there any obstacles to the collection of data (confidentiality issues, privately-owned information, etc.)? If so, please elaborate your answer.

● Please describe ongoing or planned research programmes regarding earthquake and risk and vulnerability assessment tools.

● Please describe any other method or tool used to assess earthquake risk and vulnerability.

A.1.c. Self-assessment

● How do you evaluate the Japanese population's exposure to earthquakes, taking into consideration
- The different measures implemented after the Great Hanshin Awaji earthquake

- Societal developments in the last 10 years (ageing populations, changes in population income, etc.).
- Technological developments of the last 10 years (increasing interdependence of critical infrastructures, society's dependence on telecommunications).

● In which area(s) do you feel that more information would be needed regarding the earthquake risks and the vulnerability of structures and population groups?

A.2. Principles of strategic decision-making

Main actors: Cabinet Office, Central Disaster Management Council; Affected Ministries

A.2.a. Roles and responsibilities in decision-making

● Please describe the roles and responsibilities in designing and implementing national strategies for earthquake risk reduction and earthquake vulnerability reduction (of physical structures and population groups (elderly, etc.))?

● What are the coordination and communication channels between the entities?

A.2.b. The decision-making process

● How are priorities defined and targets set at the national level?

● What are the programmes and implementation plans related to these targets?

● What are the overall public resources devoted to earthquake risk and vulnerability reduction? What is the share of these resources of the overall spending on overall natural disaster risk and vulnerability reduction?

● Which stakeholders are consulted during the decision-making process, and how?

● At what stage, if any, are the costs, benefits and risks of alternative solutions considered?

● How are financial resources allocated to the measures in support of earthquake risk and vulnerability assessment? Please make a distinction between the various levels of government (State, prefecture and municipality) and between sources of funding (State or local taxes, ear-marked funds, etc.).

A.3. Protection

Main actors: Ministry of Land, Infrastructure and Transport, Affected Ministries, in particular Ministry of Education, Culture, Sports, Science and Technology; Ministry of Health, Labour and Welfare

A.3.a. Building code policies

Please describe the roles and responsibilities for formulating and implementing building code policies in Japan.

- Please describe the way in which your organisation is structured and the resources it devotes in order to fulfil this role. In support of your reply, please provide organisational charts, statistics, activity reports and any other information deemed useful.
- Please describe recent evolutions in building code in Japan. Which are the underlying objectives for change, and what are the expected effects of a change?
- How are the formulation of building codes for buildings and physical infrastructures linked to earthquake risk assessment and lessons learnt from previous earthquakes in and outside Japan? Please indicate communication and co-ordination channels.
- What are the average delays of formulating a building code before this is translated into actual policy?
- What is the renewal rate of buildings in Japan per year?
- Which are the mechanisms for enforcing building codes in Japan? Is there a difference in the treatment of public and private buildings?

A.3.b. Land use policies

- Please describe the roles and responsibilities in designing and implementing land use policies in Japan?
- Please describe the way in which your organisation is structured and the resources it devotes in order to fulfil this role. In support of your reply, please provide organisational charts, statistics, activity reports and any other information deemed useful.
- Which are the land use criteria defined by the Ministry of Land, Infrastructure and Transport and others, in relation to earthquake risk and vulnerability?
- Please describe possible recent evolutions in land use policy in Japan. Which are the underlying objectives for change, and what are the expected effects of a change?

- How is the formulation of land use policies linked to earthquake risk assessment and lessons learnt from previous earthquakes in and outside Japan? Please indicate communication and coordination channels.
- Do these criteria refer to risk assessments elaborated by local/central authorities?
- Which are the enforcement mechanisms for land use policies?

A.3.c. Seismic retrofit

- Please describe the roles and responsibilities in designing and implementing seismic retrofit policies in Japan?
- Please describe the way in which your organisation is structured and the resources it devotes in order to fulfil this role. In support of your reply, please provide organisational charts, statistics, activity reports and any other information deemed useful.
- Please describe possible recent evolutions in seismic retrofit policy in Japan. Which are the underlying objectives for change, and what are the expected effects of a change?
- How is the formulation of seismic retrofit policies linked to earthquake risk assessment and lessons learnt from previous earthquakes in and outside Japan? Please indicate communication and co-ordination channels.
- Which are the existing policies in place to encourage the seismic retrofit of
  - Public constructions.
  - Private non-housing constructions.
  - Private housing.
  - Other constructions.
- Are these actions co-ordinated with those of other organisations? Please describe.
- Has a legislative framework been put in place to allocate responsibility and liability for seismic retrofit of buildings? If so, please describe.
- Please inform about current or planned research programmes for the seismic retrofit of buildings and the resources devoted to this activity.

A.3.d. Self-assessment

- How do you evaluate the current legislative framework in Japan concerning land use, building codes and seismic retrofit? Is the legislation "fit for purpose"?
- Are there any obstacles to the correct implementation of land use, building code and seismic retrofit policies? If so, please elaborate.

- How has the legal and regulatory framework evolved in the last 10 years, taking into consideration experiences from the Great Hanshin-Awaji earthquake, public sector decentralisation, etc.?

A.4. Information and early warning

Main actors: Japan Meteorological Agency; Cabinet Office

A.4.a. Awareness-raising among the general public

- Please describe the role and responsibilities of your organisation with regard to awareness- raising activities vis-à-vis the general public.

- Please describe the way in which your organisation is structured and the resources it devotes in order to fulfil this role. In support of your reply, please provide organisational charts, statistics, activity reports and any other information deemed useful.

- Which other actors cooperate with your organisation with regard awareness-raising activities at State level? At prefecture level? At municipal level? Please describe the coordination and communication channels.

A.4.b. Awareness-raising among public and private actors

- Please describe the role and responsibilities of your organisation with regard to awareness-raising activities vis-à-vis public (prefectures, municipalities) and private actors (infrastructure operators, etc.).

- Please describe the way in which your organisation is structured and the resources it devotes in order to fulfil this role. In support of your reply, please provide organisational charts, statistics, activity reports and any other information deemed useful.

- Which other actors co-operate with your organisation with regard to such activities at State level? At prefecture level? At municipal level? Please describe the co-ordination and communication channels.

A.4.c. Warning

- Please describe the role and responsibilities of your organisation with regard to earthquake warnings.

- Please describe the way in which your organisation is structured and the resources it devotes in order to fulfil this role. In support of your reply, please provide organisational charts, statistics, activity reports and any other information deemed useful.

- Which other actors cooperate with your organisation with regard to warning activities at State level? At prefecture level? At municipal level? Please describe the co-ordination and communication channels.

A.4.d. Self-assessment

- How you evaluate the Japanese population's preparedness for a major earthquake? Has the level of preparedness increased or decreased in the last 10 years?

A.5. Evacuation and rescue

Main actors: *Private Organisations, Fire Brigades, Police, Defence Agency, Ministry of Health, Labour and Welfare, Medical Services*

A.5.a. Roles and responsibilities

- Please describe the role and responsibilities of your organisation with regard to earthquake- induced evacuation and rescue activities.
- Please describe the way in which your organisation is structured and the resources it devotes in order to fulfil this role. In support of your reply, please provide organisational charts, statistics, activity reports and any other information deemed useful.
- Which other actors cooperate with your organisation with regard to evacuation and rescue activities at State level? At prefecture level? At municipal level? Please describe the coordination and communication channels.
- How is the formulation of evacuation and rescue plans linked to earthquake risk and vulnerability assessments and lessons learnt from previous earthquakes in and outside Japan (evacuation of particular population groups)? Please indicate communication and co-ordination channels.

A.5.b. Self-assessment

- How do you assess the response capacity of your own organisation?
- How you do assess the overall response capacity of earthquake rescue organisations in Japan?
- Do you consider that the population has changed over the last 10-20 years, and that this has consequences for earthquake disaster evacuation and rescue? Please describe.

A.6. Recovery enhancement

Main actors: Cabinet Office, Insurance Sector

A.6.a. Earthquake losses mitigation

- Please describe the efforts of your organisation to encourage the development of business continuity plans among:
  - Small and Medium-sized Enterprises.
  - Large Corporations.
  - Operators of critical infrastructures.
- Please describe the policy tools (legal incentives, tax, awareness-raising, other).
- Are there any other policies in place to mitigate economic losses of earthquake disasters? Please describe.
- Are there policies in place to encourage earthquake losses mitigation among individuals? Please describe.

A.6.b. Earthquake insurance

- Please describe the current earthquake insurance scheme in Japan (percentage of insurance penetration among Japanese households; coverage of insurance policy, insurance financing, State implication, etc.).
- Are there any policies to encourage earthquake insurance, directed towards:
  - Home owners.
  - Small and Medium-Sized Enterprises.
  - Other.

A.6.c. Compensation of victims

- Please describe the policies and legislation in place for victim compensation and reconstruction.
- Of all reconstruction costs, which share is paid by the individuals, the State and the private sector?

A.6.d. Self-assessment

- Do you consider that the current compensation system in Japan is capable of recovering from a 'mega-scale' earthquake (<M.7 in Tokyo)?
- In your opinion, is the current compensation system equitable, or does it particularly hit certain groups of the population, or business sectors?
- Has this changed in the last 10 years? How are the prospects for the next 20 years?

A.7. Feedback and organisational change

Main actors: Affected Ministries

- Please describe the role and responsibilities of your organisation with regard to feedback and organisational change.

- Please describe the way in which your organisation is structured and the resources it devotes in order to fulfil this role. In support of your reply, please provide organisational charts, statistics, activity reports and any other information deemed useful.

- Which other actors co-operate with your organisation with regard to such activities at State level? At prefecture level? At municipal level? Please describe the co-ordination and communication channels.

- Please indicate how results of this activity is integrated into existing policies in

  - The other policy layers (assessment, decision-making, etc.).

  - The different earthquake preparedness and mitigation disciplines (land use, building codes, seismic retrofit, research, etc.).

  - Are there past examples where experience feedback has led to organisational change? Please give examples.

  - How are international practices and experiences used in evaluating and elaborating Japanese earthquake preparedness policy?

  - Do channels exist for the private sector, NGOs or citizens to provide feedback on existing structures and policies? Please give examples.

B. Questionnaire to prefectures and municipalities

B.1. Risk and vulnerability assessment

- Please describe your role and responsibilities in assessing risks and vulnerabilities regarding earthquake disasters, and in communicating this information to your local and regional stakeholders, including the population.

- Of these activities, which are implementation of decisions from the central administration and the prefecture and which draw from the municipality's sole responsibility in this area?

- What is the organisational structure in place to fulfil these responsibilities?

- Please provide available data on the municipality's specific resources corresponding to these functions (grants from the central government, taxes, etc.).

- Please describe the methods and tools you use to carry out risk and vulnerability analyses. Do you receive training in conducting such analyses?

LARGE-SCALE FLOODS AND EARTHQUAKES: JAPAN – ISBN 978-92-64-05639-8 – © OECD 2009

- How do you evaluate the quality of the data used in the risk and vulnerability analyses? Who collects the data?
- How often are risk and vulnerability analyses updated?

B.2. Policy decision-making

B.2.a. Resource allocation

- Please indicate, as percentage of total budgetary spending, the resources devoted to earthquake preparedness.
- Please indicate the funding sources of your spending on earthquake prevention. Is it mainly from your own local government budget, or via central government grants? Are the latter grants (if any) earmarked (attached to predetermined measures)?
- What is the balance between prevention and emergency response policies in your budget?

B.2.b. Strategic co-ordination and supervision

- Please describe your role and responsibilities when it comes to designing and implementing prevention and preparedness policies in the area of earthquakes.
- Of these activities, which are implementation of decisions from the central administration and the prefecture and which draw from the municipality's sole responsibility in this area?
- What is the organisational structure in place to fulfil these responsibilities?
- How do the relevant services inside your municipality (rescue, buildings and infrastructures, education, social and health services, other) co-operate on earthquake disaster risk prevention and preparedness?
- Please describe the co-ordination and communication channels with other government actors when it comes to designing and implementing policy (other actors in local government, central government).

B.3. Framework conditions

B.3.a. Land use policies

- Please indicate the main principles and criteria (and existing legislation) for designing and implementing land use policies, in relation to earthquake preparedness.
- How do you assess your room for manoeuvre *vis-à-vis* central authorities when it comes to designing land use policies?

- If there are national principles and criteria of land use, how does the central government monitor their implementation at the local level (in your prefecture/municipality)?

B.3.b. Building codes

- Please indicate the main principles and criteria (and existing legislation) for designing and implementing building codes, in relation to earthquake preparedness?
- How does the central government encourage and monitor the implementation of building codes at the local level (in your prefecture/municipality)?

B.4. Protection

- Please describe the main policies of structural protection against earthquakes in your prefecture/municipality. Please indicate whether these policies have been designed at the municipality, regional or state level.
- What is the organisational structure in place to fulfil these responsibilities?
- Please provide available data on the municipality's specific resources corresponding to these functions (grants from the central government, taxes, etc.)
- Who has the responsibility for the maintenance of earthquake defence structures?

B.5. Information and early warning

- How do you get your information concerning earthquake risks, methods of organising preparedness activities, necessary prevention measures, and so on?
- Do you exchange information with other government and/or private actors on these issues, and if yes, how?

B.6. Evacuation and rescue

- Please describe your role and responsibilities with regard to evacuation and rescue of populations and structures in earthquake disasters?
- What is the organisational structure in place to fulfil these responsibilities?
- Please describe the main co-ordination and communication channels with prefectural and governmental organisations participating in evacuation and rescue.

B.7. *Self-assessment*

B.7.a.   The general situation

- What are the major challenges faced by your municipality in preventing and preparing for earthquake disasters? What are their causes?
- How has the physical and social vulnerability to earthquakes evolved in the past 10 years?
- How do you expect these vulnerabilities to evolve in the next 10 years in your municipality?

B.7.b. Own capacity

- How do you evaluate your municipality's capacity to fulfil its responsibilities regarding earthquake disaster preparedness?

ANNEX II.3

List of Institutions Interviewed

Cabinet Office

Ministry of Land, Infrastructure, Transport and Tourism
- River Bureau.
- Road Bureau.
- City and Regional Development Bureau.
- Housing Bureau.
- Government Buildings Department.

Fire and Disaster Management Agency

Ministry of Education, Culture, Sports, Science and Technology

Japan Meteorological Agency

Geographical Survey Institute

Tokyo Metropolitan Government
- Disaster Prevention Division, Bureau of General Affairs.
- Tokyo Fire Department.

Chiyoda City

Shinjuku City

The General Insurance Association of Japan

Tokyo Marine & Nichido Fire Insurance Co., Ltd

Non-Life Insurance Rating Organization of Japan

Japanese Red Cross Society

Japan Federation of Construction Contractors

Fujitsu limited

Shimizu corporation

Daido IT Co., Ltd

ANNEX II.4

Members of the Steering Group
(as of 7 November 2007)

CANADA:

Alexandre MARTEL

Agent responsable de la politique intégrée de gestion du risque

Division de la Planification Stratégique

Sécurité publique Canada

Philippe THOMPSON

Directeur

Division de la Planification Stratégique

Sécurité publique Canada

DENMARK:

Niels JACOBSEN

Head of Section

Danish Emergency Management Agency

Niels MADSEN

Senior Advisor

Danish Emergency Management Agency

Dorte JUUL MUNCH

Head of Section

Civil Sector Preparedness Division

Danish Emergency Mangement Agency

Henrik Grosen NIELSEN
Head of Division
Emergency Management Division
Ministry of the Interior and Health

Signe RYBORG
Head of Unit
Ministry of the Interior and Health

FRANCE:

Jean-Claude EUDE
Directeur
Développement et Relations extérieures
Établissement Public Loire

ITALY:

Luigi D'ANGELO
Department for Civil Protection
Prime Minister's Office

Agostino MIOZZO
Minister Plenipotentiary
Presidency of the Council of Ministers

JAPAN:

Takami ADACHI
Deputy Director, River Planning Division, River Bureau
Ministry of Land, Infrastructure and Transport

Kazuhisa ITO
Director of Second Research Department
Infrastructure Development Institute

Goro YASUDA
Counsellor for Disaster Management
Cabinet Office

NORWAY:

Hilde Bostrøm LINDLAND

Senior Engineer/Project Manager

Directorate for Civil Protection and Emergency Planning (DSB)

Ministry of Justice and the Police

SWEDEN:

Minga ORKAN

Deputy Director

Social Services

Alf ROSBERG

Project Leader

Swedish Rescue Services Agency

Jim SANDKVIST

Director

SSPA

UNITED KINGDOM:

John TESH

Deputy Director

Representing Bruce MANN

Director, Capabilities

Civil Contingencies Secretariat

Cabinet Office

UNITED STATES:

Tina GABBRIELLI (unable to attend)

Acting Director

Office of Risk Management and Analysis

National Protection and Programs Directorate

US Department of Homeland Security

Bibliography

Cabinet Office (2002), *Disaster Management in Japan*, Online document.

California Seismic Safety Commission (2001), *Findings and Recommendations on Hospital Seismic Safety*, State of California Seismic Safety Commission, Sacramento.

CalARP Program Seismic Guidance Committee (2004), *Guidance for California Accidental Release Prevention Program Seismic Assessments*, January 2004.

Central Disaster Management Council (2005), *General Principles of Measures for Dealing with Major Earthquakes Centered in Tokyo*.

Council of Local Authorities for International Relations (2004), *Local Government in Japan*.

Headquarters for Earthquake Research Promotion-HERP (2007), *Seismic Activity in Japan – Regional perspectives on the characteristics of destructive earthquakes*, online version, available at *www.hp1039.jishin.go.jp/eqchreng/eqchrfrm.htm*.

Hyogo Research Center for Quake Restoration (2005), *Lessons from the Great Hanshin Earthquake*, Kyoto, Creates-Kamogawa Publishers.

International Atomic Energy Agency (2007), *Preliminary Findings and Lessons Learned from the 16 July 2007 Earthquake at Kashiwazaki-Kariwa NPP*, Vienna: IAEA.

Kohara, M., F. Ohtake and M. Saito (2006), "On effects of the Hyogo earthquake on household consumption: A note", *Hitotsubashi Journal of Economics*, 47:2, pp. 219-228.

MEXT (2007), TITLE, *http://www.mext.go.jp/b_menu/houdou/19/06/07060507.htm* (in Japanese).

MLIT (2005), *White Paper on Land, Infrastructure and Transport in Japan*.

Netherlands Directorate-General for Public Safety and Security (2004), *Performing Together for Public Safety and Security – An Introduction*, Ministry of the Interior and Kingdom Relations, The Hague.

Okada, T. (2005), 'Improvement of Seismic Safety of Buildings and Houses', presentation at the World Conference on Disaster Reduction, Kobe, January 18-22.

OECD (2002), *Economic Survey of Switzerland*, Paris: OECD.

OECD (2003), *A Methodological Framework for Evaluating Risk Management Policies*. Background document, first meeting of the Steering Group of the OECD Futures Project on Risk Management Policies, 3 November 2003.

OECD (2005a), *OECD Recommendation Concerning Guidelines on Earthquake Safety in Schools*, Paris, OECD.

OECD (2005b), *Economic Survey of Japan*, Paris, OECD.

OECD (2006a), *Economic Survey of Japan*, Paris, OECD.

OECD (2006b), *OECD Studies in Risk Management: Japan - Earthquakes*, Paris, OECD.

RAND Corporation (2002), *Estimating the Compliance Costs for California SB1953*, California Healthcare Foundation, Oakland.

RMS (2005), *1995 Kobe Earthquake 10-Year Retrospective*, Risk Management Solutions, Inc.

Sawada, Y. and S. Shimizutani (2007), "How Do People Cope with Natural Disasters? Evidence from the Great Hanshin-Awaji (Kobe) Earthquake in 1995", *Journal of Money, Credit and Banking*, forthcoming.

Shinozuka, M. (1995), "Summary of the Earthquake", in NCEER *Response*, Special Supplement to the January 1995 Issue of the NCEER Bulletin. National Center for Earthquake Engineering Research, University of New York at Buffalo.

Spence, R. (2004), "Strengthening School Buildings to Resist Earthquakes: Progress in European Countries", OECD (2005a).

Suganuma, K. (2006), "Recent Trends in Earthquake Disaster Management in Japan", *Quarterly Review of the Science and Technology Foresight Center*, No. 19.

Tenth Year Restoration Committee (2005), *Report of the 10-Year Reconstruction*, The Great Hanshin-Awaji Earthquake Memorial Research Institute, Kobe.

Uitto, J. I. (1998), "The geography of disaster vulnerability in megacities", *Applied Geography*, Vol. 18, No. 1.

United States Geological Survey (2007), *Earthquake "Top 10" Lists and Maps*, *http://earthquake.usgs.gov/eqcenter/top10.php*, accessed 5 October 2007.

Whittaker, A., J. Moehle and M. Higashimo (1998), *Evolution of Seismic Building Design Practice in Japan: The Structural Design of Tall Buildings*, 7:2, pp. 93-111.

Yamamoto, S. (2005), "Great Earthquakes Disaster-Prevention Measures for Houses and Buildings", presentation at the World Conference of Disaster Reduction, Kobe, January 18-22.

OECD PUBLICATIONS, 2, rue André-Pascal, 75775 PARIS CEDEX 16
PRINTED IN FRANCE
(03 2009 03 1P) ISBN 978-92-64-05639-8 – No. 56597 2009